SG24-6115-00

IBM International Technical Support Organization

Magstar Peer-to-Peer Virtual Tape Server Planning and Implementation Guide

December 2000

AF779481

Take Note!

Before using this information and the product it supports, be sure to read the general information in Appendix G, “Special notices” on page 271.

First Edition (December 2000)

This edition applies to the Magstar Peer-to-Peer Virtual Tape Server, including the 3494-AX0 Virtual Tape Controller, for use with OS/390.

Comments may be addressed to:
IBM Corporation, International Technical Support Organization
Dept. 471F Building 80-E2
650 Harry Road
San Jose, California 95120-6099

When you send information to IBM, you grant IBM a non-exclusive right to use or distribute the information in any way it believes appropriate without incurring any obligation to you.

© Copyright International Business Machines Corporation 2000. All rights reserved.
Note to U.S Government Users – Documentation related to restricted rights – Use, duplication or disclosure is subject to restrictions set forth in GSA ADP Schedule Contract with IBM Corp.

Contents

© Copyright IBM Corp. 2000

Figures

© Copyright IBM Corp. 2000

Tables

© Copyright IBM Corp. 2000

Preface

This IBM Redbook discusses enhancements to the Magstar VTS in the area of automated tape copying for OS/390 systems.

These enhancements broaden the usage of the VTS extensively and make the VTS a possible replacement product for any existing OS/390 tape solution. However, they also add another level of complexity in terms of planning for and implementing the Peer-to-Peer VTS solution.

Starting with a detailed description of the architecture and the design of the Peer-to-Peer VTS, we give you a comprehensive overview of all the planning tasks, provide guidance on a wide variety of possible configuration choices, and discuss several possible recovery scenarios as well as considerations for day-to-day operations.

A fairly good knowledge of the IBM virtual tape technology is assumed.

The team that wrote this redbook

This redbook was produced by a team of specialists from around the world working at the International Technical Support Organization San Jose Center (Figure 1).

© Copyright IBM Corp. 2000

Figure 1. The Peer-to-Peer VTS redbook team

Matthias Werner is responsible for tape and tape library projects at the International Technical Support Organization, San Jose Center. His function is to plan and run residencies to build and maintain high quality redbooks for use with IBM's leading tape library products in the field. This is a pivotal function between the development labs and the professionals at customers, Business Partners and within IBM. He also regularly teaches technical workshops and sessions at conferences and seminars.

Babette Haeusser works for the Advanced Technical Support team in EMEA and is located in Germany. She has contributed to various tape redbooks in the past.

Tom Koudstaal is a Certified IT Specialist working for Integrated Technology Services (ITS) in IBM Netherlands. He joined IBM in 1969 as a systems programmer. He is currently working as a technical consultant and project leader in systems and storage management projects with a focus on tape related implementations. He was involved with most of the 3495 and 3494 installations in the mainframe area in the Netherlands.

Taisei Takai is an I/T Specialist, and has been working as the leader of tape and tape library technical support in the Asia/Pacific region Advanced Technical Support organization for 5 years. Before, he has been working in other positions for storage products support after joining IBM back in 1990.

Marco Ceresoli is an I/T Specialist working for IBM Italy ITS (Integrated Technology Services). He has ten years of experience in storage products implementation in S/390 environment. His area of expertise includes IBM 3494 and VTS implementations, DFSMSrmm migrations, and offerings development in tape storage environments. He has contributed to several other IBM Redbooks.

Nigel Morton is responsible for tape projects at the International Technical Support Organization, San Jose. He joined IBM UK in 1977 and has worked on storage software and hardware for 20 years.

Thanks to the following people for their invaluable contributions to this project:

Don Lockett, Bill Travis, Dan Lindseth, Jesse Thrall, Bill Greeley, Justin Hildebrandt, Kathy Eldred, J.D. Metzger, Jon Peake, Erika Dawson, Linda Schiltz, and many more
IBM Tucson

Aare Onton, Bill Warren
IBM San Jose

John Martin
IBM Canada

Horst Boerner, Martin Berger, Thorsten Altmannsberger
IBM Germany

David B. Petersen
IBM Gaithersburg

Particular thanks are due to Yvonne Lyon and to Emma Jacobs, both of the San Jose ITSO Center, who edited this book and graphics.

Comments welcome

Your comments are important to us!

We want our Redbooks to be as helpful as possible. Please send us your comments about this or other Redbooks in one of the following ways:

- Fax the evaluation form found in "IBM Redbooks review" on page 285 to the fax number shown on the form.
- Use the online evaluation form found at **ibm.com**/redbooks
- Send your comments in an Internet note to redbook@us.ibm.com

Chapter 1. Introducing the Magstar Peer-to-Peer VTS

The Magstar Peer-to-Peer Virtual Tape Server, an extension of the Magstar Virtual Tape Server, builds on a proven base configuration to provide even greater benefits for tape processing and operations. By enhancing data backup and recovery capabilities, the Magstar Peer-to-Peer Virtual Tape Server is specifically designed to enhance data availability. It accomplishes this by providing dual volume copy, remote functionality, and automatic recovery and switchover capabilities. With a design that reduces single points of failure — including the physical media where logical volumes are stored — the Magstar Peer-to-Peer Virtual Tape Server improves system reliability and availability, as well as data access. To help protect current hardware investments, existing Magstar Virtual Tape Servers can be upgraded for use in this new configuration (Figure 2).

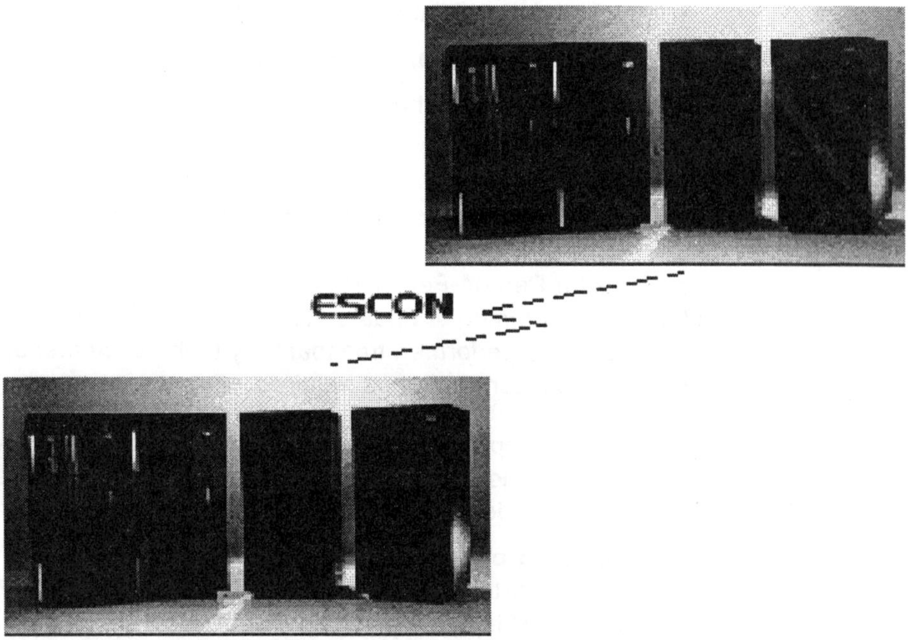

Figure 2. Peer-to-Peer configuration

The Magstar Peer-to-Peer Virtual Tape Server consists of new models and features of the Magstar 3494 Tape Library that are used to join two separate Magstar Virtual Tape Servers into a single interconnected system. The two virtual tape systems can be located at the same site or at different sites which

© Copyright IBM Corp. 2000

are geographically remote. This provides a Remote Copy capability for remote vaulting applications.

The Magstar Peer-to-Peer Virtual Tape Server appears to the host S/390 processor as a single automated tape library with 64 virtual tape drives and up to 250,000 virtual volumes. The configuration of this system has up to 3.5 TB of Tape Volume Cache native (10.4 TB with 3:1 compression), up to twelve Magstar 3590 tape drives, and eight host ESCON channels.

The new models require no additional host processor resources, and provide the dual copy function transparently to the host processor.

Advantages from this new configuration include:

- Automated outboard data copying of virtual volumes between two Magstar Virtual Tape Servers
- Remote data copying between two ESCON connected Magstar Virtual Tape Servers
- Improved data availability by eliminating single points of failure
- Concurrent maintenance capabilities
- Workload balancing between the two connected Magstar Virtual Tape Servers

1.1 Design

The Magstar Peer-to-Peer Virtual Tape Server automatically creates a copy of any newly created or updated tape volume in both Virtual Tape Servers. This process is performed transparently to the customer application and with no host processor resources required.

Either volume copy can then be used to satisfy a specific customer mount. This copy of all new or updated virtual volumes can be created using one of two possible modes of operation.

Immediate Copy - creates a copy of the logical volume in the companion connected Virtual Tape Server prior to completion of a Rewind/Unload command. This mode provides the highest level of data protection.

Deferred Copy - creates a copy of the logical volume in the companion connected Virtual Tape Server as activity permits after receiving a Rewind/Unload command. This mode provides protection that is superior to most currently available backup schemes.

A Magstar Peer-to-Peer Virtual Tape Server configuration is built from the following components:

- The Magstar 3494 Model AX0 Virtual Tape Controller
- The Magstar 3494 Model CX0 Auxiliary Frame
- The Magstar 3494 Model B18 Virtual Tape Server attached to a 3494 tape library
- Peer-to-Peer Copy features

1.2 Component functions

The function of the new models and features of the Magstar Peer-to-Peer Virtual Tape Server is described in this section. Figure 3 introduces some new terms used to describe the Peer-to-Peer configuration which are explained later on.

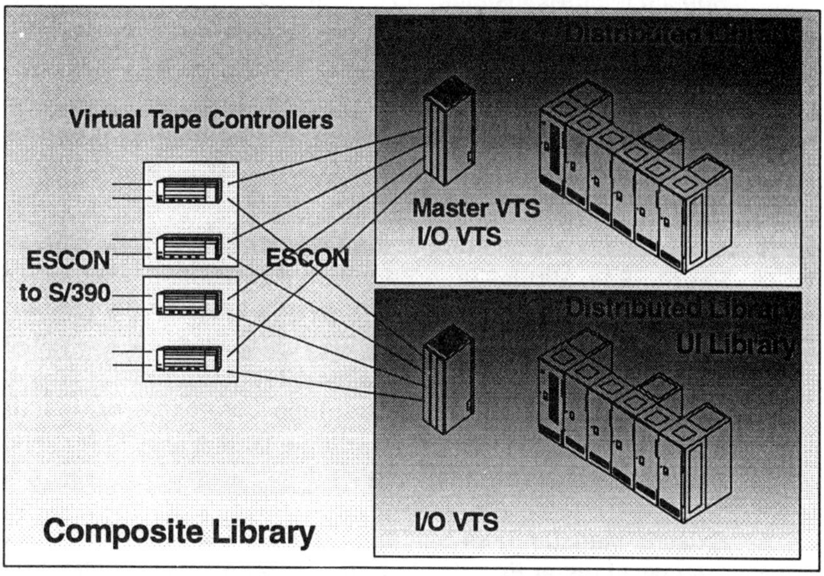

Figure 3. VTS Peer-to-Peer components

1.2.1 Magstar 3494 Model AX0 Virtual Tape Controller

The Model AX0 provides interconnection between two Magstar 3494 Model B18 Virtual Tape Servers with the Peer-to-Peer Copy features. It also provides two ESCON host attachments for sixteen drives of the Magstar Peer-to-Peer Virtual Tape Server. There must be four Magstar 3494 Model AX0 controllers in the configuration with each attaching to both 3494 Model B18s, giving a total of 64 virtual drives.

Each Magstar 3494 Model AX0 maintains synchronization of the copy of logical volumes, creates logical volume copies using large block transfers of compressed logical volumes, balances workload between the two Magstar Virtual Tape Servers, directs specific volume mounts to the Magstar Virtual Tape Server with a cached copy of the requested virtual volume, and displays the status and current configuration of the Peer-to-Peer VTS through a Web-based browser interface accessed through an Ethernet local area network connection.

1.2.2 Magstar 3494 Model CX0 Auxiliary Frame

The Model CX0 provides the housing and power for up to four Magstar 3494 Model AX0 Virtual Tape Controllers. Each Model CX0 can be configured with two or four Model AX0s.

1.2.3 Peer-to-Peer Copy features

Special features installed on both Magstar 3494 Model B18s in a Peer-to-Peer configuration provide automatic copies of virtual volumes. These features can be installed on existing VTS systems to upgrade them to a Peer-to-Peer VTS.

1.3 Independence and investment protection

In the instance when one of the Magstar Virtual Tape Servers in a Magstar Peer-to-Peer Virtual Tape Server configuration is taken off-line for maintenance, routine service, or even a system upgrade, all activity will be directed to the remaining Magstar Virtual Tape Server. When the Magstar Virtual Tape Server that was taken off-line returns to service, each of the Magstar 3494 Model AX0 Virtual Tape Controllers will resume copy operations to bring the logical volume copies in both Magstar Virtual Tape Servers back into synchronization.

Existing Magstar 3494 Model B18 Virtual Tape Servers can be upgraded to the new Magstar Peer-to-Peer Virtual Tape server configuration by adding the incremental hardware and a second Model B18 with the Peer-to-Peer Copy features. This protects the investment that many customers have already made in IBM Magstar technology.

1.4 A new way to improve tape operations

The Magstar Virtual Tape Server or the Magstar Peer-to-Peer Virtual Tape Server resides between a host processor and a Magstar 3494 Tape Library. To the host processor's operating system, either device appears to be a series of automated 3490E tape drives. The use of virtual drives significantly reduces the number of real drives needed to support the processing environment. Unlike real tape drives, however, the Magstar Virtual Tape Server uses RAID 5 disk arrays to cache data, then efficiently fills tape cartridges and files them in the Magstar 3494 Tape Library. All data transfers with the host processor are performed to or from the Tape Volume Cache at disk access speeds.

In addition, utilizing the full capacity of the Magstar 3590 cartridges can significantly reduce the requirement for additional tape drives, automation devices, media, and floor and shelf space.

1.4.1 Maximized data access

The Magstar Peer-to-Peer Virtual Tape Server is a major step in dealing with the ever-increasing need to maintain access to data 24 hours a day, 7 days a week, 365 days a year. Key components of the Magstar Peer-to-Peer Virtual Tape Server are duplicated to reduce single points of failure — a design that helps ensure that data remains accessible after a failure, during planned maintenance, or during system upgrades (Figure 4 shows a logical view of this concept).

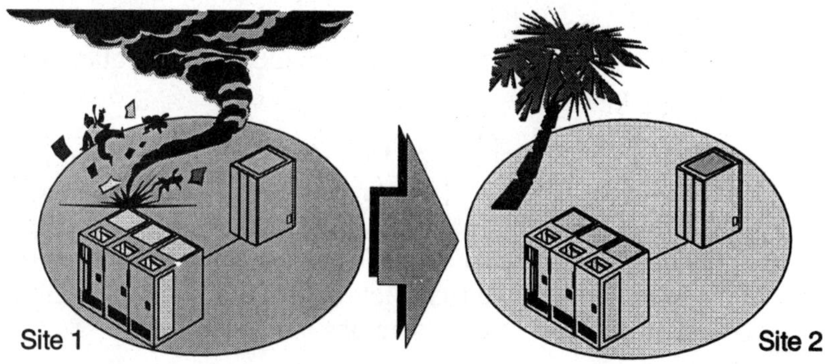

Figure 4. Peer-to-Peer design, logical view

Each Magstar 3494 Model B18 in a Magstar Peer-to-Peer Virtual Tape Server configuration continues to operate during scheduled or unscheduled service of the other Model B18. After a repair action, the system initiates the creation of second copies to bring both Magstar Virtual Tape Servers back into synchronization.

1.4.2 Electronic vaulting and remote operation

Because one of the Magstar Virtual Tape Servers can reside in a geographically separate location from the other, operations can continue even if either the local or remote facility is not operational. This design can virtually eliminate the need to physically transport data for disaster backup. The connections within a Magstar Peer-to-Peer Virtual Tape Server use ESCON channels, so Magstar Virtual Tape Servers can be physically separated by as much as the ESCON architecture allows. Refer to 4.6, “Peer-to-Peer VTS ESCON configurations” on page 72, for further discussion of the ESCON distance.

1.4.3 Software support

The Magstar Peer-to-Peer Virtual Tape Server operates in the OS/390 environment. Support is provided as a Small Programming Enhancement (SPE) for DFSMS/MVS 1.4 and 1.5 and for DFSMS 2.10. Toleration PTFs are provided for DFSMS/MVS 1.2 and higher.

At least one attached host must be running DFSMS/MVS 1.4 or higher with the Peer-to-Peer full support PTFs to enable the software's reliability and serviceability features. All other hosts attached to a Magstar Peer-to-Peer Virtual Tape Server must have a minimum level of DFSMS/MVS 1.2 with toleration maintenance.

A Peer-to-Peer VTS may be attached to VM/ESA or VSE/ESA guests of VM/ESA as long as there is also an OS/390 host attached, with the full support installed.

You monitor and control the Peer-to-Peer VTS using existing, standard host console commands and displays, the 3494 library manager panels, and, as additional tools, the IBM 3494 StorWatch Peer-to-Peer Specialist which provides Web-browser accessed pages for monitoring the Peer-to-Peer configuration and the IBM StorWatch Enterprise Tape Library Expert for detailed analysis of trends across many libraries.

Chapter 2. Peer-to-Peer VTS concepts

A single Model B18 VTS presents itself to the host as one logical library containing 32 or 64 virtual 3490E tape drives, if it is not integrated into a Peer-to-Peer configuration. In this book, we call a single Model B18 VTS that is not part of a Peer-to-Peer configuration a *stand-alone* Model B18 VTS.

The Peer-to-Peer VTS also presents itself to the host as one logical library containing 64 virtual 3490E tape drives, although the underlying hardware and the software implementation are different from the stand-alone Model B18 VTS. It is essential that you understand the terminology, the general concepts, and the process flow to allow for detailed installation planning, easy implementation, and full integration of the Peer-to-Peer VTS into your disaster recovery plans.

In this chapter, we describe the technical details and the internal logic of the Peer-to-Peer Virtual Tape Server. We explain the hardware components introduced with Peer-to-Peer VTS. We also give an overview of where the components of a Peer-to-Peer VTS can be located and which configurations are supported. We describe, in detail, new terms and expressions which are introduced with the Peer-to-Peer VTS and are used to describe the components and processes that allow for automated dual copy of virtual volumes in the VTS. We discuss these processes as well as the control points that allow you to influence the Peer-to-Peer VTS internal processing. Finally, we summarize performance considerations specific for the Peer-to-Peer VTS.

For details about hardware features and software implementation of the Peer-to-Peer VTS, see Chapter 5, “Preinstallation planning” on page 91. For a detailed description of the VTS feature codes related to a stand-alone Model B18 VTS, please refer to *IBM Magstar Virtual Tape Server: Planning, Implementing, and Monitoring*, SG24-2229, and the *Magstar IBM 3494 Tape Library Introduction and Planning Guide,* GA32-0279.

2.1 Hardware overview

Every VTS is always integrated into an IBM 3494 tape library which provides all necessary elements to manage automated cartridge and physical tape drive handling. All the components needed for automation are integrated in the IBM 3494-L1x Control Unit Frame. In addition to the Model L1x frame, the minimum configuration of a stand-alone Model B18 VTS consists of these hardware components:

© Copyright IBM Corp. 2000

- One 3494-D12 frame installed inside an IBM 3494 tape library, including the Magstar 3590 tape drives for exclusive use of the VTS. Three to six Magstar 3590 Model B1A or Model E1A can be installed in the D12 frame.
- One 3494-B18 frame installed up to 14m away from the IBM 3494 tape library. The tape volume cache, the VTS controller, and the ESCON and/or SCSI channel adapters are all located in the B18 frame.

In a Peer-to-Peer VTS environment, two VTSs residing in two different IBM 3494 libraries must be interconnected to build the Peer-to-Peer configuration. Additional hardware components are required to allow for automated dual copy of virtual volumes which are written to the Peer-to-Peer VTS.

2.1.1 Peer-to-Peer VTS hardware components

Figure 5 shows all the hardware components required for a Peer-to-Peer VTS installation.

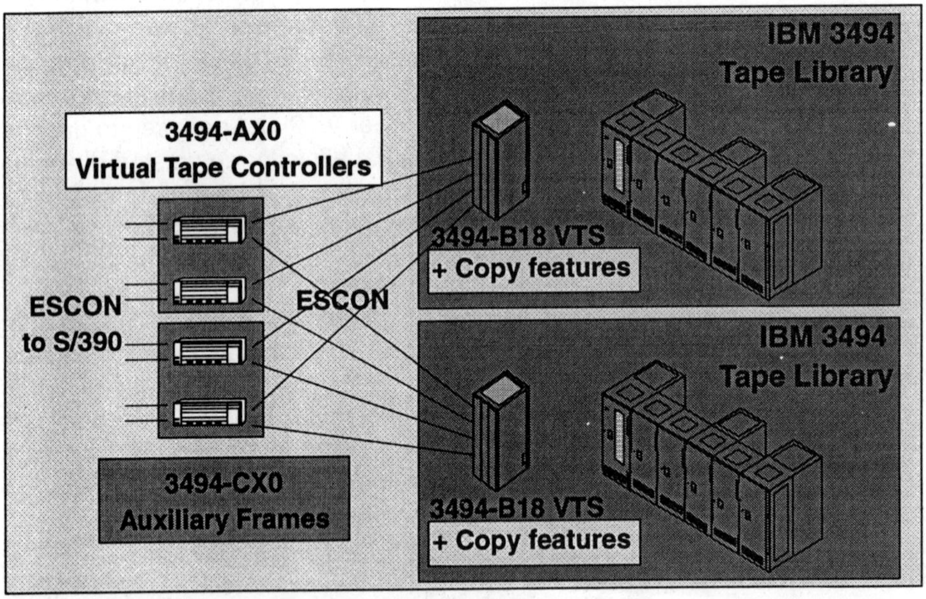

Figure 5. Peer-to-Peer VTS hardware components

The two boxes on the right-hand side of Figure 5 show the elements that are also required for the stand-alone Model B18 VTS. The *Copy Features* plus the components shown on the left-hand side of Figure 5, are required to integrate two stand-alone Model B18 VTSs into a Peer-to-Peer VTS. A Model B18 VTS with the Peer-to-Peer Copy features installed is an independently operating distributed server node in a Peer-to-Peer VTS.

The minimum configuration of a Peer-to-Peer VTS consists of:

- Two IBM 3494 tape libraries, each of them containing one B18 VTS, which has the Peer-to-Peer Copy features installed, and one D12 frame dedicated to each of the Model B18 VTS
- Four IBM 3494 Model AX0 Virtual Tape Controllers (VTC)
- One or two IBM 3494-CX0 Auxiliary frames

2.1.2 Model B18 Peer-to-Peer Copy features

The Peer-to-Peer Copy features enable the Model B18 VTS to operate in a Peer-to-Peer VTS configuration. For installation of the Copy features, each Model B18 VTS in the Peer-to-Peer configuration must fulfill these requirements:

- Each Model B18 VTS must be installed in a separate IBM 3494 library.
- The Extended High Performance Option (EHPO) and the Performance Accelerator feature (PAF) must be installed.
- Four Extended Performance ESCON channels are required. Additional ESCON channel attachments or SCSI attachments are not supported.
- The tape volume cache must have a capacity of 144 GB or 288 GB, if 9-GB disks are installed in the drawers. If 36-GB disks are installed, the TVC capacity can be 216 GB, 432 GB, 864 GB, or 1,728 GB. For more details on the available TVC configurations, please refer to 5.2.1.4, “Tape volume cache” on page 95.
- Four to six Magstar 3590 tape drives must be installed in the associated Model D12 frame.
- SCSI attachment on the Model B18 VTS is not supported and, if installed, needs to be removed for migration to a Peer-to-Peer VTS.
- The Import/Export function provided as part of the Advanced Function feature (feature #4000) on the Model B18 VTS is not supported for a Peer-to-Peer VTS and, if installed, is disabled during migration to the Peer-to-Peer VTS.

In addition, it is strongly recommended that the two VTSs have the same cache size, same number of physical drives and same model of physical drives.

The Peer-to-Peer Copy features enhance the functionality of the Model B18 VTS by providing the capabilities described below:

- Both Model B18 VTSs in a Peer-to-Peer configuration store and manage the data (known as *tokens*) required to keep track of the status of a virtual volume.
- Additional internal control commands enable the Model B18 VTS to process these tokens and to enable message broadcasting between the Model AX0 controllers.
- Additional data transfer commands allow compressed large block transfers for the copy operation
- Additional virtual devices are defined internally to be used for message broadcasting and copy operations.
- Tape volume cache usage is enhanced by providing expedited copying to the stacked volumes of the secondary copy, thus freeing up space in the tape volume cache.

One of the Model B18 VTSs in a Peer-to-Peer configuration functions as a focal point for commands relating to volumes and drives in the Peer-to-Peer VTS. For more details, see Section 2.3, “Terminology and definitions” on page 16.

2.1.3 Model AX0 Virtual Tape Controller

The IBM 3494 Model AX0 Virtual Tape Controller is a new component introduced with Peer-to-Peer VTS. Figure 6 highlights the fact that the Model AX0 controller is not installed in the B18 frame, but rather in a separate CX0 frame.

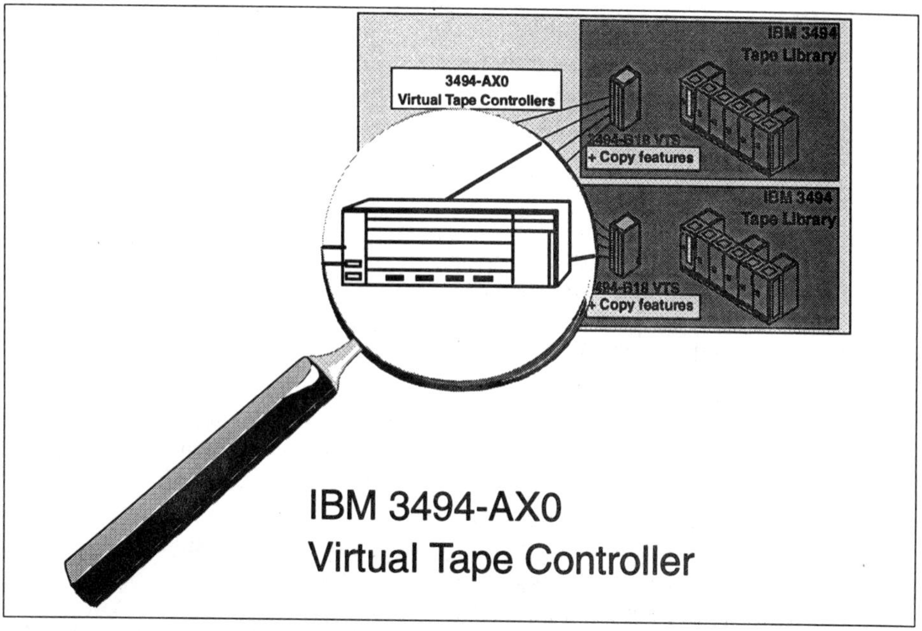

Figure 6. IBM 3494 Model AX0 Virtual Tape Controller

Each Model AX0 Virtual Tape Controller provides a total of four ESCON channel attachments:

- Two ESCON channels attach to the host systems. The host systems no longer attach directly to the B18 VTS, but instead to the AX0 controllers.
- Two ESCON channels attach to two Model B18 VTSs in the Peer-to-Peer configuration. Each B18 VTS attaches to each of the AX0 controllers through one ESCON channel.

A single Model AX0 controller presents itself to the host as one 3490E tape control unit with sixteen 3490E tape drives. In order to allow a single host to allocate all 64 virtual device addresses of a Peer-to-Peer VTS, the host must be attached to all four Model AX0 controllers in the Peer-to-Peer configuration. The attachment options are:

- Direct attachment
- Attachment through ESCON directors
- Attachment using EMIF channels

All communication between the OS/390 host systems and the Peer-to-Peer VTS (including the distributed libraries) is through the Model AX0 controller ESCON channel attachments. The Model AX0 controllers combine the status of the underlying physical libraries to provide a logical view of the Peer-to-Peer VTS to the host.

The Model AX0 controllers use a broadcast mechanism to communicate with the other Model AX0 controllers in the Peer-to-Peer VTS configuration. The communication is through the Model B18 VTSs. Each controller periodically broadcasts heartbeat information to the other controllers.

Each Model AX0 controller in a Peer-to-Peer VTS:

- Maintains synchronization of the dual copies of logical volumes and maintains volume integrity between the two Model B18 VTSs.
- Creates logical volume copies using chained 64 KB block transfers of compressed logical volumes.
- Selects, for each mount request, which VTS will process that mount request from the host.
- Operates in non-preferred or in preferred mode when selecting the VTS on which to mount a virtual volume in response to a host mount request. The Model AX0:
  - Balances workload across both Model B18 VTSs by directing host mounts to the VTS which is least busy, when operating in non-preferred mode.
  - Directs the mount to the specified VTS when operating in preferred mode.
- Directs all activity to the remaining VTS, if one of the Model B18 VTS is offline.
- Resumes dual copy operation to synchronize both Model B18 VTSs after one of the VTSs has been brought online.

In addition to the tasks which each single Model AX0 controller performs, there are some tasks which require more than one Model AX0 controller. All Model AX0 controllers in a Peer-to-Peer VTS, as a group:

- Elect one of the VTSs to be the focal point or master VTS of the Peer-to-Peer VTS.
- Control the switchover to the other VTS, if the master VTS fails.

- Work in the same mode of operation for creation of secondary copies:
  - In *immediate copy mode*, where the secondary copy of a virtual volume is created, before completion of rewind/unload of the primary copy of the virtual volume.
  - In *deferred copy mode*, where the secondary copy of a virtual volume is scheduled after completion of rewind/unload of the primary copy of the virtual volume.

We explain the copy modes in detail in Section 2.4, "Creating the secondary copy of a virtual volume" on page 19

Each Model AX0 controller is an independently operating distributed node within the Peer-to-Peer VTS and continues to operate during the planned or unplanned outage of another Model AX0 controller. For uninterrupted data access, at least one of the AX0 controllers must be active.

2.1.4 Model CX0 Auxiliary Frame

The IBM 3494 Model CX0 Auxiliary Frame has the same dimensions as a Model B18 frame and contains two power control compartments (PCC) each with its own power cord to allow connection to two power sources. The Model CX0 frame provides power and housing for two or four Model AX0 controllers.

Depending on whether all components of the Peer-to-Peer VTS are installed in one location or in two different locations, one or two Model CX0 frames are required. If one Model CX0 frame is used, all four Model AX0 controllers are installed in this frame. With two Model CX0 frames, each of them contains two Model AX0 controllers. Figure 7 illustrates these two different installation options.

2.2 Peer-to-Peer VTS location considerations

The Model AX0 controllers in a Peer-to-Peer configuration can be located up to 43 km away from the hosts. The B18 VTSs can be located up to 26 km away from the Model CX0 frames with the installed AX0 controllers. Based on the distance specifications, two basic installation options are available:

Local installation:

Both VTS subsystems and all four Model AX0 controllers are installed locally. All Model AX0 controllers are installed in one CX0 Auxiliary frame. All hosts systems attach to all Model AX0 controllers.This scenario is shown in the top part of Figure 7.

Remote installation:

The Peer-to-Peer configuration is installed in two separate sites. Each site has one VTS subsystem, one Auxiliary frame, and two Model AX0 controllers installed. Host systems attach to the Model AX0 controllers installed at their site. This scenario is shown in the bottom part of Figure 7. For details on ESCON channel attachment options of the Peer-to-Peer VTS, please see 4.6, “Peer-to-Peer VTS ESCON configurations” on page 72 and Appendix A, “ESCON configurations” on page 217.

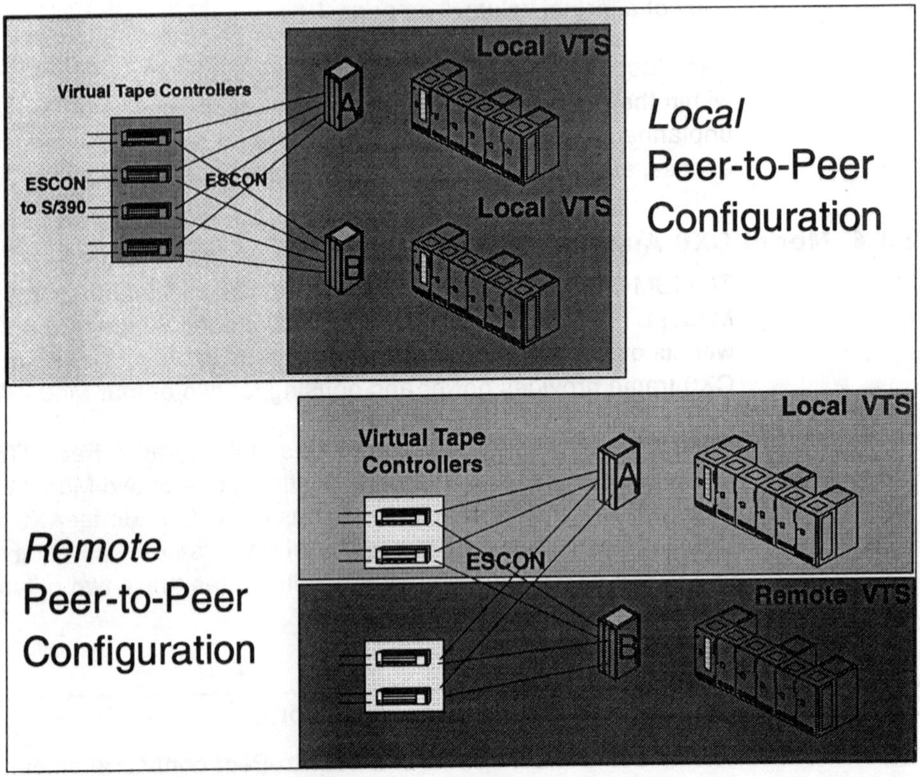

Figure 7. Local and remote Peer-to-Peer configuration

It is very likely that, in a remote Peer-to-Peer-configuration, a host system from one location is only attached to the Model AX0 controllers installed on site. If a host system only attaches to one Model AX0, only 16 virtual tape drives are available to this host system, and the AX0 becomes a single point of failure. If the host system attaches to both Model AX0 controllers on site, 32 virtual tape drives are available to the host.

Note

For availability reasons, every host system using a Peer-to-Peer VTS should always attach to more than one Model AX0 controller.

A single IBM 3494 tape library supports up to two VTS subsystems. The two scenarios shown in Figure 7 are *single Peer-to-Peer configurations*. For *dual Peer-to-Peer configurations*, one IBM 3494 tape library may include up to two VTS subsystems, as shown in Figure 8.

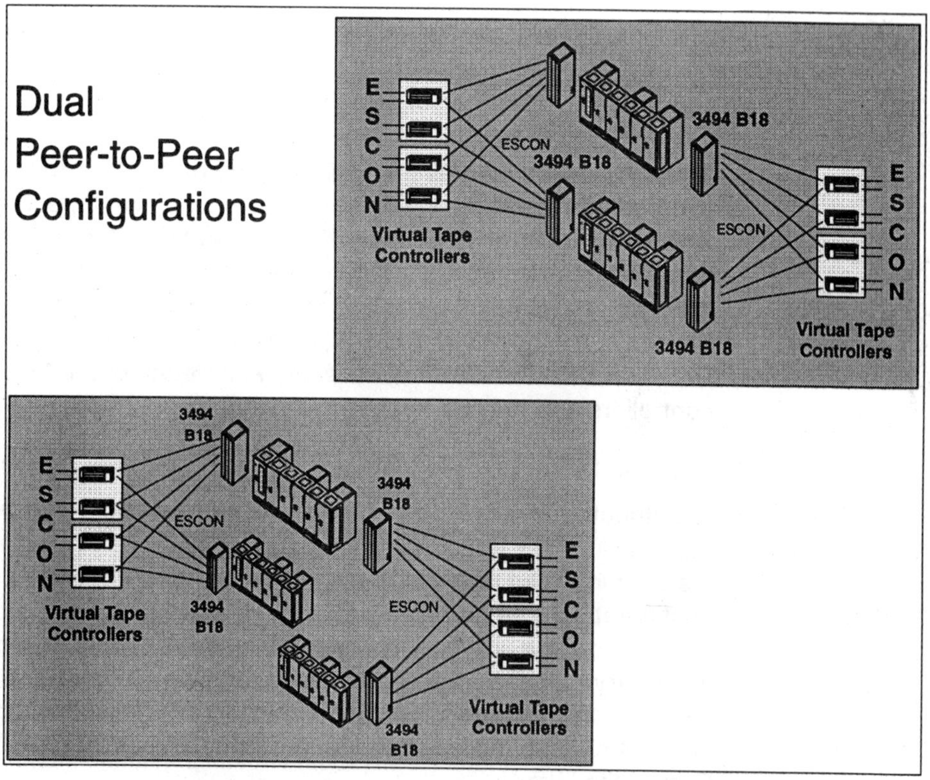

Figure 8. Dual Peer-to-Peer configurations

The installation option to choose depends on a variety of criteria such as, for example, the organization of your data center, the number of different locations, the distance between data centers, and data availability and disaster recovery requirements.

For details about integration of the Peer-to-Peer VTS configuration into existing disaster recovery and high availability implementations, please refer to Chapter 4, "Availability configurations" on page 63.

2.3 Terminology and definitions

With the introduction of the Peer-to-Peer VTS, new processes and mechanisms are required to ensure virtual volume and data integrity as well as resynchronization of the Peer-to-Peer VTS after planned or unplanned outages of the different components. In this section we explain the new terms that are used with the Peer-to-Peer VTS.

The terms used with the Peer-to-Peer VTS and shown in Figure 9 on page 18 are listed and defined below.

Composite Library:

The composite library is the logical image of the Peer-to-Peer VTS which is presented to the host. The host sees one logical tape library with four 3490E tape control units, each of them with 16 IBM 3490E tape drives and attached through two ESCON channel attachments. The composite library presents the same image to the MVS host as a single VTS does. It is defined to the host in a similar way to the definition of a stand-alone VTS. Note that the host does not have any knowledge of the Model AX0 controllers and they do not need to be defined to the host.

Distributed Library:

A distributed library (or distributed VTS) is a physical IBM 3494 library in the Peer-to-Peer VTS which includes a Model B18 VTS with the Copy features installed. Two distributed libraries are required in a Peer-to-Peer configuration. The host has sufficient knowledge about the distributed libraries to allow appropriate console message handling of messages from the library manager of a distributed library. On the host, the distributed library is only defined to SMS. It is defined using the existing ISMF panels and has no tape devices defined; the tape devices were defined for the Composite library.

Master VTS:

The master VTS is one of the Model B18 VTSs in a Peer-to-Peer configuration. The designation of a master VTS is necessary to serialize access to logical volumes within the Peer-to-Peer VTS. Certain commands must be sent to the master VTS to ensure data integrity and volume consistency within the subsystem.

These commands are referred to as *master required commands*:

- Commands that cause a volume to be queued for a mount
- Commands that change the library manager volume category assignment of a volume
- Commands that change the device category assignment
- Requests for volume or device data

The master VTS is the focal point for synchronizing the mounting of volumes to virtual drives, and for the selection of a volume serial number (volser) from a scratch category in response to a scratch mount request. Most display commands from the host are also directed to the master VTS, except for commands that are processed by the UI Distributed Library (insert category data). The master VTS is determined at initialization of the Peer-to-Peer VTS by the Model AX0 virtual tape controllers. If one of the commands above cannot be processed through the master VTS, a successful switchover must be completed and the command issued to the *new* master before the command can be completed.

I/O VTS:

The I/O VTS is the Model B18 VTS that processes the host I/O commands (such as read and write commands) for a certain virtual volume. The I/O VTS is determined by the Model AX0 controller during mount processing (load balancing function). Both VTSs may operate as I/O VTSs for different sets of volumes, determined at mount time for a logical volume. Hence, one VTS may be the I/O VTS for one mount of a logical volume and the other VTS could be chosen as the I/O VTS for a later mount, assuming that the volume is no longer in cache.

UI Distributed Library:

The User Interface (UI) Distributed Library is the distributed library that allows you to insert logical volumes into a Peer-to-Peer VTS. The time and date of all Model AX0 controllers is synchronized with the date and time of the library manager of the UI distributed library. The UI distributed library is defined at installation time and can be either of the distributed libraries; typically, it would be the local library.

Figure 9 shows an example of how these terms apply to the hardware components of the Peer-to-Peer VTS.

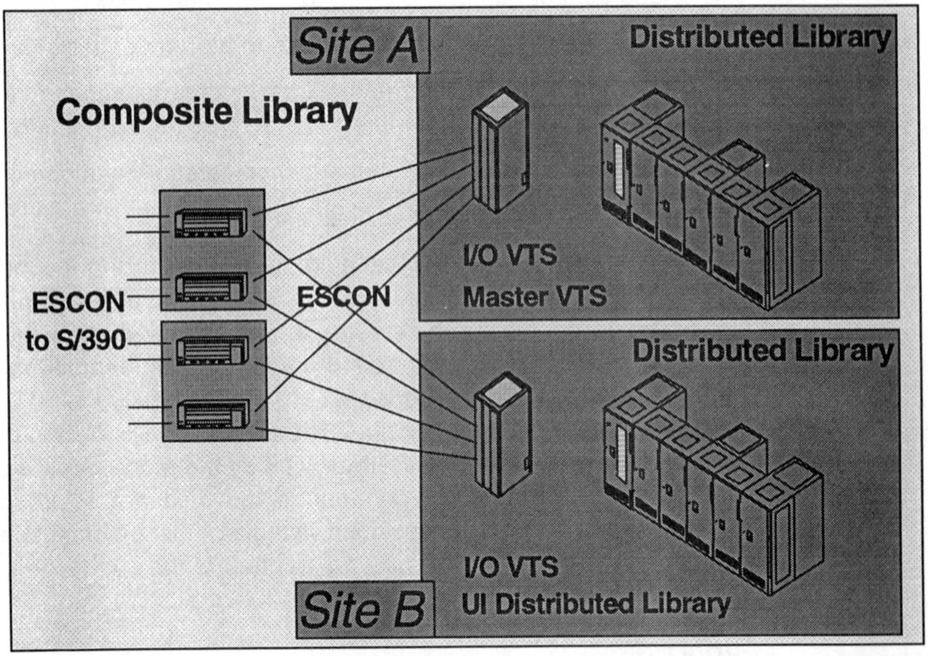

Figure 9. Peer-to-Peer VTS specific terms

The example in Figure 9 shows that the *distributed libraries,* located at *Site A* and *Site B,* are connected in a Peer-to-Peer VTS configuration. The Model AX0 controllers present the logical view to the host as one *composite library.* The distributed library located at Site B has been defined to function as the *UI distributed library.* The *distributed VTS* at Site A has been determined to be the *master VTS*. Both distributed VTSs are working as *I/O VTS.*

In addition to the terms shown in Figure 9, the following definitions are used when describing the processes and components of a Peer-to-Peer VTS configuration:

Broadcast Device:

In each distributed VTS, four internal device addresses are defined and used by the Model AX0 controllers to send broadcast messages via the distributed VTS. All Model AX0 controllers together use one shared pool of four broadcast devices per distributed VTS.

Copy Device:

In each distributed VTS, twelve internal device addresses are defined and used to perform the volume copies. Each Model AX0 controller has three out of a total of twelve available copy devices assigned. Copy devices are not shared between the Model AX0 controllers.

Token:

A token is the data which is stored in the databases of both distributed VTSs, and which is used to keep track of the level and status of each volume within the Peer-to-Peer VTS.

Token reconciliation:

The process to compare tokens stored in each VTS to determine required copy updates and token synchronization, is called token reconciliation. Token reconciliation is performed at power up and at periodic intervals.

Hot Token List:

The hot token list is held by each Model AX0 controller. A hot token is created when a change has occurred to a virtual volume and the token could not be updated on one of the distributed VTSs. The hot token list is maintained to ensure that the latest version of a virtual volume is used even if one of the distributed VTSs is not operational. Refer to 7.3.7, "Logical volume status" on page 165 for a sample display of this information.

Token Protected:

A set of data transfer and tape control commands that cannot be performed until the tokens on both distributed VTSs have been updated. This prevents the Peer-to-Peer VTS from using a down level version of a logical volume if a failure or switchover has occurred.

Disconnected Volume:

A disconnected volume is a virtual volume that is in the progress of having data on it changed, which causes a version of it on one distributed VTS to be down level until a secondary copy has been created.

2.4 Creating the secondary copy of a virtual volume

The Peer-to-Peer VTS allows you to select when to create the secondary copy of a virtual volume: immediately during close processing (immediate copy mode), or asynchronously at a later time. Immediate or deferred copy mode of operation are configured by the IBM service representative during setup of the Model AX0 controllers.

The default mode, set when the Model AX0 controllers are shipped, is immediate copy mode. The mode of operation may be changed at any time; however, this must be done by a service representative using a service interface to a Model AX0 controller.

All Model AX0 controllers in one Peer-to-Peer VTS must use the same mode of operation. A mode change requires that all of the virtual devices of each Model AX0 controller must be varied offline to allow the service representative to bring down a Model AX0 controller, change the mode, and restore the Model AX0 controller to normal operation. Although all the AX0 controllers must use the same mode, only one controller's mode is changed at a time.

2.4.1 Volume close and copy process

The following example shows how the secondary copy of virtual volume V00001 is created. We assume that the primary copy of V00001 was directed to VTS0.

1. The host completes writing to V00001 and close processing starts. As part of close processing, the host issues a rewind unload command.
2. The model AX0 controller to which the virtual drive allocated on the host is defined issues a rewind unload command to both distributed VTSs.
3. After receiving EOV complete from both distributed VTSs, the Model AX0 controller adds V00001 to one of its copy queues, depending on the copy mode.
4. In deferred copy mode, the Model AX0 controller presents rewind unload complete to the host at this point. In immediate copy mode, the copy process is started.

In Figure 10, we show the communication between the VTS components during close processing. The numbers on the arrows refer to the step numbering used in the list above.

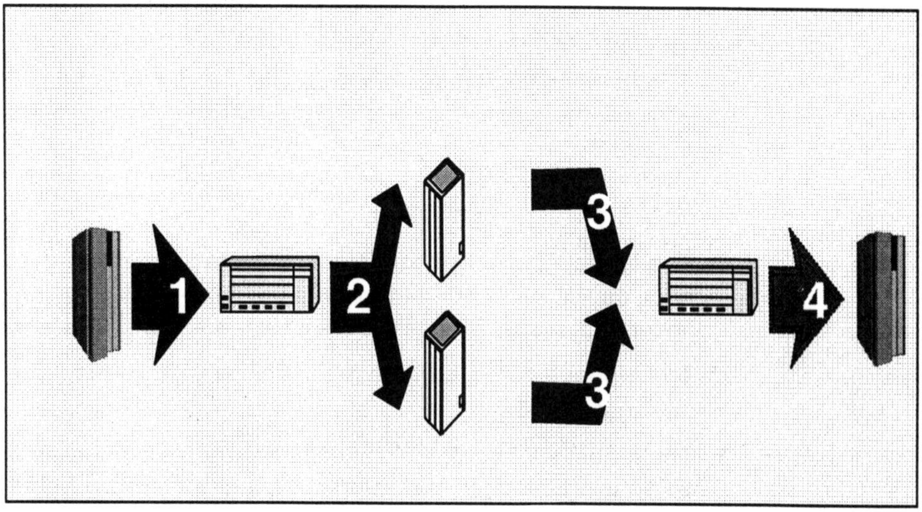

Figure 10. Volume close process

The steps to create the secondary copy of a virtual volume are shown in Figure 11.

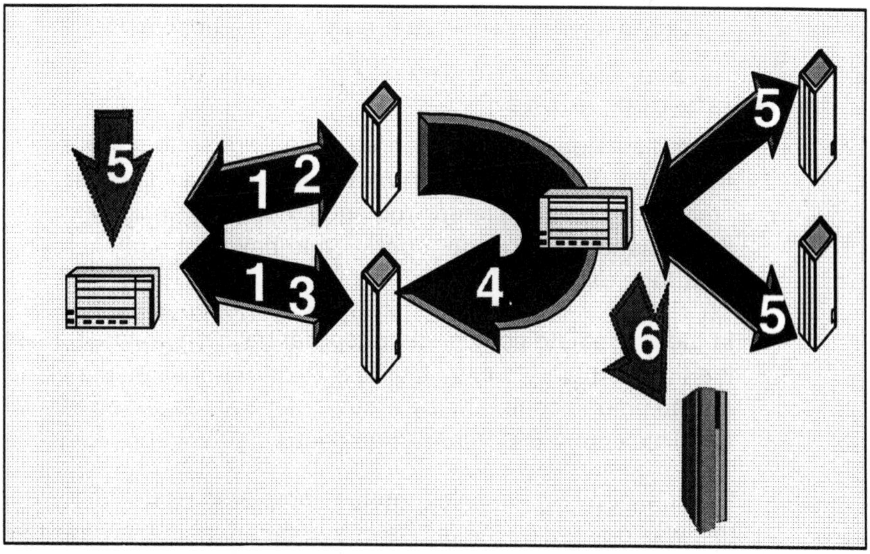

Figure 11. Volume copy process

The process to create the secondary copy of virtual volume V00001 is started by the Model AX0 controller which processed the mount command for that virtual volume if in immediate copy mode. In deferred copy mode, any AX0 may initiate the copy. Creating the secondary copy involves the steps outlined in Figure 11, and which are described below:

1. The Model AX0 controller checks with both distributed VTSs regarding whether the tokens for volume V00001 are valid. The tokens must indicate that VTS0 has the most recent copy of V00001 and that this one should be used as a source. If the tokens do not reflect the need for a copy, then the copy process is terminated.
2. The Model AX0 controller establishes read access to volume V00001 on a copy device of VTS0. If the volume is currently being copied to a stacked volume, the copy process to the stacked volume is terminated.
3. The Model AX0 controller establishes write access to V00001 on a copy device in VTS1.
4. The Model AX0 controller begins copying the content of V00001 from VTS0 to VTS1. After the volume content has been copied, the Model AX0 controller disables its access to the virtual volumes on both VTSs.
5. The Model AX0 controller initiates the updates of the token for volume V00001 on both VTS0 and VTS1.
6. In immediate copy mode, the Model AX0 controller presents rewind/unload complete to the host when the copy process completes. This is signaled whether the copy is successful or not.

2.4.2 Immediate copy mode

Immediate copy mode of operation ensures that, under normal conditions, two identical copies of a virtual volume exist, as soon as the rewind unload command has completed. You should consider using immediate copy mode, if it is mandatory for your operation to have the highest level of protection for your tape data.

In the immediate copy mode of operation in an unconstrained environment, the time required to copy a virtual volume will delay the completion of the rewind unload command by around 80 seconds, for an 800 MB volume that is full. This time will increase in a constrained environment.

If a dual copy operation cannot be completed immediately, it is very likely that this was caused by the failure of a component in the Peer-to-Peer VTS. Upon a component failure, the immediate copy mode may operate as if in deferred copy mode until the failing component has been brought back online. For details on the possible recovery scenarios, please refer to Chapter 7, "Operating and using the Peer-to-Peer VTS" on page 153.

If a dual copy operation is delayed, the host is notified with a warning message (CBR3787E) that indicates that immediate copy mode operations are deferred in a specific composite library. The warning message is retained until all the immediate mode copy operations that were deferred have completed.

Once the failing component has been brought back online, the outstanding copies are processed to synchronize both distributed VTSs as soon as possible.

2.4.3 Deferred copy mode

In deferred copy mode, the secondary copy is created at some time after the host finished processing the primary copy. When a deferred copy operation is processed, the amount of channel bandwidth it is given between the Model AX0 controller and the distributed VTSs is such that it has minimal interference with host channel bandwidth requirements. Host bandwidth requirements are given priority over copy bandwidth needs. This allows the host to use maximum bandwidth during peak periods and the Peer-to-Peer VTS to catch up on the copies during periods of low host activity.

The AX0 controller, which has the task of making a copy of a particular deferred volume, checks the time which has elapsed since completion of the host rewind/unload operation for the volume. If this elapsed time is greater than the Deferred Copy Priority Threshold, the copy operation will occur with a priority which allows equal contention for processing cycles with current host I/O activity. The resolution of the elapsed time comparison is one minute. If the elapsed time is less than the Deferred Copy Priority Threshold, the copy will proceed with the normal deferred copy priority. During periods of high host activity, deferred copy operations are performed slowly, and the number of queued copy operations grows. When the host workload decreases, the performance of the deferred copies increases, and the number of queued copy operations will decrease.

The low priority for copy operations continues until the space occupied by virtual volumes in the tape volume cache of a VTS reaches a certain threshold. To avoid virtual volumes being removed from the tape volume cache before they have been copied to the other VTS, the deferred copy operations will be given higher I/O priority.

Figure 12 illustrates two reasons for increasing the copy priority when operating in deferred copy mode of operation:

- If the tape volume cache reaches a certain threshold for the space occupied by virtual volumes which have not had a dual copy made in the other VTS, the completion of the rewind/unload commands following host write operations is delayed. This effectively throttles host writes and allows more dual copies to be completed. This is indicated on the left-hand side of Figure 12.

While the bandwidth available for host I/O operations is decreased during this time, copy operations continue at a higher priority until a lower threshold is hit which removes the throttling delay described above.

- The copy priority for a single virtual volume is increased after the time defined for the *deferred copy priority threshold time* has passed. This is indicated on the right-hand side of Figure 12.

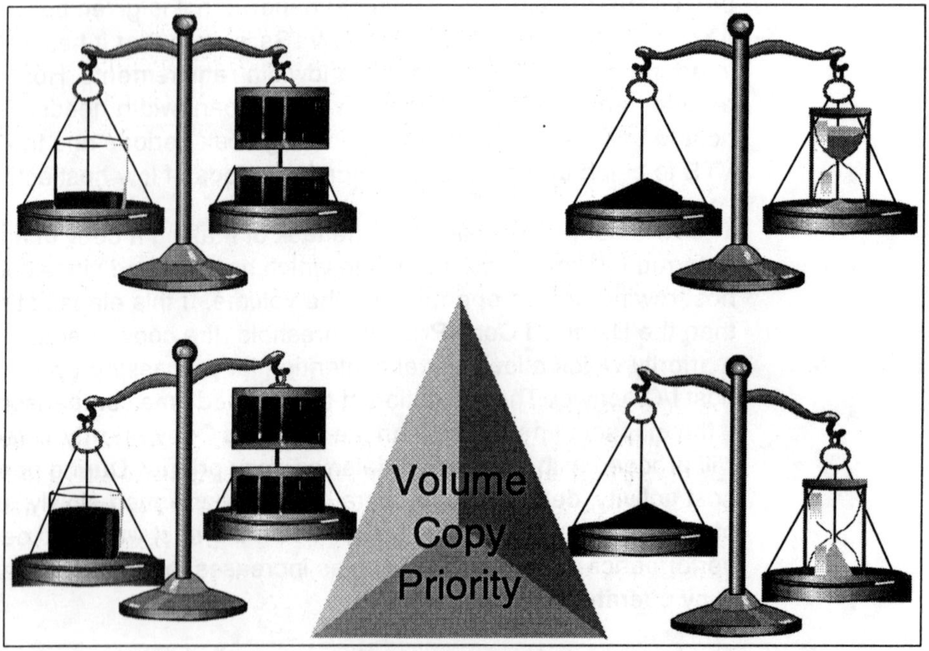

Figure 12. Increasing volume copy priority

The default for the deferred copy priority threshold time, indicated by the hourglass in Figure 12, is 8 hours. It is set by the service representative during setup of the Model AX0 controllers and cannot be changed dynamically.

You can select a value of 0 to 24 hours for the deferred copy priority threshold. This value is set by the service representative.

In order to avoid recalls for virtual volumes which have not yet been copied, the size of the tape volume cache should be configured to be large enough to allow all virtual volumes written or modified during the peak period to stay in the tape volume cache. If the TVC size is too small, this may decrease the overall host Peer-to-Peer VTS throughput.

2.5 Workload balancing and VTS preferencing

Workload balancing in a Peer-to-Peer VTS is performed on two levels:

1. On the host system, when allocating a tape drive. This allocation determines which Model AX0 controller is used to perform the mount. We explain the allocation algorithm in 2.5.1, "Host based workload balancing" on page 25.
2. On the Model AX0 controller, when selecting the I/O VTS to process this mount. This selection determines where the primary copy of a virtual volume is written to. We explain the selection algorithm, and how you can influence it, in 2.5.2, "Peer-to-Peer VTS workload balancing" on page 29.

The overall objective of workload balancing is to maximize the overall throughput of the subsystem from the using host's perspective. The workload to be considered within the Peer-to-Peer VTS is the workload from and to the host as well as the copy operations between both distributed VTSs.

2.5.1 Host based workload balancing

The host allocation algorithm is important for a Peer-to-Peer VTS. With a stand-alone VTS, it is not necessary to distribute the mounts evenly across all defined virtual tape devices and tape control units to achieve the maximum throughput because all tape drives are available though all defined channel paths. Any control unit path can access the total bandwidth available from the stand-alone VTS. Figure 13 shows the logical view for the stand-alone VTS.

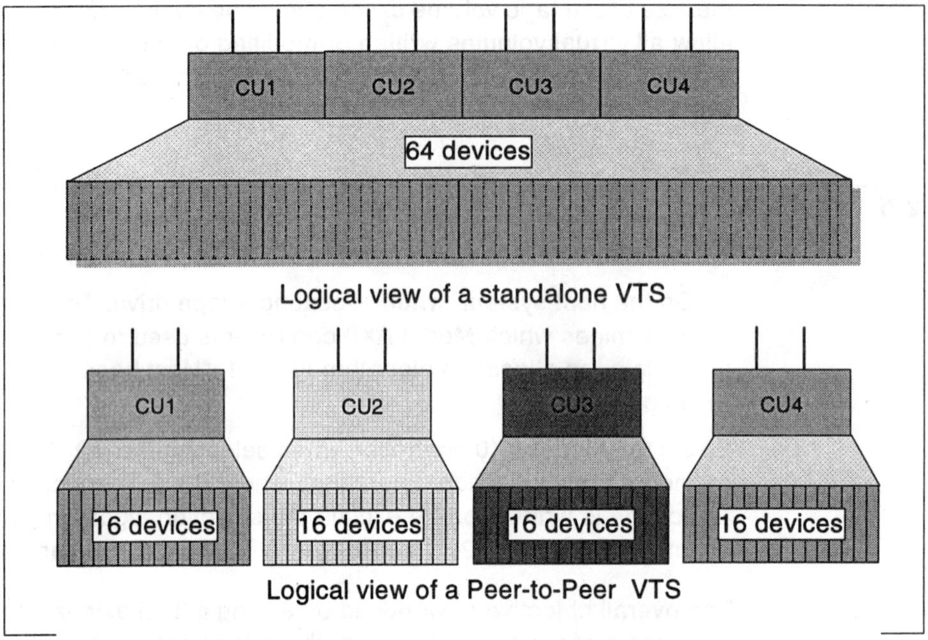

Figure 13. Standalone and Peer-to-Peer VTS virtual CUs and devices

In comparison to the logical view for the stand-alone VTS, Figure 13 shows the boundaries in a Peer-to-Peer VTS configuration. Each Model AX0 controller represents a single 3490 tape control unit with two channel paths and 16 tape drives, and only has access to a quarter of the total VTS bandwidth. In order to allow the peak performance of the Peer-to-Peer VTS, the workload must be distributed evenly across the four Model AX0 controllers. The Peer-to-Peer VTS, in this respect, is similar to four physical tape control units, each of them having their own tape devices and channel paths. Therefore, the host allocation algorithm is important for the overall performance of the Peer-to-Peer VTS. We will look at the implications for JES2 and JES3 environments.

2.5.1.1 Tape allocation in JES2 environments

Under DFSMS/MVS with JES2 or JES3 with MVS managed (non-JES3 managed) devices, MVS allocation routines are used for tape drive allocation.

For scratch mount requests, MVS allocation attempts to randomize the use of the drives in a library. For the Peer-to-Peer VTS, this refers to all 64 virtual device addresses.

For specific mount requests, subsystem affinity is used in the Peer-to-Peer VTS. The example shown in Figure 14 summarizes the process to direct a specific mount request to the Model AX0 controller with the least drives currently used.

The first Model AX0 controller (CU1) currently has five virtual drives allocated. It is the last one in the list, because it has the most drives allocated.

The second and the fourth Model AX0 controllers (CU2 and CU4) each have four drives allocated. They are listed in sequence, because they have the same number of virtual drives currently allocated.

The third Model AX0 controller (CU3) has three drives allocated. It is the first in the list because it has the fewest virtual tape drives allocated at this point in time.

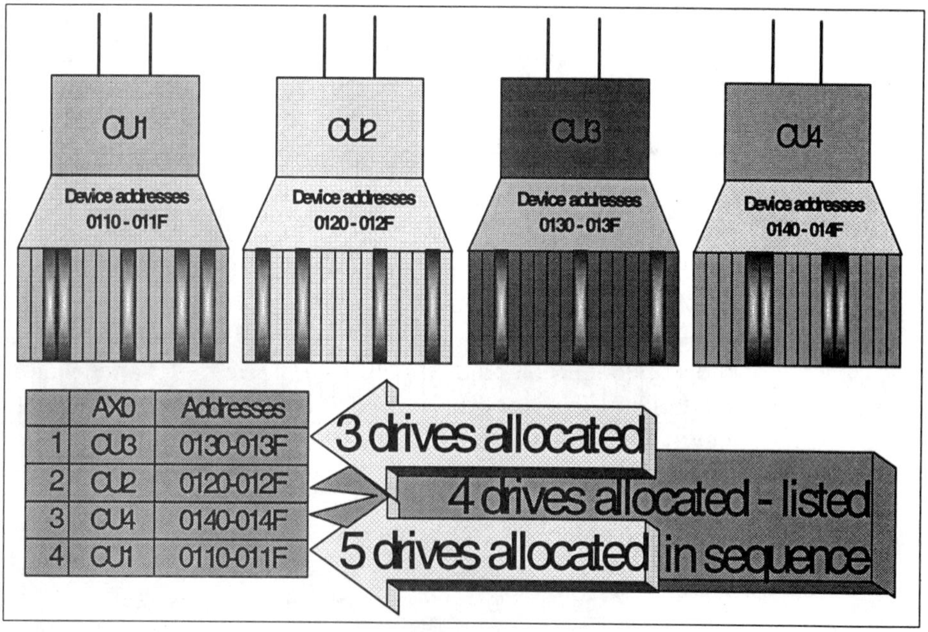

Figure 14. Subsystem affinity usage for a JES2 environment

Prior to issuing the mount request for a specific volume, the host obtains a subsystem affinity list of the composite library. The Model AX0 controller processing the request builds the subsystem affinity list based on the current workload of each Model AX0 controller.

The Model AX0 controller with the least number of mounted devices is the first subsystem in the list. MVS will then try and allocate a device from the first subsystem in the list. If a device from that subsystem is not currently available, MVS allocation will try to allocate from the next subsystem in the list. Figure 14 shows an example of the order in which the Model AX0 controllers are reported to the host. Device addresses are not reported to the host, only the subsystem IDs representing the Model AX0 controllers. Device addresses as listed in the table of Figure 14 are shown for clarification only.

2.5.1.2 Tape allocation in JES3 environments

In a JES3 environment, where MVS allocation is not used, JES3 attempts to spread scratch mount requests across all library devices.

For specific mounts, subsystem affinity cannot be used. In a JES3 environment, where JES3-managed devices get assigned at pre-execution time before MVS allocation is invoked, a different approach can be used. JES3 can be setup, through definition of ADDRSORT=NO in its INISH deck, to use the devices in the defined order, evenly distributing workload across the AX0 controllers. Figure 15 shows the order in which JES3 DEVICE statements must be defined.

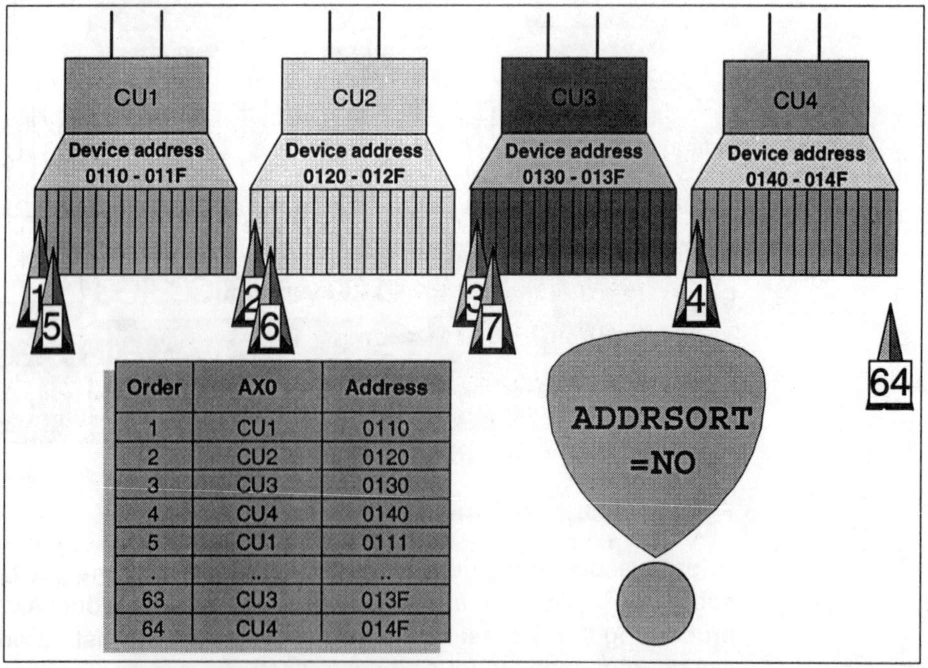

Order	AX0	Address
1	CU1	0110
2	CU2	0120
3	CU3	0130
4	CU4	0140
5	CU1	0111
.	..	..
63	CU3	013F
64	CU4	014F

Figure 15. JES3 device order for specific mounts

As shown in Figure 15, the first device address in the list is 0110 from the first Model AX0 controller, the second device address in the list is 0120 from the second controller, and so on. The last device address in the list is 014F for the highest device address of the fourth Model AX0 controller. Based on this setup, specific mounts are spread across all Model AX0 controllers as the device allocation starts from the top of the list until it finds one that is available.

For detailed information on defining the JES3 INISH deck, please refer to Section 6.3.2, "JES3 initialization deck definition" on page 128.

2.5.2 Peer-to-Peer VTS workload balancing

During processing of a mount request, the Model AX0 controller selects one of the distributed VTSs as the I/O VTS which results in the primary copy of a virtual volume being directed to the selected distributed VTS. The selection of the I/O VTS is based on the following information in the listed order:

1. **Component availability**

   If a distributed VTS or a path to a distributed VTS is not available, then the Model AX0 controller will select the remaining VTS, if it has valid data on it. This selection criteria will apply, if, for example, one of the distributed VTSs is in service preparation mode.

2. **Volume tokens**

   The token data is read from both distributed VTSs as soon as the volser to be mounted is known. If one token indicates that it is the most current one, or that it is the only valid one, then the distributed VTS with this token is selected. If both distributed VTSs have the same level of the virtual volume, then the distributed VTS which has the virtual volume residing in the tape volume cache will be favored.

3. **Peer-to-Peer VTS preferencing**

   Please refer to Section 2.5.3, "I/O VTS preferencing" on page 30, where we explain in detail how you can influence the selection of the I/O VTS by preferring one distributed VTS over the other one.

4. **VTS loading factor**

   A VTS loading factor is passed to the Model AX0 controllers from each distributed VTS together with the token. The VTS loading factor is broken into three ranges:

   - Idle
   - Not idle and not throttling
   - Throttling

The loading factors for both distributed VTSs are compared to see which one is less busy and should attempt more of the work.

5. **Count of mounts requiring recall**

   Each Model AX0 controller keeps track of the number of mounts requiring recalls which are in progress on each of the distributed VTSs. If a mount request is for a specific volser, and the volser is not in the cache on either VTS, then the mount will be considered a recall mount, and the distributed VTS having the least recall mounts in progress will be favored.

6. **Count of total mounts**

   Each Model AX0 controller keeps track of the total number of mounts it has in progress or completed on each of the distributed VTSs. Based on the information from its own count, the Model AX0 controller favors the VTS with the least number of mounts in progress as the I/O VTS.

2.5.3 I/O VTS preferencing

In remote Peer-to-Peer VTS configurations, you may wish to direct the primary copies of virtual volumes from a host at one site to the distributed VTS at either the same site, or to one at the other site. Although all Model AX0 controllers of one Peer-to-Peer VTS must be operating in the same copy mode of operations, they can be set up differently for VTS I/O preferencing.

Each Model AX0 controller can be set up by the service representative to operate with no-preference or with preference of either VTS0 or VTS1 as the I/O VTS.

If all components of the Peer-to-Peer VTS are available, and if both distributed VTSs have a valid copy of the virtual volume, and if none of them or if both of them have a copy in the tape volume cache, the I/O VTS will be selected based on the VTS preferencing setup you choose for the Model AX0 controller.

2.5.3.1 No-preference selection

In this case, no specific distributed VTS is chosen. The next selection criterion applies which allows the selection of the distributed VTS which is less busy.

No-preference mode allows the spreading of the workload across both distributed VTSs and thus allows the maximum performance for the Peer-to-Peer VTS. This mode should be chosen for Peer-to-Peer VTS configurations where both distributed VTSs are located at the same distance from the Models AX0 controllers and the hosts. This applies to local and remote configurations and is shown in Figure 16.

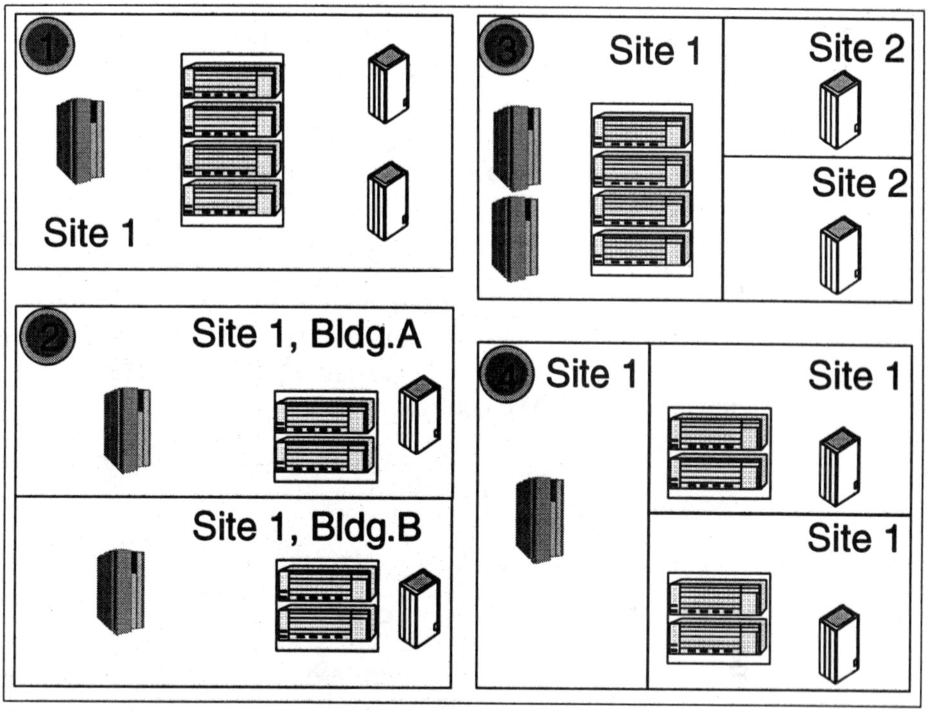

Figure 16. Scenarios for non-preferred VTS I/O selection

The scenarios shown in Figure 16 are theoretical scenarios that we describe to illustrate in which situations we would recommend using no-preference I/O VTS selection:

1. In the first scenario, all components are located on the same site, basically in the same building such that no performance degradation because of ESCON distance can be expected.
2. In the second scenario, components are split into two locations on the same site, still within a distance that does not cause ESCON distance related performance degradation.
3. In the third scenario, the host and all Model AX0 controllers are installed at one site, whereas both distributed VTSs are installed at another site in different buildings in about the same distance from the host.

4. In the fourth scenario, the host is located at the same distance from both distributed libraries. The components are located in different rooms or buildings on the same site.

Where there are significant differences in distance between the components, using no-preference I/O VTS selection may not be the best choice.

2.5.3.2 Preferred VTS selection

Preferring one VTS over the other may be suitable in remote Peer-to-Peer configurations, where the distances from an AX0 controller to the two distributed libraries are significantly different. Taking into account that ESCON performance degradation is expected to be close to 2% per kilometer of ESCON distance, and that the primary copy of a virtual volume is created sending uncompressed data to the distributed VTS, the overhead may be significant, if the remote distributed VTS was selected as the I/O VTS from the local Model AX0 controllers.

Figure 17 shows two scenarios where preferred I/O VTS selection may be suitable.

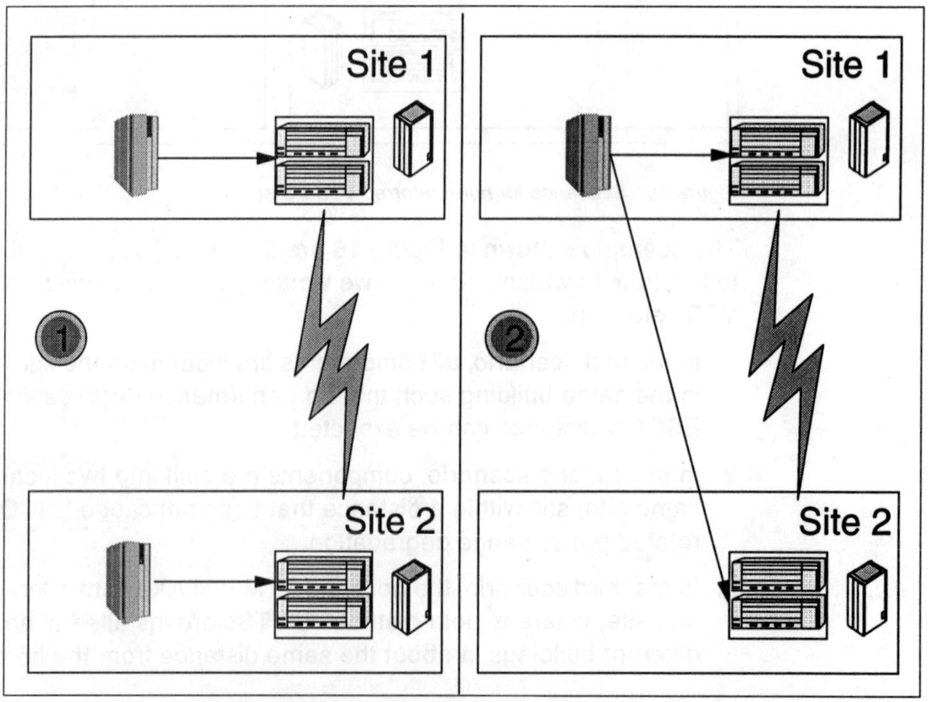

Figure 17. Scenarios for preferred I/O VTS selection

In both scenarios shown in Figure 17, we assume that the distance between the two locations is close to the maximum of 26 km.

1. The first scenario shows a split configuration, basically a mirrored data center, where the host at each of the sites is only connected to the Model AX0 controllers at the same location.

   The deferred copy mode of operation is recommended. If the secondary copy is created at a remote location, the ESCON distance may increase the time until rewind unload completes, and it may prolong job run times significantly.

2. The second scenario shows one host connected to all Model AX0 controllers at both the local site and the disaster recovery site. The same considerations as in the first scenario apply. You may consider using preferred I/O VTS selection (preferring the local distributed VTS) and using the deferred copy mode of operation.

2.6 Peer-to-Peer VTS management

In this section we summarize the mechanisms of the Peer-to-Peer VTS that allow for continuous data availability and operation. The internal management includes, for example, the decisions made during initialization, actions to be taken in case of a failure, synchronization between the components, and optimized usage of available resources.

2.6.1 Initializing the Peer-to-Peer VTS configuration

If all components are powered off, the initialization of the Peer-to-Peer VTS can only start after both distributed VTSs and distributed libraries and at least one of the Model AX0 controllers are available. Establishing the Peer-to-Peer VTS is done through the Model AX0 controllers.

The power on and initialization (POI) sequence ensures that the Model AX0 is correctly configured within the Peer-to-Peer VTS, determines the overall status, and brings the devices controlled by this Model AX0 controller to a known state before the tape control unit and the composite library are brought online to the attached host systems. The initialization steps are performed by each Model AX0 controller in a defined sequence. The defined sequence guarantees the integrity of the overall Peer-to-Peer VTS.

As part of the POI sequence, the clock synchronization based on the UI distributed library and the selection of the master VTS are performed.

2.6.1.1 Clock synchronization

The system clocks within the Peer-to-Peer VTS are synchronized to allow logs (which may be used for problem resolution) to show consistent time-stamps. The time setting does not affect the operation of the Peer-to-Peer VTS.

The time of the Model AX0 controllers is synchronized with the time of the distributed VTS in the UI distributed library. If it is not available, the time of the distributed VTS in the other distributed library is used.

2.6.1.2 Selecting the master VTS

As part of the POI sequence of the Peer-to-Peer VTS, the master VTS is selected. To be selected as the master VTS, all operational Model AX0 controllers must be able to communicate with the distributed VTS and the distributed library, requiring its library manager to be online.

If both distributed VTSs meet the selection criteria, the distributed VTS of the UI library is selected as the master VTS. It is most likely that the distributed VTS on the local site has been defined as the UI distributed library.

2.6.2 Master VTS switchover

In the Peer-to-Peer VTS, the master VTS needs to be available for normal processing. It is the focal point to which library commands that update a volume are initially directed. If the master VTS fails, or if the connection between one or more Model AX0 controllers and the master VTS is interrupted, a switchover from the original master VTS to the other VTS is initiated.

The switchover is initiated by the Model AX0 controller that detects that it can no longer communicate with the master VTS. At least three of the Model AX0 controllers are required to perform a master VTS switchover. In a remote installation where both Model AX0 controllers on one site are no longer available, or if for any reason less than three Model AX0 controllers are operational, the switchover is not performed automatically. In this situation, the service representative can initiate a Master VTS switchover.

In case of an unsuccessful master VTS switchover, the Model AX0 controller enters the *Master Disabled* state until the communication with the current master VTS has been re-established or another switchover attempt has completed successfully.

2.6.3 Token processing

Data integrity in the Peer-to-Peer VTS is guaranteed by means of tokens which are stored in a database in each distributed VTS and synchronized upon every update. In addition, token data is stored with each logical volume when it is written onto physical tape.

Note

The existence of these tokens is the major reason why a distributed library cannot be used as a standalone VTS (for example, after a disaster at one site) and later be re-integrated into a Peer-to-Peer VTS: The tokens would be completely out-of-synchronization.

The token data for a virtual volume includes information:

- That indicates whether a virtual volume resides in the tape volume cache of the distributed VTS or has already been copied to a stacked physical cartridge. The Model AX0 controllers direct the mount request to the distributed VTS with the cached copy to improve recall efficiency.
- That indicates whether the distributed VTS contains a valid copy of a virtual volume. This prevents using an outdated version of a virtual volume.
- That prevents using the same I/O VTS again if a read operation has encountered an error. Subsequent mount requests for this virtual volume will be directed to the other distributed VTS.
- That indicates whether the copy of a virtual volume still needs to be created.
- That can be displayed by the StorWatch Peer-to-Peer Specialist to provide up-to-date information about the logical volumes in a Peer-to-Peer VTS.

Tokens are initially created:

- During insert processing of a virtual volume.
- When migrating an existing stand-alone VTS into a Peer-to-Peer VTS

During a recall of a virtual volume from physical tape into the TVC, the token stored with the virtual volume on tape and the token data in the token database are compared to ensure that the latest version of a virtual volume is used.

2.6.4 Dynamic device reconfiguration

Host dynamic device reconfiguration (DDR) functions are used to allow jobs to continue execution after a failure in the Peer-to-Peer VTS when the host is reading data, and in some cases, even if only one valid copy of the data exists.

Data availability in a Peer-to-Peer VTS is dependent on there being a valid copy of the virtual volume and on the re-run of a job which abended due to a failure. When jobs which were abended are re-run, the Peer-to-Peer VTS is able to provide access to the virtual volume by bypassing the failed component, such as the Model AX0 controller, the distributed VTS, or the connection between the Model AX0 controller and the distributed VTS.

Existing MVS host DDR capabilities are used to try to avoid job re-runs. Upon operator approval of DDR, the virtual volume is demounted, and another tape drive is allocated for retry of the read operation. If the mount is successful, the job will continue to run. If the mount cannot be satisfied, for example because the I/O VTS containing the only valid copy has failed, the job will abend, indicating `valid volume not accessible`.

Table 1 summarizes the cases when a mount is successful and when it is unsuccessful.

Table 1. DDR scenarios

Original failure	Copy available		Copy not available	
	Same AX0	**Other AX0**	**Same AX0**	**Other AX0**
Connection from AX0 to I/O VTS	Mount successful on other VTS	Mount successful on either VTS	Mount failed	Mount successful, selecting VTS with valid copy
I/O VTS	Successful on VTS other than original I/O VTS		Mount failed	

When the mount is successful after a DDR attempt, and the volume label is validated, the read command is retried after the DDR function positions to the block which previously failed.

2.6.5 Tape volume cache management

Tape volume cache management in the Peer-to-Peer VTS has three functions:

1. Keeping the host input operations and the copying of virtual volumes to stacked volumes in balance
2. Expediting the removal of the secondary copy of a virtual volume from the TVC (a process known as *fragmenting*)
3. Preventing the removal of a virtual volume from the TVC if it has not yet been copied to the other distributed VTS.

Note that the tape volume cache management functions described in Appendix E, “VTS tape volume cache management” on page 263 also apply to a Peer-to-Peer VTS.

2.6.5.1 Balance host input and stacked volume copies

The tape volume cache in the distributed VTSs is managed in the same manner regarding throttling as the TVC in a stand-alone Model B18 VTS with the Performance Accelerator Feature installed. If the distributed VTS has been running for some time at peak throughput rate, then the background operations (such as copying the virtual volumes from the TVC to the physical stacked volume) may require higher bandwidth to keep up with the data that is written from the host. To allow higher bandwidth for the background processes, host input is throttled. This in indicated in Figure 18.

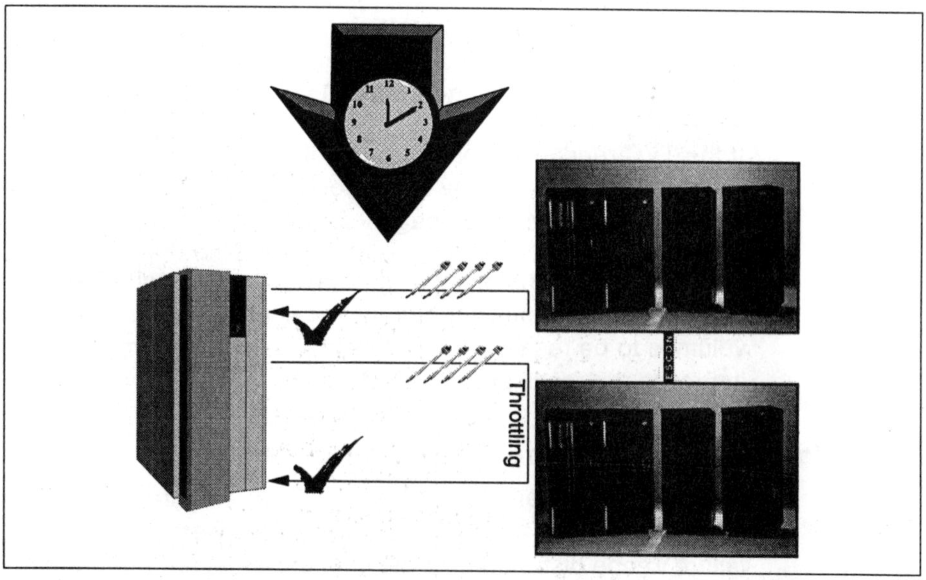

Figure 18. Host input throttling

Throttling is a fixed delay imposed on host write operations to allow the process of copying to stacked volumes to keep up with incoming data and hence prevent the TVC from filling. The first write operation indicated by the pencils in Figure 18 does not show throttling. The second write operation in the lower part of the diagram shows throttling as the time between starting the I/O and signaling completion has been increased by the throttling delay.

For a detailed discussion of VTS performance management and host throttling algorithms, please refer to *IBM Magstar Virtual Tape Server: Planning, Implementing, and Monitoring*, SG24-2229.

2.6.5.2 Expedite deletion of the secondary copy

Removal of the primary copy from the TVC (fragmentation) follows the same rules as in a stand-alone VTS, using the *least-recently used (LRU)* algorithm to keep the virtual volume in the TVC as long as possible. The secondary copy is removed from the cache as soon as possible.

This is achieved by adding the secondary copy to the top of the queue of volumes to be removed, thus allowing primary copies to stay longer in the TVC and improve recall efficiency.

2.6.5.3 Prevent removal from cache before copy

In deferred copy mode, virtual volumes which have not yet been copied to the other distributed VTS are preferentially held in the TVC to prevent them from being fragmented and later on recalled for copy. This is done to improve the overall performance of the Peer-to-Peer VTS.

If the TVC reaches a certain threshold of space occupied by uncopied virtual volumes, the copy priority is temporarily changed as explained in 2.4.3, "Deferred copy mode" on page 23.

If virtual volumes have been removed from the cache before the secondary copy has been created, a special recall process allows multiple virtual volumes to be recalled from the same stacked volume in one operation. This improves the recall performance.

2.6.6 Distributed and composite library states

When all components of the Peer-to-Peer VTS are fully functional, the distributed libraries and the composite library are in *normal* state. In case of a failure in one distributed library, it changes its state according to the failure. Multiple states can be active at the same time.

If *any* of the distributed libraries is in a state as listed below, the composite library also is in this state:

- Automated mode operation
- Degraded operation
- Safety Interlock open

If *all* distributed libraries are in one of the states listed below, the composite library is also in the same state:

- Paused mode operation
- Manual mode operation
- Vision system non-operational
- Library manager Check 1 condition
- All storage cells full
- Out of cleaner volumes
- Dual write disabled
- Out of mount resources
- Library manager switchover in progress
- Out of empty stacked volumes

Based on Model AX0 controller status, the following states can exist for the composite library.

Copy operation disabled:

If all of the Model AX0 controllers only have paths to one of the distributed libraries.

VTS operations degraded:

If one of the components of the Peer-to-Peer VTS is not operational.

Immediate copy completions deferred:

If one of the model AX0 controllers has outstanding secondary copies queued while operating in the immediate copy mode of operation.

Service preparation:

If a distributed library is in the service preparation state. See 2.7, "Service considerations" on page 40 for more details.

The state of the distributed and the composite library, as well as of all four Model AX0 controllers, can be displayed using the StorWatch Peer-to-Peer Specialist (see 7.3, "Monitoring the Peer-to-Peer VTS" on page 155) as well as using the host console display commands (see 7.3.2.2, "Host commands" on page 158).

2.6.7 Special AX0 operational modes

An IBM product specialist can, in exceptional circumstances, override the normal minimum configuration requirement to allow operation with one VTS and a minimum of one VTC. There are two special operational modes that may be chosen:

Read/write disconnected mode

Logical volumes may be read, modified, or rewritten unless the volumes are known not to be valid. This mode may only be set for one VTS; even if all links between two sites have been lost, you must not operate both sites in read/write disconnected mode.

When the second VTS is brought back into the configuration, the VTCs will then reconcile tokens, resume normal operations, and schedule logical volume copies.

Read-only mode

Logical volumes may be read unless they are known not to be valid. The host is prevented from writing to the volumes or from changing their category assignment (for example, private, scratch, or insert).

After other components have been repaired or made accessible, the virtual drive addresses currently being used must be taken offline again before discontinuing read-only mode.

These modes can only be activated by the IBM product support specialists, for example, in cases when, after a complete shutdown of the Peer-to-Peer VTS, only one VTS can be brought back online, or if all Model AX0 controllers are in the master-disabled state. All the virtual drive addresses must be varied offline at the host systems before read-only or read/write disconnected mode may be set.

2.7 Service considerations

In this section, we cover the considerations related to Peer-to-Peer VTS service, including microcode upgrades of the various components. The key objective for the Peer-to-Peer VTS is to provide continued access to data stored within the configuration. In the event of service of a component of the Peer-to-Peer VTS, the component will be unavailable to perform any work; however, other components of the configuration will continue to provide full access to data.

2.7.1 Service preparation

When a B18 VTS component of the Peer-to-Peer VTS needs to be serviced, the service representative must initiate the Service Preparation state. The mode selected determines the impact on host operations. Service Preparation does not apply to the AX0 controllers, although any one AX0 may be used for the initiation of the action.

2.7.1.1 Model AX0 controller

In the Peer-to-Peer VTS, the Model AX0 controller presents itself to the host as an IBM 3490 tape control unit with 16 devices. Preparing the Model AX0 controller for service is the same as preparing any tape control unit for service.

The following steps are performed by the service representative and the customer operator to prepare the Model AX0 controller for service:

- At the hosts attached to the Model AX0 to be serviced, vary offline the tape drive addresses associated with the AX0. Drives which are not allocated will go offline and allocated drives will become offline pending.
- Allow currently running jobs to complete or have the operator cancel them.
- For long running jobs, swap the virtual tape drives being used to drives on another AX0 using the SWAP command.
- Verify that all of the virtual drives are unloaded and not ready.
- Change the state of the AX0 to offline.

In order to allow permanent access to data, a single host should *always* be attached to multiple Model AX0 controllers. If one Model AX0 controller needs to be taken offline, the data can be accessed through the devices of another Model AX0 controller.

2.7.1.2 B18 VTS

When an operational B18 VTS has to be taken offline for service, the Peer-to-Peer VTS must first be prepared for the loss of the resources involved. The main operational changes in the Peer-to-Peer VTS as it is prepared for service of a distributed VTS or library are:

- Direct workload to the remaining distributed VTS.
- Expedite data copies where the only valid copy is on the distributed VTS to be serviced.

Service preparation for the VTS is initiated by the service representative through one of the Model AX0 controllers. Based on the type of service which is required, and based on the urgency of having it performed, the service representative selects the service mode. Only one B18 VTS of a Peer-to-Peer VTS can be prepared for service at any time. Four service modes are provided. During the service preparation process, the mode may be changed to a more restrictive mode.

Normal mode:

This mode is used when service or microcode update is to be performed on the distributed VTS or the distributed library with the least impact on performance of the Peer-to-Peer VTS. The following actions are taken:

- If in Immediate copy mode, copy operations in progress which target the distributed VTS to be serviced, complete normally.
- Subsequent rewind unload commands on the distributed VTS which is not to be serviced are treated as if in deferred copy mode.
- Subsequent rewind unload commands for modified volumes on the VTS to be serviced are treated as in immediate mode, and rewind unload completes after the copy has been created. Copy operations compete with host I/O operations equally for bandwidth priority.
- The VTS which is not to be serviced is selected as the I/O VTS for all workload except for when the only valid copy of a virtual volume is in the VTS to be serviced.
- Copy operations from the distributed VTS to be serviced to the other VTS are selected prior to those that have the distributed VTS to be serviced as the target.
- Copy operations to the VTS to be serviced are suspended.

Expedite mode:

This mode is used when the time to do service preparation has to be minimized, but continued access to data is required. The difference from normal mode is that copy operations from the distributed VTS to be serviced to the other VTS, are processed with a bandwidth priority *equal* to host I/O operations. Some impact to the Peer-to-Peer performance may be experienced.

Immediate mode:

This mode is used when there is an urgent need to service or perform an offline operation with the distributed VTS or its associated distributed library. The actions described under normal mode are changed, so that:

- All virtual volumes currently open on the distributed VTS to be serviced are allowed to process to completion.

- All workload is routed to the VTS which is not to be serviced. If the only valid copy of a virtual volume which is subsequently required is in the VTS to be serviced, the job terminates abnormally with *valid volume inaccessible.*
- All copy operations are suspended.

Forced mode:

This mode is used only after the other modes have failed to complete or if the jobs in progress could not be terminated to free up the virtual devices.

Paths to the distributed VTS are terminated immediately regardless of copy and device status. Devices may be left in use and volume copies may fail. This mode is for emergency hardware service only and is not expected to be used for microcode upgrades.

Once a service mode has been selected, all attached hosts are notified of the state change. After service preparation has completed, each of the Model AX0 controllers notifies the attached hosts. The service representative can then perform the normal steps for service of the distributed VTS or the distributed library.

During the time, a VTS is being prepared for service, and for the duration of the service, host operations to the Peer-to-Peer VTS are degraded as listed for the different service modes. In addition, some host commands are restricted, such as `Library Volume Audit`, `Library Volume Eject` and logical volume insert processing. These commands will not be performed. The Model AX0 controller receiving the command will indicate `Function Incompatible` to the host.

The service representative can request information about the service preparation process in progress from any of the Model AX0 controllers. The information received includes, for example:

- The time required to complete the copies
- The percentage complete of the dual copy work
- The virtual drives in use by a host

The service representative may request that the operator issue a SWAP command to the same tape drive address. This will terminate the operation on the VTS being prepared for service and continue on the other VTS. In this manner, long running jobs can be moved to the VTS which is not being prepared for service.

2.7.1.3 Distributed library

If a distributed library requires service, the associated VTS must first be prepared for service. Once the VTS has completed service preparation, the service representative can continue the normal procedures for servicing of the tape library. When other tape drives or a VTS which is not part of the Peer-to-Peer VTS are installed in a tape library, other activities may need to be performed before servicing the tape library.

2.7.2 Microcode installation and activation

Customers who prefer and are able to halt all usage of the Peer-to-Peer VTS for microcode updates may find that the total process is simpler and less demanding of operations and service representative communications and interaction. It will avoid:

- Continued build up of volumes to be copied
- Reduced performance during upgrade and after components are returned for use

Microcode upgrades should be considered a form of service, and a service preparation process as described in 2.7.1, "Service preparation" on page 41 will be performed by the service representative. Access to all logical volumes will be provided while microcode upgrades are performed.

If necessary, the Peer-to-Peer VTS may be returned to the customer at any time for data access without completing the microcode upgrades of all components.

2.7.3 Resuming operation after service

After the service activity has been completed, the component which was being serviced is brought back online again. If a Model AX0 controller has been serviced, the virtual drives associated with this controller can be varied online again.

After service is completed for a VTS in a Peer-to-Peer VTS configuration, either because service was required on the distributed VTS itself or on the associated library, the Peer-to-Peer VTS will proceed to synchronize and perform copy operations which may have been suspended during the service period. While recovering to normal operational states, access to all virtual volumes is granted. Some impacts to Peer-to-Peer performance may be experienced due to accumulated workload of volumes to be copied. The amount of pending secondary copies is reported in field S94CLLVC of the SMF record 94 and can be displayed using the StorWatch Peer-to-Peer Specialist.

The VTS recovery processing steps include:

- Verify that the library manager is online.
- Resolve the hot token list. Tokens that have been created during the time of service are synchronized on both distributed VTSs.
- Change the distributed VTS availability state to *available*.
- Notify the host that the Peer-to-Peer VTS operation is no longer degraded.
- Synchronize the mounts with the other VTS.
- Check whether there are volumes in the insert category of the UI distributed library and generate an attention message if required.

2.8 Host related processes

In this section we describe how host or operator initiated processes are performed in the Peer-to-Peer VTS, for example scratch mount requests from the host or the definition of virtual volumes at the library manager console.

2.8.1 Inserting logical volumes

In a Peer-to-Peer VTS, logical volume ranges can only be defined from the library manager console of the UI distributed library. For details on other definitions on the library manager console, such as defining physical volume serial ranges for the distributed VTS, please refer to Chapter 6, “Implementation and migration” on page 117.

After virtual volumes are added in the UI distributed library during host insert processing, the virtual volume is first created in the other distributed library. Subsequently the volume category is changed in the master VTS and in the other VTS to PRIVATE or SCRATCH, depending on the host request, and the tokens for the virtual volume are created.

If either distributed library is not operational, no virtual volumes can be inserted. After both distributed libraries are operational again, the host is automatically informed about volumes in the insert category and the normal insert processing is performed.

2.8.2 Mount processing

The processing of mount requests in the Peer-to-Peer VTS depends on whether it is a specific or a scratch mount request. Writing data to a VTS, either standalone or Peer-to-Peer, you should use scratch mount processing to benefit from fast virtual mount times. `DISP=MOD` and `DISP=OLD` processing may require a recall of the volume into the TVC, unless the virtual volume still resides in the TVC.

Scratch mount and specific mount processing is summarized in the sections below.

2.8.2.1 Scratch mount processing

A scratch mount request is first sent to the master VTS which selects the next volume from the requested scratch category (MEDIA1 or MEDIA2).

After the mount is complete on the master VTS and the validity of the volume in both distributed VTSs has been confirmed, the Model AX0 controller selects the I/O VTS based on the criteria described in Section 2.5.2, "Peer-to-Peer VTS workload balancing" on page 29.

A specific mount request is then sent to the non-master VTS, using the Fast-Ready attribute to prevent recalling the virtual volume into the tape volume cache, and the host is notified via sending device end.

In the Peer-to-Peer VTS, it is not required that you define the Fast-Ready attribute for the scratch categories: however, we strongly recommend that you define the Fast-Ready attribute for scratch categories; otherwise, eject processing of virtual volumes will fail. A scratch mount request will automatically include the Fast-Ready indication and prevent the recall of volumes into the TVC even if they are newly written.

2.8.2.2 Specific mount processing

When a specific mount request from the host is sent to the Peer-to-Peer VTS, the model AX0 controller processing this request selects the I/O VTS based on the selection criteria described in Section 2.5.2, "Peer-to-Peer VTS workload balancing" on page 29.

2.8.3 Ejecting logical volumes

Eject processing results in deleting the logical volume from both distributed libraries. Therefore, eject processing requires both distributed libraries and VTSs to be operational in order to process the eject request.

Ejecting virtual volumes from the Peer-to-Peer VTS requires the virtual volume to be in the scratch category. The Fast-Ready attribute must be defined for the scratch category; otherwise, the eject will fail.

A maximum of 1000 eject requests can be issued at a time. Additional eject requests will fail.

2.8.4 Creating Peer-to-Peer VTS statistics

The statistical data for a standalone Model B18 VTS and for an IBM 3494 tape library with only native tape drives installed, is presented once an hour to the attached hosts. If enabled on the host, an SMF type 94 record is written. One SMF type 94 record is written per logical library.

With the Peer-to-Peer VTS, the process to present statistical data to the attached hosts is different than for a stand-alone Model B18 VTS. For the Peer-to-Peer VTS, three different SMF type 94 records are created:

- One record for each of the two distributed libraries containing the statistics of the physical library
- One record for the composite library containing the statistics for the Peer-to-Peer configuration

For details about Peer-to-Peer VTS statistics and about monitoring and reporting in the Peer-to-Peer environment, please see Chapter 8, "Monitoring and reporting" on page 193.

Chapter 3. Peer-to-Peer VTS performance

The Peer-to-Peer VTS shares many of the performance characteristics of a stand-alone VTS. The performance of the individual VTSs in a Peer-to-Peer VTS configuration is affected by the same factors that govern the performance of a stand-alone VTS:

- Physical configuration:

  For example, the tape volume cache size or the number of physical drives

- Data characteristics:

  For example, compressibility or block size

- Internal cache management algorithms:

  For example, internal thresholds or throttling

For a discussion of stand-alone VTS performance, see *IBM Magstar Virtual Tape Server: Planning, Implementing, and Monitoring*, SG24-2229.

The Peer-to-Peer VTS is also creating, copying, and managing a duplicate copy of every logical volume; therefore, it must perform a greater amount of work to process the same amount of host data as a stand-alone VTS. For this reason, and because of the basic architecture of the Peer-to-Peer VTS, it has unique performance considerations.

The most significant Peer-to-Peer VTS performance consideration is the mode of operation, either Immediate Copy Mode or Deferred Copy Mode. The choice of mode has, in addition to significant availability ramifications, a very considerable impact on the throughput capability of the Peer-to-Peer VTS. Much of the following discussion will be devoted to a detailed examination of the effect of Deferred Copy Mode on Peer-to-Peer VTS performance.

Note

For a detailed discussion of Peer-to-Peer performance models and measurements, please refer to the *Peer-to-Peer Performance White Paper* which is available from:

```
http://www.ibm.com/support/techdocs
```

The performance information discussed in this chapter is based on modeling and on initial laboratory performance measurements. Specific customer environments may experience different results. Please also note that performance characteristics can be changed by microcode changes.

© Copyright IBM Corp. 2000

3.1 Peer-to-Peer operational modes

Before discussing performance measurements in detail, we will briefly review the Peer-to-Peer VTS operational modes.

Immediate Copy Mode: The copy of the new or modified logical volume to the other VTS (the peer-to-peer copy) is made prior to the completion of the rewind/unload of the original logical volume. When the volume completes close processing, the Peer-to-Peer VTS has completed performing the copy of the logical volume. No further peer-to-peer copy processing is required. The impacts on throughput are:

- The elongation of the job time
- The reduction in potential host bandwidth due to the resources consumed by the copy work being performed

Deferred Copy Mode: The peer-to-peer copy of the new or modified logical volume is queued, and occurs some time after the volume completes close processing. When the peer-to-peer copy is performed depends on several factors, including:

- The current VTS workload
- The length of time since the original volume was created or modified
- The amount of uncopied data in the Tape Volume Cache of the VTS which contains the original volume

The impact on throughput is reflected in a reduction of host bandwidth when the copy process is ultimately performed.

It is important to note that, regardless of the operational mode, the Peer-to-Peer VTS will perform as much of the background work (peer-to-peer copies and copies to physical stacked volumes) as possible with the resources available at the time.

This should be kept in mind when considering some of the information in the following sections, especially the information concerning Deferred Copy Mode. In Deferred Copy Mode, although the peer-to-peer copy is initially placed on a lower priority queue than host work, the Peer-to-Peer VTS will perform the copy as soon as resources are available.

3.1.1 Peer-to-Peer VTS basic measures of performance

The basic measure of performance for the Peer-to-Peer VTS is the same as for a stand-alone VTS: maximum throughput in MB/second. The following charts compare the maximum throughput measurements for the Peer-to-Peer VTS to the measurements for stand-alone Model B18 VTS with EHPO installed and the stand-alone Model B18 VTS with the Performance Accelerator feature installed.

3.1.1.1 Maximum write data rate

Figure 19 shows the maximum data rate that can be achieved for different VTS configurations if 100% of the I/O activity is write activity. The measurements are based on a compression ratio of 3:1, a 32760-byte block size, 800-MB volumes, and BUFNO=20 specified in the JCL.

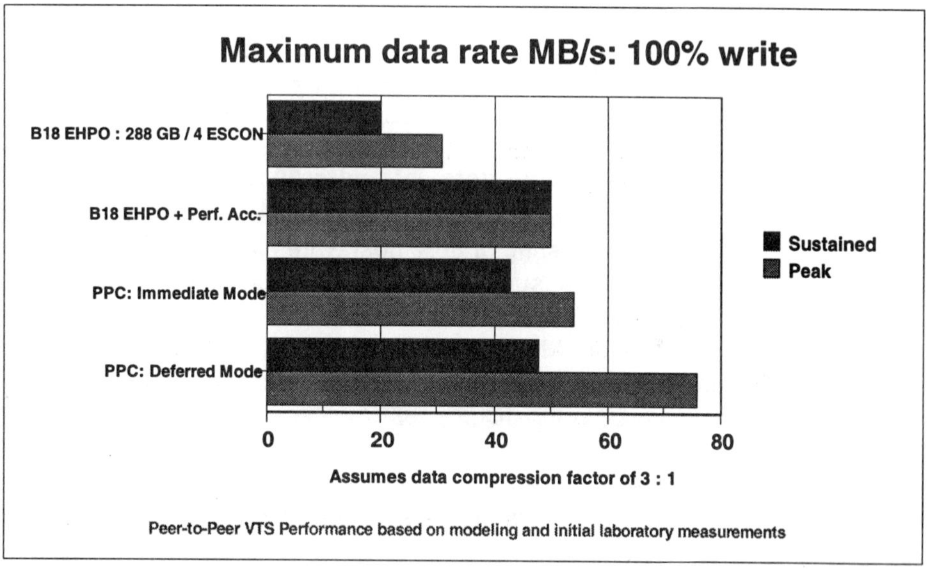

Figure 19. Maximum data rate at 100% write

The bars shown in Figure 19 indicate the maximum achievable data rate, if the Peer-to-Peer VTS is operating with balanced workload distribution using all four Model AX0 controllers equally and without ESCON distance penalty. Note that workload skew between AX0s would reduce the maximum data rates that we would expect.

Additional measurements were made for both read hit and read miss (recall from a stacked volume) performance. Those measurement results, along with the Peak and Sustained Write results, are consolidated in Figure 20.

Data Rates with 32K Blocks and 3:1 Compression	Peak Writes MB/s	Sust. Writes MB/s	Read Hits MB/s	Read Misses MB/s
EHPO	31	20	26	18
PAF (4-ESCON)	50	50	38	38
Peer-to-Peer Deferred Copy	76	42	64	50
Peer-to-Peer Immediate Copy	54	42	64	50

Figure 20. Maximum data rate comparison

3.1.1.2 Maximum data rate with 60% writes

Figure 21 shows the maximum data rate that can be achieved with a mixed workload consisting of 60% host writes and 40% host reads, where 50% of the reads are assumed to be cache hits. The measurements for the Peer-to-Peer VTS were for an all-local environment with a balanced workload across all four Model AX0 controllers. The numbers are based on a compression ratio of 3:1, a 32760-byte block size, 800-MB volumes, and BUFNO=20 in the JCL.

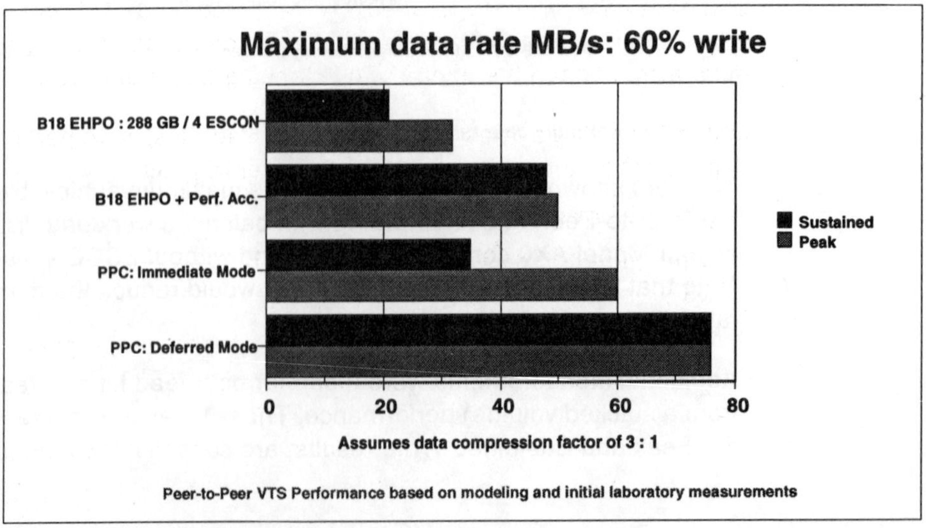

Figure 21. Maximum data rate at 60% write

3.1.2 Peer-to-Peer host write throughput in Immediate Copy Mode

The behavior of Peer-to-Peer VTS write throughput in Immediate Copy Mode is similar to that of a stand-alone VTS. In practical terms, the level of host write performance is dependent upon a single threshold, the amount of data in the tape volume cache which has not been copied to stacked volumes.

Assuming a continuous maximum host write workload, and beginning with a cache whose volumes have all been previously copied to physical tape, there are two distinct performance data rates: a peak rate and a sustained rate.

During the initial period, the *peak rate* is achieved since no resources are being used for copying logical volumes to stacked volumes. Tape volume cache space is created for new volumes by fragmenting (removing from cache) those volumes which were already copied to stacked volumes. The duration of this peak rate period will depend on the host write activity, the data compression achieved, and the size of the cache.

The *sustained* rate occurs when the uncopied data threshold is exceeded. This will cause older logical volumes in the cache to be copied to physical tape. The sustained rate can continue indefinitely, with the host write activity that is allowed, balancing the copying of logical volumes to stacked volumes.

Note that the peer-to-peer copy process is being performed through both the peak and sustained rate periods.

3.1.3 Peer-to-Peer host write throughput in Deferred Copy Mode

The behavior of Peer-to-Peer VTS write throughput in Deferred Copy Mode is more complex than for Immediate Copy Mode because the Peer-to-Peer VTS must also manage the queue of outstanding deferred copies.

Instead of a single threshold, the Peer-to-Peer host write performance level is dependent on three separate thresholds or triggers:

1. The *Deferred Copy Priority Threshold*
2. The amount of data in the tape volume cache not yet copied to the other VTS
3. The amount of data in the tape volume cache not yet copied to stacked volumes

3.1.3.1 Deferred Copy Priority Threshold

The Deferred Copy Priority Threshold, or *hours* threshold, is selected by the customer and set by the service representative when the Peer-to-Peer VTS is installed. Once this age (expressed in hours) has been reached for a logical volume in the tape volume cache and it has not yet been copied to the other VTS, its priority for being copied will be increased. The default threshold is eight hours.

3.1.3.2 Peer-to-Peer Copy Threshold

The Deferred Copy Mode peak rate will begin at a higher level than the Immediate Copy Mode peak rate since the peer-to-peer volume copy activity is being deferred. This peak rate period will continue until the amount of data that has not yet been copied to the other VTS exceeds the peer-to-peer copy threshold.

When the peer-to-peer copy threshold is exceeded, the Peer-to-Peer VTS will begin to copy new and modified logical volumes from each VTS to the other VTS in a manner similar to Immediate Copy Mode. At the same time, the priority of the peer-to-peer copy process will be raised. At this point, the host write rate will be reduced since additional bandwidth is being devoted to the peer-to-peer copy process.

Once the amount of uncopied data falls below the peer-to-peer copy threshold, the VTS will lower the priority of the peer-to-peer copy process, and host throughput will increase to the peak rate. However, if the host write demand continues at a high level, the peer-to-peer copy threshold will again be exceeded. Thus, the Peer-to-Peer VTS will alternate between the peak and reduced performance level until the host write throughput demand drops.

3.1.3.3 Tape Volume Cache Copy Threshold

When the amount of data in a tape volume cache in a Peer-to-Peer VTS configuration that has not been copied to stacked volumes exceeds the uncopied data threshold, then that VTS, just like a stand-alone VTS, will cause logical volumes in the cache to be copied to physical tape. This will also cause a reduction in the host write data rate that can be achieved. This is referred to as the *Deferred Copy Mode sustained rate,* since it can continue indefinitely, with the host write activity that is allowed balancing the copying of logical volumes to stacked volumes.

As can be seen, the level of throughput of the Peer-to-Peer VTS in Deferred Copy Mode is dependent on a complex set of conditions. If you choose to run the Peer-to-Peer VTS in Deferred Copy Mode, you need to consider several factors.

3.1.4 Deferred Copy Mode considerations

When running in Deferred Copy Mode, we must consider:

- How long our peak period lasts
- What the Peer-to-Peer VTS must do after the peak period.

3.1.4.1 Deferred Copy Mode peak rate duration

Deferred Copy Mode provides the highest write peak rate. However, the duration of the peak rate is not unlimited. The duration will primarily depend on tape volume cache size, with larger caches affording longer peak rate duration, but at some point, the uncopied data will have to be copied. When this occurs, the host bandwidth capability will be significantly reduced. Figure 22 illustrates this effect.

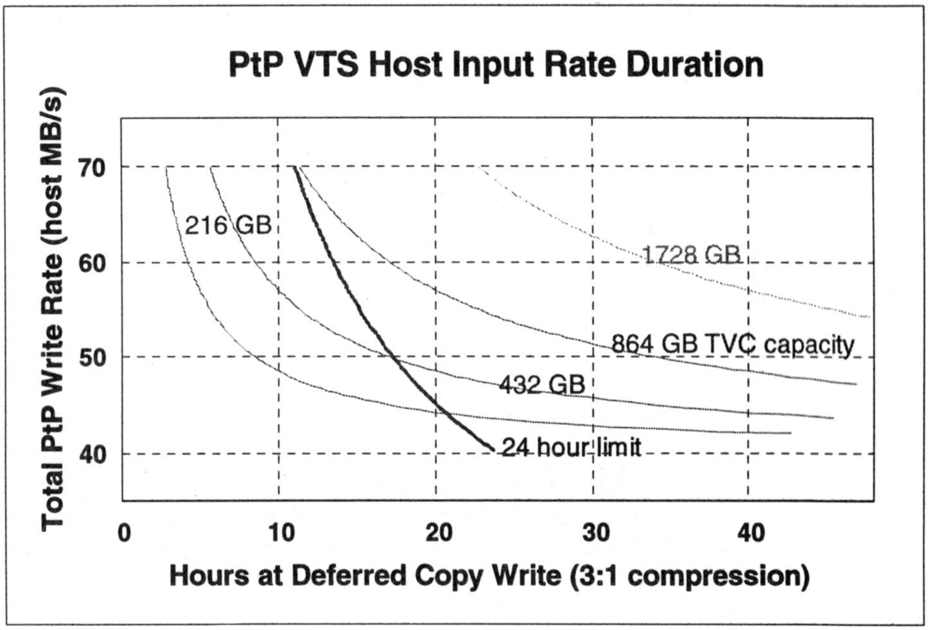

Figure 22. Deferred copy mode peak rate duration

Figure 22 shows, for four tape volume cache sizes (physical GB per VTS), the length of time that the Peer-to-Peer VTS can be operated in Deferred Copy Mode at the peak rate before the peer-to-peer copy threshold is exceeded. For example, the Peer-to-Peer VTS can be operated at the maximum write rate of 76 MB/second host input (assume a data compressibility of three to one), for over eleven hours if the tape volume cache capacity is 864 GB per VTS.

At lower input rates, the time to fill the tape volume cache to the maximum allowed uncopied data level is extended. For example, if the average deferred copy write rate is 60 MB/second, then the capacity criterion for the 864 GB tape volume cache allows the accumulation of the input for about 17 hours. Note that these curves include an estimate of how much background peer-to-peer copy work is getting done at any given input rate.

In estimating the hours at a 60 MB/second deferred copy write input rate from Figure 22, we start at the 60 MB/second level on the vertical axis and proceed to the right until we intercept the tape volume cache size of the Peer-to-Peer VTS configuration being assessed. Note that, if the tape volume cache size is 864 GB, we first cross the line labeled *24 hour limit* at about 13.5 hours. This limit means that if we want to manage the Peer-to-Peer VTS installation in such a way that there is no un-copied data remaining at the end of a twenty-four hour cycle, then we have to stop host input entirely at 13.5 hours for there to be enough time for all the un-copied data to be copied to the peer VTS in the remaining time of that twenty-four hour cycle.

The corresponding *24 hour limit* at the maximum deferred copy write input rate of 70 MB/second is at about 11 hours, somewhat before the maximum uncopied data limit of the 864 GB cache has been reached.

Note that, at a deferred copy write rate of about 40 MB/second, there is no net accumulation of uncopied data in the tape volume cache.

3.1.4.2 Deferred Copy Mode recovery time

Figure 23 illustrates the relationship between the duration of the peak write rate and the amount of off-peak (or recovery) time required at various off-peak write rates. If there is some write activity during the off-peak time, the peak deferred copy write window under a twenty-four hour recovery constraint is reduced. For example, if the average write rate is expected to be about 20 MB/second during the off-peak time, then the maximum allowable peak period rate should be no more than about 7 hours.

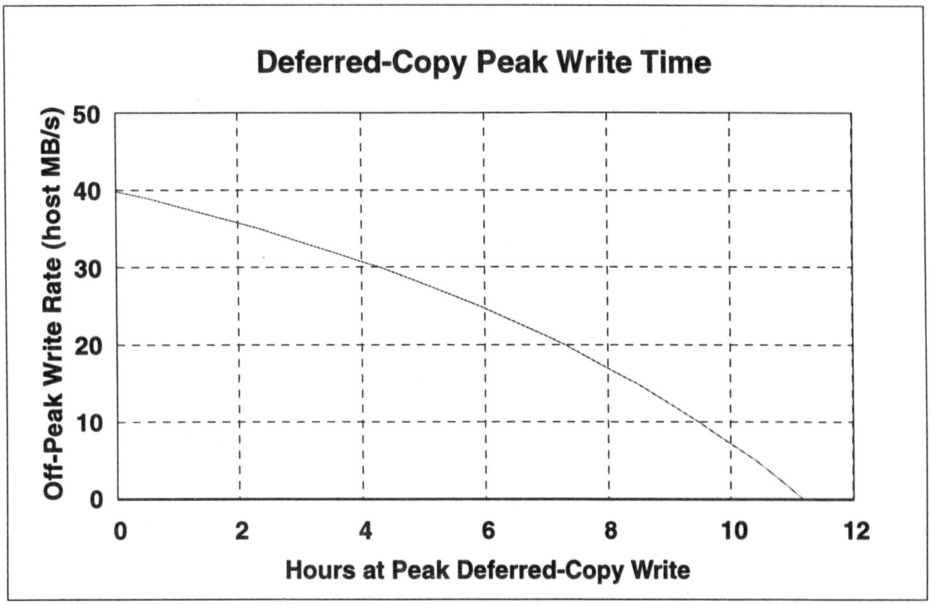

Figure 23. Effect of write activity on copy resynchronization

Note

Because of the need for recovery time, it is imperative that Deferred Copy Mode be used only in workload environments that have a definite peak vs. average data rate profile (i.e. a peak rate two or three times the average data rate), so that the Peer-to-Peer VTS has sufficient time to make a dual copy all the logical volumes before the next workload peak.

3.1.4.3 Setting the Deferred Copy Priority Threshold

Another parameter affecting deferred-copy write performance is the Deferred Copy Priority Threshold (in integral hours in the range 0 to 24 hours). The way it can affect performance is that, when the hours threshold is reached, the copy load is added to the existing host I/O load. For example, if the Peer-to-Peer VTS is operating in Deferred Copy Mode and uncopied data in the tape volume cache reaches the specified hours threshold, the observed write rate will drop because of the additional copy load.

> **Recommendation**
>
> For best performance, the Deferred Copy Priority Threshold (hours) parameter should be set to exceed the anticipated critical peak write requirement period duration.

3.2 Preferred VTS for I/O

When a Peer-to-Peer configuration is being installed, you may either choose to prefer one VTS for I/O, or you may express no-preference and allow the Peer-to-Peer VTS to balance the work in order to make best use of the resources available. We will discuss how to decide which mode to choose, both for a single host site and for split host sites.

3.2.1 Preferred versus non-preferred selection — single host site

In Peer-to-Peer configurations where the host(s) and one VTS are located at one site, and the other VTS is located at a remote site, the decision of whether the AX0s will be set up to prefer a VTS, or have no-preference, is a consideration.

When the host issues a mount for a logical volume and both VTSs are online and available, the AX0 will select a VTS for the I/O VTS. If the mount is for a scratch volume, or if the mount is for a specific volume, and both or neither of the VTSs has a copy of the specific volume in cache, the AX0 will select the I/O VTS based on the preference setting. If only one VTS has a cache copy, it will be selected as the I/O VTS.

When a VTS has been preferred, the AX0 will always direct the mount of a scratch logical volume to that VTS. The VTS which will be preferred is determined by the customer and set by the service representative at the time of the AX0 installation.

When no-preference has been made, the AX0 balances the selection between the two VTSs by directing the mount to the VTS that has the fewest logical volumes currently mounted, regardless of whether the VTS is local or remote to the AX0.

In a remote configuration, an additional component of the total system performance is the ESCON propagation delay due to distance. We might think that we should configure an AX0 to prefer a local VTS for remote configurations to avoid this effect. However, measurements for distances up to 25 km clearly show that this effect is outweighed by the ability of a

Peer-to-Peer VTS to maximize the use of internal resources when configured for no-preference.

Recommendation

We would generally recommend that no-preference be configured for single host site configurations.

Figure 24 illustrates this and shows estimated host throughput rates for a Peer-to-Peer VTS with data with a compression ration of 3:1 for various distances.

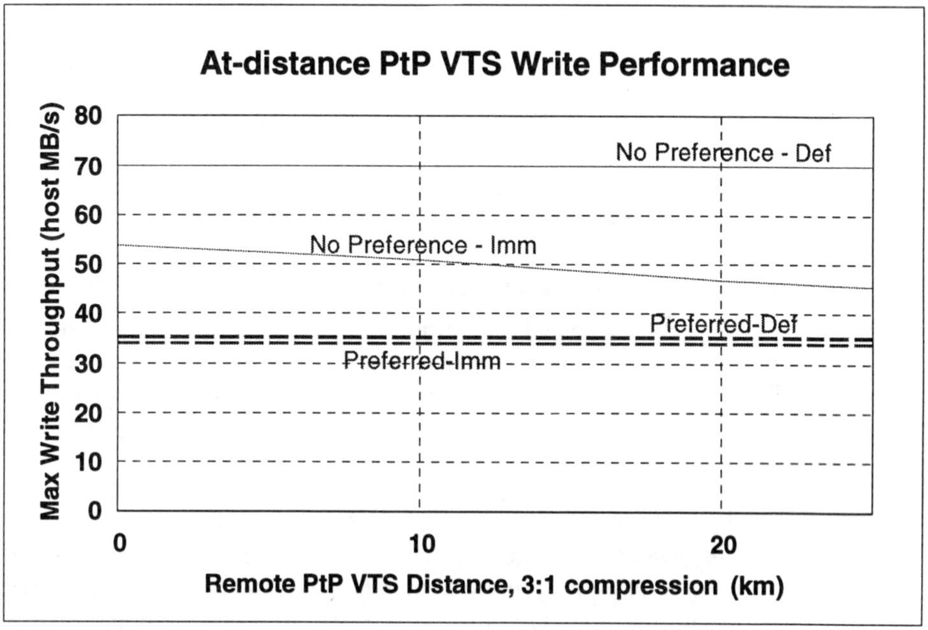

Figure 24. ESCON distance and host data rate, write workload

Figure 25 shows similar measurements for a different workload, this time comprising 60% writes and 40% reads.

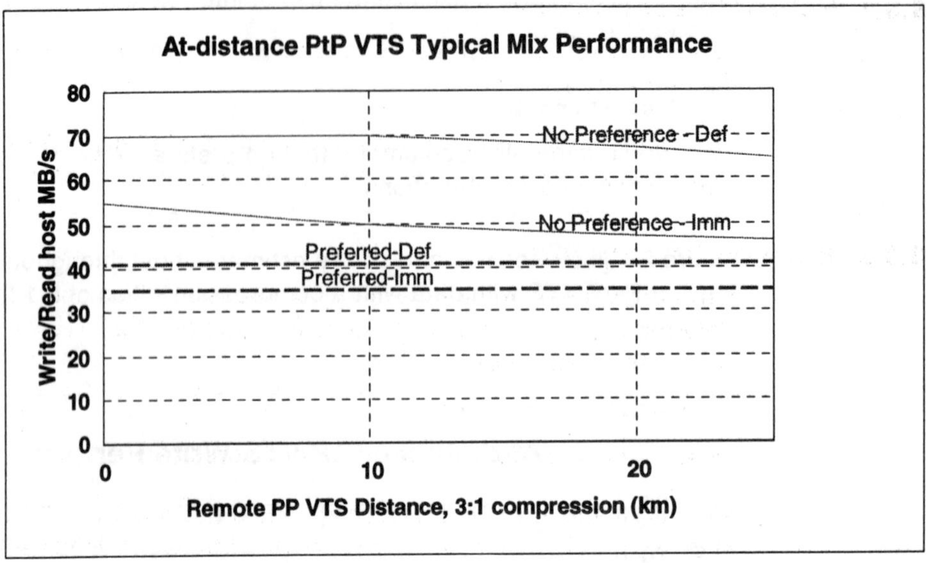

Figure 25. ESCON distance and host data rate, mixed workload

3.2.2 Preferred versus no-preference selection — split host sites

In Peer-to-Peer VTS configurations where host(s) and one VTS are located at one site, and other host(s) and the other VTS are located at a remote site, the decision of whether the AX0s will be configured for preference of a particular VTS or for no-preference is more complex.

Modeling has shown that, even in a split site configuration, no-preference will theoretically provide the highest host write data rate. However, there will be a response time advantage when a VTS is configured to be preferred. By having all tape I/O served locally, the Deferred Copy Mode writes and reads will be more likely to have a shorter open time. In this environment, the requirement for throughput should be weighted against the need for faster mount time, and the preference set accordingly.

3.3 Other performance considerations

We have concentrated on the throughput of a Peer-to-Peer configuration. However, there are some further performance differences between Peer-to-Peer and stand-alone configurations which we discuss in this section.

3.3.1 Return to scratch time

The time taken to return volumes to scratch is greater for a Peer-to-Peer VTS than for a stand-alone VTS.

Laboratory measurements showed that a stand-alone VTS returned volumes to scratch at about four times the rate of a Peer-to-Peer VTS.

3.3.2 Elapsed time for jobs

Laboratory measurements show an increase in job elapsed time for both deferred copy mode and immediate copy mode. The increase is most noticeable when there is:

- A small number of jobs
- An imbalance between the workload across AX0s

Measurements with 64 drives active and a balanced workload across AX0s show a small elapsed time increase in deferred copy mode and, as expected, a larger increase in immediate copy mode.

3.3.3 Mount times

Measurements of a laboratory workload show that the fast ready mount time for a virtual volume is about 3 seconds for a stand-alone VTS using 64 drives concurrently. In a Peer-to-Peer VTS, the additional processing needed elongates this mount time to about 6 seconds.

3.3.4 AX0 configuration and channel throughput limitation

In a stand-alone VTS, all virtual drives are accessible through all channel adapters. The MVS I/O definition at the host, for example, is coded as if all the virtual control units were daisy-chained on the same ESCON channels. This means, in effect, that the throughput of the VTS is not dependent on which virtual control units or drives are in use - the total bandwidth of all the ESCON channels is available to all drives.

In the Peer-to-Peer VTS, however, the virtual drives are associated with individual AX0s, each AX0 having 16 virtual drives, and 2 physical ESCON channel attachments (see 5.3.1.4, “Sharing and partitioning with multiple hosts” on page 108.) The effect of this architecture is that only one quarter of the total Peer-to-Peer VTS bandwidth is available to each AX0 and its associated virtual drives. In addition, in order for a host to achieve maximum throughput to an AX0, both channel attachments must be utilized.

In cases where multiple hosts will be attached to the Peer-to-Peer VTS, careful consideration must be made to insure that each host has channel attachments to a sufficient number of AX0s to provide for the peak throughput requirements of that host.

Chapter 4. Availability configurations

In this chapter we describe how you can use a Peer-to-Peer VTS to improve the data availability in your data center. Data availability is a key issue for any organization. Your current information and communication technology (ICT) infrastructure already has been implemented with data availability as an important design objective.

Data availability has many aspects. They range from outages for software maintenance to interrupts caused by hardware failures. Before we describe the new opportunities that you have with the Peer-to-Peer VTS, we will discuss and clarify the continuous availability terminology in use in the first part of this chapter.

Disaster recovery adds another dimension to continuous availability. There are several levels of disaster recovery distinguished based on the level of data loss and service loss. The relationship between disaster recovery and continuous availability is also discussed. For an in-depth discussion on these topics, see the *Continuous Availability System Design Guide,* SG24-2085 and the *Continuous Availability S/390 Technology Guide,* SG24-2086. We hope that these discussions will help you to decide what level of availability you wish to seek and how you might begin to achieve your availability objectives for tape by implementing a Peer-to-Peer VTS.

The Peer-to-Peer VTS uses ESCON connections between its components. It is important that the technical details of ESCON and its consequences are well understood before you plan a configuration. We use three theoretical ESCON examples to show the role of ESCON in a Peer-to-Peer environment. More information on ESCON can be found in Appendix A, “ESCON configurations” on page 217.

We describe three single site configurations and four dual site configuration in more detail. For each configuration we document the availability targets, the configuration details and the configuration considerations in detail. The configurations may assist you in determining the preferred configuration for your environment.

A Peer-to-Peer VTS helps you to improve your data availability for tape data. As a consequence, it can result in changing your current implementation in terms of infrastructure and daily procedures.

© Copyright IBM Corp. 2000

4.1 Continuous availability concepts

Computer outages are less and less accepted in today's data centers. More and more business applications have to be online for 24 hours a day and 365 days per year. Outages can have a serious impact on the performance of an enterprise and should be kept to a minimum.

Sometimes outages are caused by hardware, software, and data maintenance work which needs to be performed at regular intervals. Such *planned* outages are usually scheduled at a period of low activity.

Sometimes outages are caused by faulty hardware, software, and procedures. Such *unplanned* outages have become quite rare in recent years with advanced multi-user systems.

Today, an increasing number of enterprises require that both types of computer outages, planned and unplanned, be eliminated or substantially reduced. An advanced computer system is not a single box, but a complex assembly of such components as processors, peripherals, networks, operating systems, and application software. Consequently, an outage-free system cannot be bought from the shelf. It requires an appropriate systems design, using elements such as redundant and fault tolerant components and appropriate systems management.

4.2 System availability terms

We use three terms to describe the concept of system availability: *high availability*, *continuous operation*, and *continuous availability*. These terms are explained in the following sections.

- **High availability**

  This is the ability of a system to provide service to its users during defined service periods, at an acceptable or agreed level.

  These service periods, as well as the definition of an "acceptable" service level, are either stated in a service level commitment by the service provider, or in a service level agreement between end users and the service provider.

  Typically, a service level above 99.7% is accepted as high availability. High availability is maintained by avoiding or reducing any unplanned outages.

- **Continuous operation**

  This is the ability of a system to provide service to its users at all times, day and night, without scheduled outages to perform system and data maintenance activities.

  It is obviously difficult to perform change and maintenance work on a system that is supposed to be in continuous operation. However, without preventative maintenance, a system can be in continuous operation, but its availability may not be as high as it should be since it may suffer unscheduled outages more frequently.

  Even if true continuous operation turns out to be impossible to implement for some applications, a realistic goal might be to increase the defined service period; for example, from 14 hours per day to 18 hours per day.

- **Continuous availability**

  This is the property of a system that provides both high availability and continuous operation at the same time. The system must be designed so users experience neither scheduled nor unscheduled outages.

  This goal seems difficult to achieve, as hardware and software components are usually not entirely error-free and maintenance-free, and large computer systems undergo frequent component additions and changes. The solution is to employ hardware components, software, and operational procedures that mask outages from the user. This solution usually requires that recovery from an outage must be performed so quickly that the user does not perceive it as an outage. It also frequently requires the use of redundant components, so that an alternate component can be used in case of a permanent component failure, or while a component is in maintenance.

An additional term, which you often hear used with high availability and which is sometimes erroneously used instead of high availability, is *fault tolerant*.

Many major components of today' s computer systems are fault tolerant to some degree, which means they will tolerate some faults. These components may have:

- Redundant sub-components
- Error checking and correction for data
- Retry capabilities for basic operations
- Alternate paths for I/O requests
- Duplexed data facilities on DASD and tape

However, they may also have a single point of failure which, despite the fault tolerance, can cause them as components to fail. Similarly, if one important component in a system is not fault-tolerant, then the system is not fault-tolerant even though all other components are.

Note

A set of fault-tolerant components or products does not necessarily make a fault-tolerant system. A fault-tolerant system design will make a fault-tolerant system only if it is implemented and managed properly.

Figure 26 illustrates the relationship between the components of continuous availability.

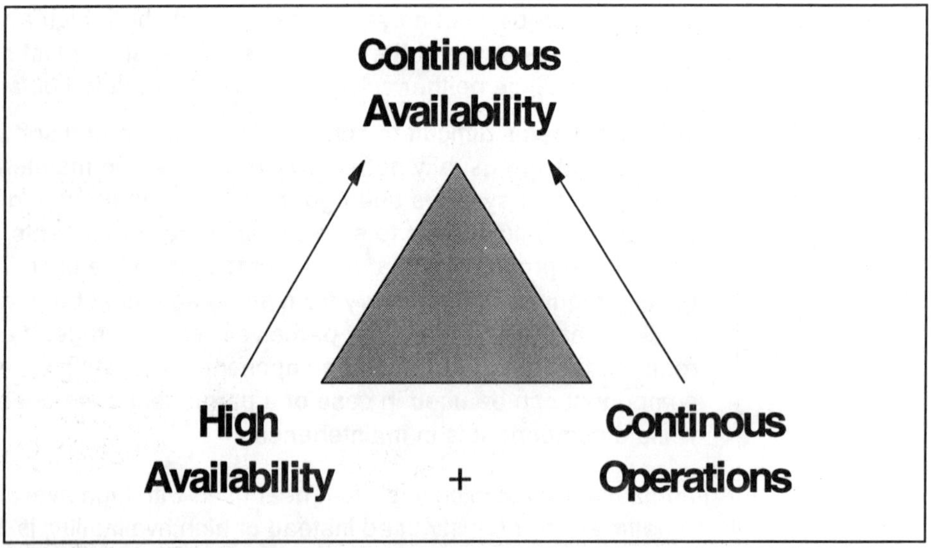

Figure 26. Components of continuous availability

4.3 Disaster recovery

Disaster recovery is the process of reacting to a disaster by being able to provide computing services from another location. In most cases, the countermeasures you employ to be able to recover from a disaster are entirely different from the solution you use to achieve continuous availability.

In a disaster situation, users normally are aware that an outage has happened to the central computer facility, and the duration of the outage is mainly dependent on the recovery solution.

Usually this duration is measured in two different components:

- Data loss:

  This represents the loss of data you have, that is, how much work you must re-execute once your system is recovered,

- Service loss:

  This represents the loss of computing you experienced from the moment of disaster up to the moment when your system has been recovered.

At SHARE 78 held in Anaheim in 1992, session M028, the *Automated Remote Site Recovery Task Force* presented seven tiers of recoverability, which were ranked based on the recovery method and recovery time. The following sections describe these tiers.

4.3.1 Tier 0 — No offsite data

This tier provides no preparation in saving information, determining requirements, establishing a backup hardware platform, or developing a contingency plan (Figure 27).

> **Typical recovery time**: The length of time for recovery is unpredictable. Indeed, you cannot be sure of being able to recover at all.

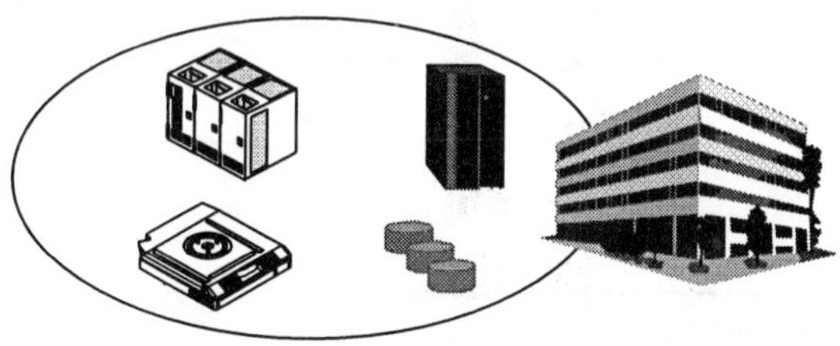

Figure 27. Tier 0: no recovery solution

4.3.2 Tier 1 — Pickup truck access method (PTAM)

To be at tier 1, an installation would need to develop a contingency plan, back up required information and store it in contingency storage (off-site location), determine recovery requirements, and optionally establish a backup platform supporting a conditioned facility without processing hardware (Figure 28).

> **Typical recovery time**: The length of time till recovery is usually more than a week.

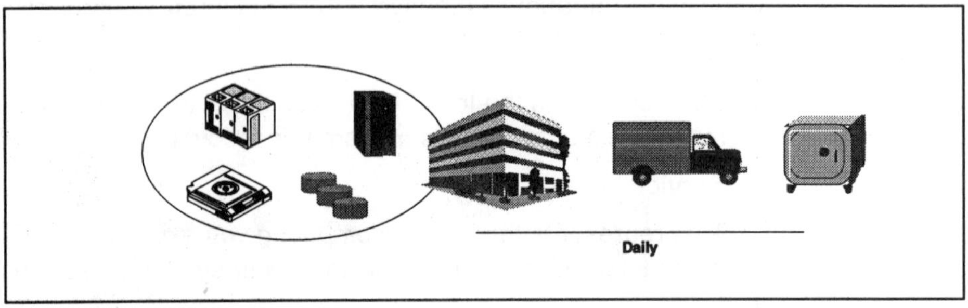

Figure 28. Tier 1 recovery solution

4.3.3 Tier 2 — PTAM with hot site

Tier 2 encompasses all requirements of tier 1 and also requires a backup platform to have sufficient hardware and network to support the installation's critical processing requirements. Processing is considered critical if it must be supported on hardware that exists at the time of the disaster (Figure 29).

Typical recovery time: The length of time for recovery is usually more than one day.

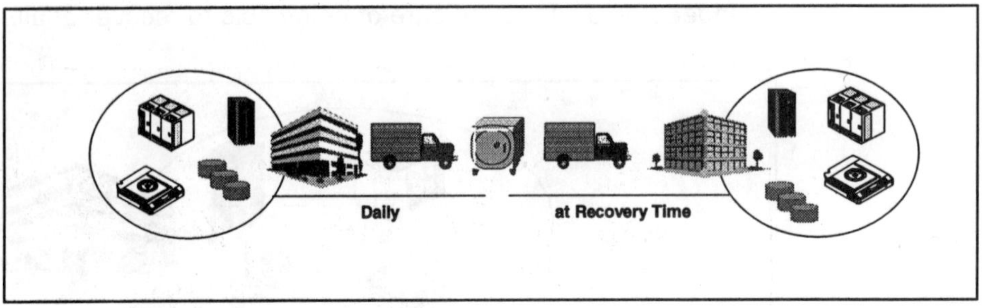

Figure 29. Tier 2 recovery solution

4.3.4 Tier 3 — Electronic vaulting

Tier 3 encompasses all the requirements of tier 2 and, in addition, supports electronic vaulting of some subset of the information. The receiving hardware must be physically separated from the primary platform and the data stored for recovery after the disaster (Figure 30).

Typical recovery time: The length of time till recovery is usually about one day.

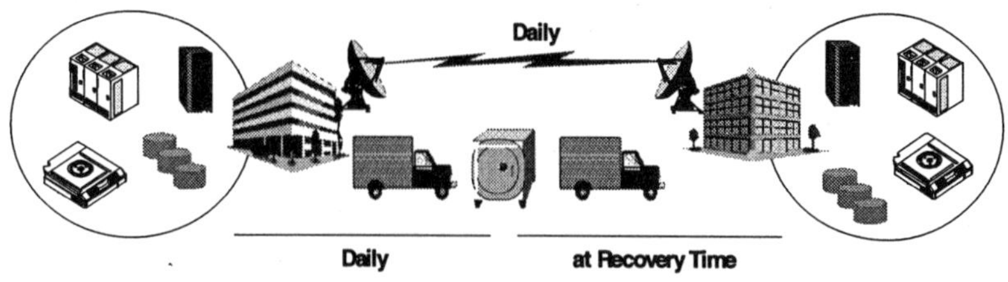

Figure 30. Tier 3 recovery solution

4.3.5 Tier 4 — Active secondary site

Tier 4 introduces the requirements of active management of the recovery data by a processor at the recovery site, and bi-directional recovery. The receiving hardware must be physically separated from the primary platform (Figure 31).

Typical recovery time: The length of time for recovery is usually up to one day.

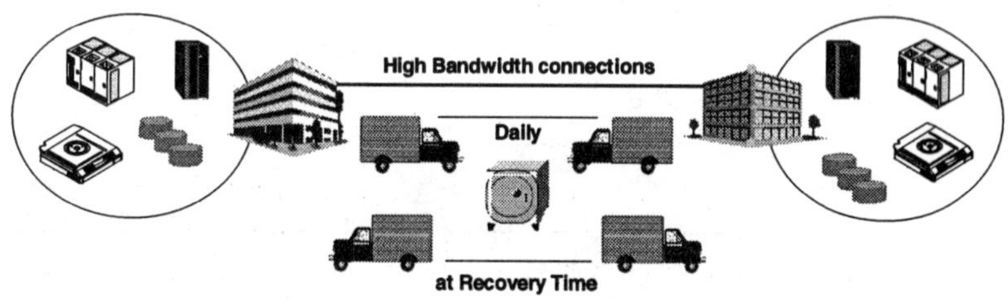

Figure 31. Tier 4 recovery solution

4.3.6 Tier 5 — Two-site two-phase commit

Tier 5 encompasses all the requirements of tier 4 and, in addition, will maintain selected data in image status (updates will be applied to both the local and remote copies of the databases within a single commit scope). Tier 5 requires both the primary and secondary platforms' data to be updated before the update request is considered satisfied. Tier 5 requires partially- or fully-dedicated hardware on the secondary platform, with the capability to automatically transfer the workload to the secondary platform (Figure 32).

Typical recovery time: The length of time for recovery is usually less than 12 hours.

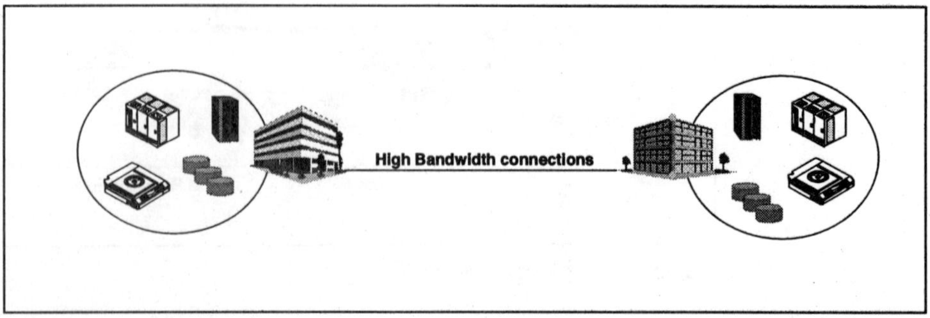

Figure 32. Tier 5 recovery solution

4.3.7 Tier 6 — Zero data loss

Tier 6 encompasses zero loss of data and immediate and automatic transfer to the secondary platform. Data is considered lost if ENTER has been accepted (at the terminal), but the request has not been satisfied (Figure 33).

Typical recovery time: The length of time for recovery is usually a few minutes.

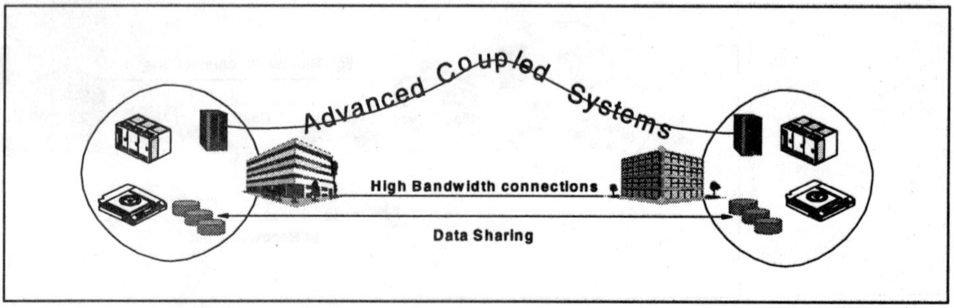

Figure 33. Tier 6 recovery solution

4.4 Data loss and service loss

The typical recovery time associated with each tier is just a rough indication of the time that an installation usually needs to restore its computing services. However, in a disaster situation, there are many other points to consider.

For example, some installations can tolerate resuming their services after longer periods of time, but with maximum data currency. Other installations must resume their services as soon as possible, regardless the currency of their data. Still others need both a short recovery time and maximum data currency (Figure 34).

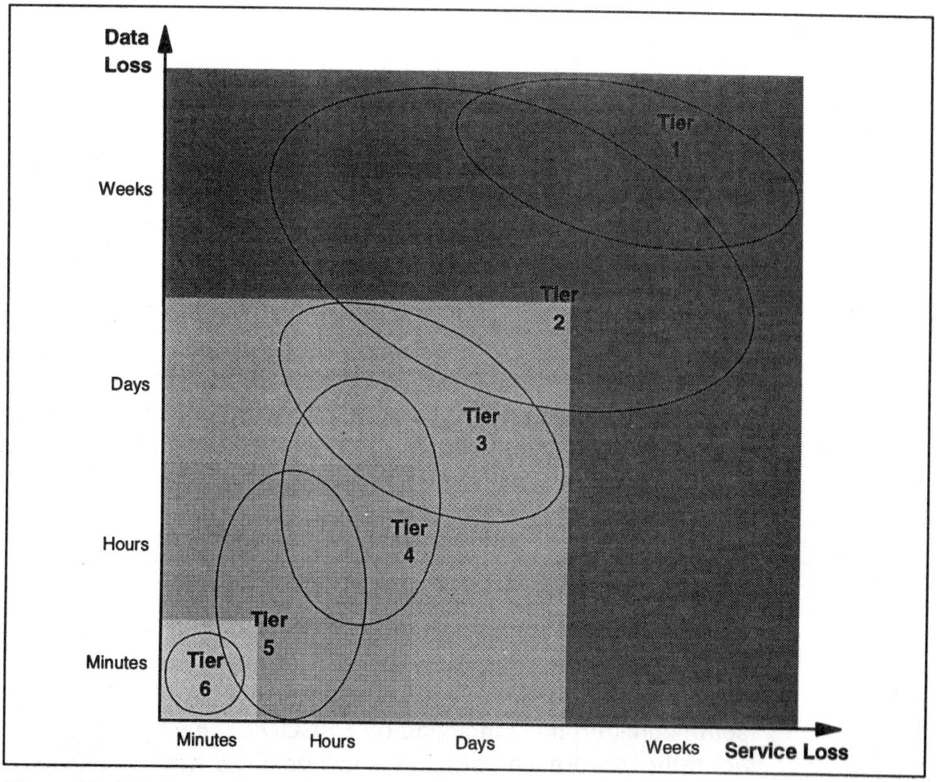

Figure 34. Data loss and service loss

4.5 Relating continuous availability and disaster recovery

All the components that make up continuous availability in a computer system are usually situated in the same building. Therefore, the building itself can represent a single point of failure. In this case, and despite all the continuous availability you have designed into the system, a disaster could cause you to lose all your computing services.

While you must of course be prepared to react to a disaster, the solution you would apply in this case may be more of a recovery solution than a continuous availability solution. A recovery solution can be defined by making a trade-off among implementation costs, maintenance costs, and financial impacts resulting from performing a business impact analysis of your business.

Furthermore, as you can see from the tier definitions, only a disaster recovery tier 6 solution can be compared to a continuous availability solution, although currently there is limited technology available that fully fulfill that definition.

However, with the current S/390 technologies, it is possible to achieve a tier 6 workload transfer if you have enough time to do it in a controlled fashion before all computing capabilities are lost in a disaster at your production site.

A combination of S/390 technologies such as Parallel Sysplex, ESCON channel technology, IBM RAMAC Virtual Array (RVA) with Extended Remote Copy (XRC), Peer-to-Peer Remote Copy (PPRC), and Snapshot functions, IBM Enterprise Storage Server (ESS) with XRC, PPRC and Flashcopy functions, and IBM Peer-to-Peer VTS, together with a good set of system automation products that include site and environmental control, can allow you to approach a tier 6 disaster recovery solution.

4.6 Peer-to-Peer VTS ESCON configurations

ESCON is the technology in use for the connections between the components of the Peer-to-Peer VTS. A well-designed ESCON configuration is important in reaching your availability targets. Therefore, we now present some configurations focusing on ESCON connections. These configurations are rather theoretical, but they show possible ways to exploit ESCON technology. For a better understanding of ESCON, you will find more information in Appendix A, “ESCON configurations” on page 217.

The following three configurations are described:

- A configuration with only direct connections.
- A configuration with ESCON directors.
- A configuration with ESCON channel extenders and remote channel extenders.

4.6.1 Configuration with direct connections

Figure 35 shows a direct point-to-point connection with or without shared channels using the ESCON Multiple Image facility (EMIF), between the host and the Model AX0 controllers. There are also point-to-point connections between these controllers and the Model B18 VTSs. The connections can only be multimode connections. Depending on the fibers in use, the maximum distance is 2 km (if 50/125 μ fibers are used) or 3 km (if 62.5/125 μ fibers are used). The total distance between the S/390 server and the distributed Model B18 VTSs amounts to 6 km (4 km with 50/125 μ fibers) as a maximum.

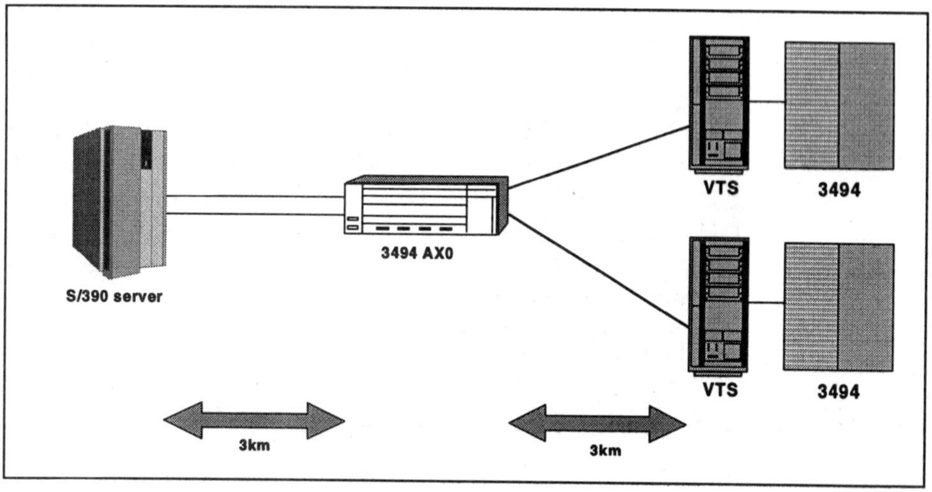

Figure 35. Sample configuration with direct connections

4.6.2 Configuration with ESCON directors

Figure 36 shows a connection through the maximum allowed number of IBM 9032 ESCON directors. The maximum distance are provided for (62.5/125 μ fibers). The distances for 50/125 μ fibers are given in brackets. The (numbers) in the following list refer to the numbers in the figure.

It is unlikely that there will be as many ESCON directors in a real life situation. However, this diagram allows us to explain what the maximum distances are.

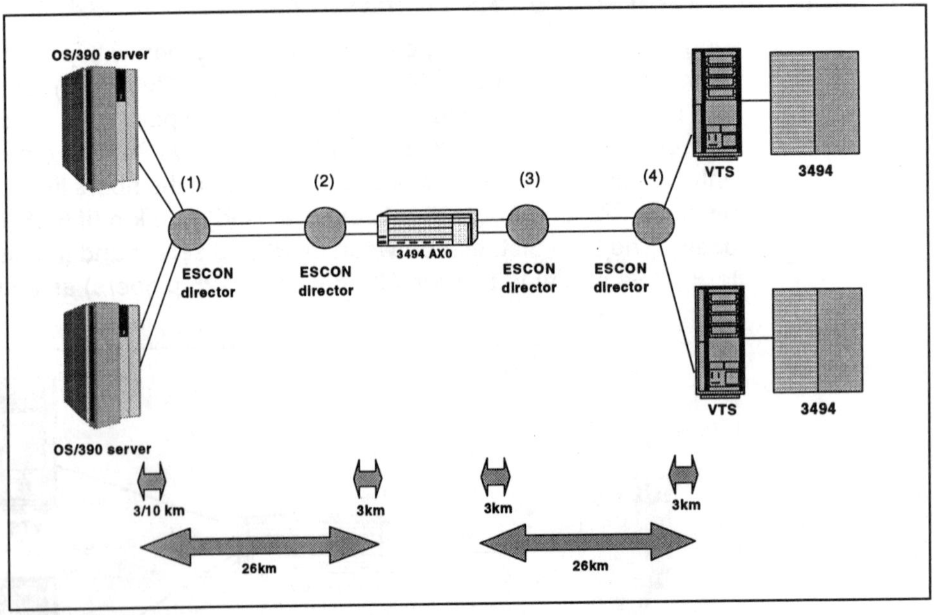

Figure 36. Sample configuration with ESCON directors

- The maximum distance between the S/390 server and the ESCON director (1) is dependent on the ESCON channel in use. The maximum for ESCON channels is 3 km (2 km). The maximum for FICON channels is 10 km (20 km by RPQ). This requires the FICON bridge adapter card in the ESCON director.
- The maximum distance between the ESCON director (1) and the ESCON director (2) is 3 km (2 km) if LED ports are used for the interconnection and 20 km if XDF ports are used.
- The maximum distance between the ESCON director (2) and the Model AX0 controller is 3 km (2km). The total distance between the S/390 server and the Model AX0 controller determines the throughput achieved between those components. Taken into account a reduction of about 1.9% per km, a maximum data rate on a ESCON channel will be reduced from 17 MB/sec to 10.3 MB/sec (10.7 MB/sec).
- The maximum distance between the Model AX0 controller and the ESCON director (3) is 3 km (2 km).
- The maximum distance between the ESCON director (3) and the ESCON director (4) is 3 km (2 km) if LED ports are used for the interconnection and 20 km if XDF ports are used.

- The maximum distance between the ESCON director (4) and the distributed Model B18 VTSs is 3 km (2 km). The total distance between the Model AX0 controller and the distributed Model B18 VTSs impacts not only the data rate between the host and those Model B18 VTSs but also the data rate of the copy activity between the Model B18 VTSs and the throughput of the control commands flowing between the Model AX0 controller and the distributed Model B18 VTSs.

As mentioned in some of the previous points, extended length channels don't come free. Before you design a configuration with long ESCON channels we advise you to calculate the expected data rate in your peak periods and evaluate if your planned configuration is able to handle this load. For more information see Chapter 7, "Operating and using the Peer-to-Peer VTS" on page 153.

4.6.3 Configuration with channel extenders

Figure 37 shows a connection using ESCON channel extenders. The maximum distance are provided for (62.5/125 μ fibers). The distances for 50/125 μ fibers are given in brackets. The numbers in parentheses in the following list refer to the numbers in the figure.

Also, this configuration is theoretical. It is unlikely that there will be as many extenders in a real situation.

In both cases you have to decide where you want to place the Model AX0 controllers. They can be placed in your main location near the S/390 server or near the distributed libraries in your remote location. This decision is not only driven by the characteristics of the technology but also depends on other items like the location of your computer sites, the installed infrastructure, your disaster recovery strategy and the method of duplicating your DASD data.

Note

The vendors of channel extenders must modify and validate their products in order to handle additional ESCON commands and command sequences used between the 3494 model AX0 virtual tape controllers and the 3494 model B18 virtual tape servers.

Please contact the vendors for information on the certification of their products in a Peer-to-Peer VTS environment.

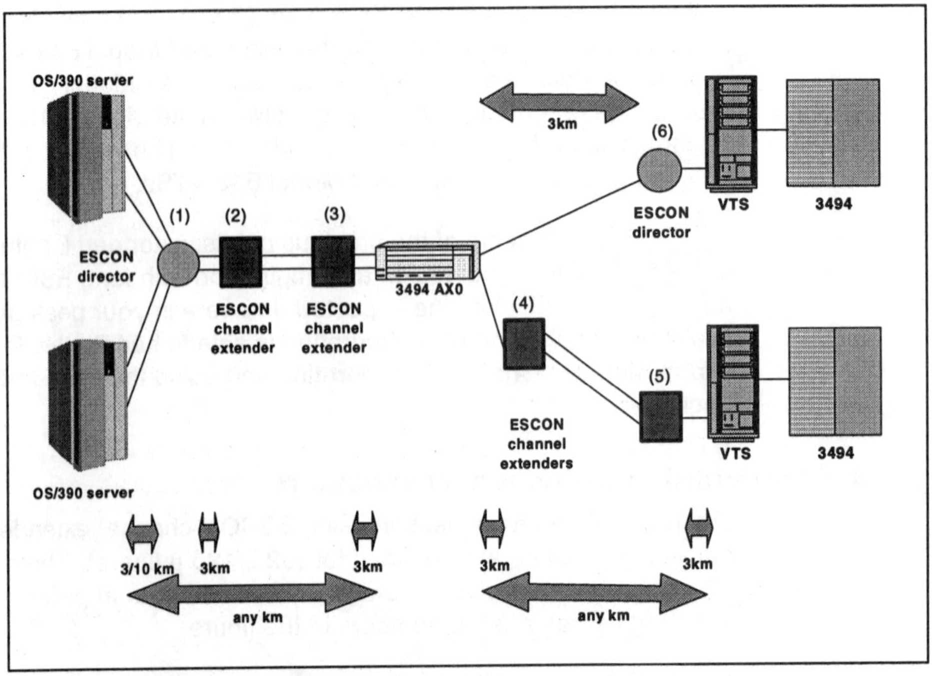

Figure 37. Sample connection with channel extenders

- The advantage of having an ESCON director between the hosts and the controllers is the configuration flexibility it provides. A director allows you to make changes in your configuration during your primary service hours. It is easy to add, remove, or change the connections between the I/O controller and the host by changing the configuration of the cross-points in the director.

  The maximum distance between the S/390 server and the ESCON director (1) is dependent on the ESCON channel in use. The maximum is for ESCON channels 3 km (2 km). The maximum for FICON channels is 10 km (20 km by RPQ). This requires the FICON bridge adapter card in the ESCON director.

- The maximum distance between the ESCON director (1) and the ESCON channel extender (2) with LED ports is 3 km (2 km). It may be possible that there are further limitations prescribed for the extender equipment. You should verify the documentation provided by the vendor.

- Also the maximum distance between the ESCON extender channel boxes (2) and (3) without using a repeater is determined by the functional characteristics of the equipment. The ESCON channel extender uses single mode fiber for the connection. Depending on the situation in your country, you may provide them yourself or you may get them from your data carrier.

- The maximum distance between the ESCON channel extender (3) and the Model AX0 controller is 3 km (2km). Again, the total distance between the S/390 server and the Model AX0 controller determines the throughput achieved between those components. The total throughput reduction is the sum of the reduction caused by the ESCON connection length, the delay caused by the channel extender equipment and the connection delay between the extenders. For the ESCON connections you can estimate using a 1.9% reduction per km.
- The maximum distance between the Model AX0 controller and the channel extender (4) is 3 km (2km). Verify the documentation of the channel extender equipment for any additional limitations.
- The maximum distance between the channel extenders (4) and (5) is determined by the functional characteristics of the equipment.
- The maximum distance between the channel extender (5) and the lower distributed Model B18 VTS is 3 km (2 km).

  It is unlikely that both distributed Model B18 VTSs are connected via a channel extender. In Figure 37 we gave the upper distributed Model B18 VTS an ESCON connection to the Model AX0 controller. (Note that we also show an ESCON director which is solely for configuration flexibility rather than being required by the Peer-to-Peer configuration). The connection between the Model AX0 controller and the ESCON director (6) and the connection between this director and the upper distributed library have both a maximum length of 3 km (2 km) because they use LED technology.
- The total distance between the Model AX0 controller and the distributed Model B18 VTSs impacts not only the data rate between the host and those Model B18 VTSs but also the throughput of the copy activity between the Model B18 VTSs and the speed of the control commands flowing between the Model AX0 controller and the distributed Model B18 VTSs.

  The overall performance of the data traffic between the upper distributed Model B18 VTS and the lower distributed Model B18 VTS can differ considerably. This should be well understood when designing the total data availability configuration.

  The gap between the theoretically maximum throughput and required throughput based on your peak load should be large enough to handle additional delays caused by a unequal distributed library configuration.

Calculating the total performance of complex environments is not an easy task. Ensure that you have enough spare capacity before you start using your Peer-to-Peer VTS configuration. Real life measurements help you to determine the additional load the Peer-to-Peer VTS can handle in your environment. Refer to 7.3, "Monitoring the Peer-to-Peer VTS" on page 155.

4.7 Peer-to-Peer VTS configurations

This section deals with some sample configurations of a Peer-to-Peer VTS.

You must design a configuration that suits your requirements before you can plan and implement a Peer-to-Peer VTS. There is no single solution for all possible situations. Each organization has different requirements. And even with the same set of requirements, you can design various configurations depending on physical factors like the location of your computer sites and the possibility of using the currently available infrastructure.

Tape data is a part of your total data infrastructure. Any solution for your tape data must be in line with the measures you have taken or plan to take for your other data. Do you plan to use PPRC or XRC in your DASD environment? Did you take any measures for your optical data? As said before, tape data availability is a part of your data availability strategy and should be evaluated accordingly.

The basic elements for design depend on the level of continuous availability you want to achieve for your daily operations and the tier level of the disaster recovery solution you want to implement for your tape data.

The configuration samples in this section are designed to help you distinguish the differences between them. For each scenario, we describe the configuration, the options advised, and the considerations related to that scenario. In most of the configurations, the ESCON connections are presented as lines only. This includes the possibility of using ESCON directors. Remote connections are explicitly indicated, because the use of remote channel extenders impacts the use and the performance of the configuration considerably. ESCON configuration examples are given in section 4.6, "Peer-to-Peer VTS ESCON configurations" on page 72. General information on ESCON can be found in Appendix A, "ESCON configurations" on page 217.

Configurations can be grouped as follows:

- Single site configurations
- Dual site configurations

4.7.1 Single site configurations

Here, we describe the following scenarios:

- Single Peer-to-Peer VTS
- Multiple Peer-to-Peer VTSs
- Mixed configuration

4.7.1.1 Single Peer-to-Peer VTS

Figure 38 represents a single Peer-to-Peer VTS in a single location.

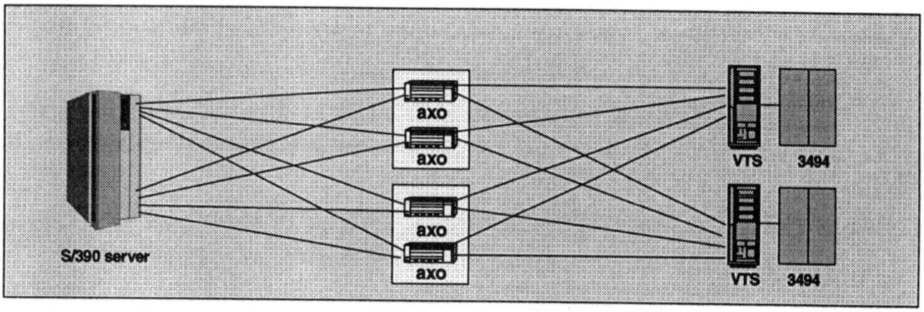

Figure 38. Single Peer-to-Peer VTS configuration

Availability targets

- This configuration addresses the need for high data availability in the day to day operation. Tape data availability in both distributed libraries must be guaranteed. It can be compared with a request for a "RAID 1 solution" in the DASD environment. This configuration may be required if applications rely heavily on tape data.
- This configuration is not intended for disaster recovery — you need to address disaster measures separately. That can be done by making additional copies of your tape data on real volumes that are transported to another site (a tier 1 or tier 2 solution) or sent via telecommunication lines to the disaster location (a tier 3 solution).

Configuration description

- The S/390 servers represent one or more OS/390 images. These images can share in an SMSplex or partition the composite library as is presently available on stand-alone Model B18 VTSs.
- Figure 38 shows two channel connections per Model AX0 controller to the host. The controller allows you to use only one ESCON channel connection rather than two, but you should be aware that you have configured a single point of failure if you do so.

- The four Model AX0 controllers can be housed in one Model CX0 frame or split over two Model CX0 frames. Two frames offer a slight advantage over one frame because the AX0s can be located in different places.
- Each Model CX0 frame has two power sources.

Configuration considerations

- The use of immediate mode of operation for the composite library ensures that the copy is available at completion of rewind/unload of the tape.
- The use of one ESCON channel connection per Model AX0 controller limits the requirement for the number of ESCON channels available in the host. However, it also limits availability of the Model AX0 controller. If the ESCON connection fails, you lose 16 virtual addresses.
- Neither of the Model B18 VTSs is defined as the preferred VTS. Non-preferred I/O provides the best performing option.
- One of the distributed 3494 libraries must be assigned as the UI Distributed Library. It is likely that it will be the library closest to the operator console bridge.

4.7.1.2 Dual Peer-to-Peer VTS

Figure 39 shows a dual Peer-to-Peer VTS in a single location. Compared to the previous scenario, there is a Peer-to-Peer VTS added in the same location.

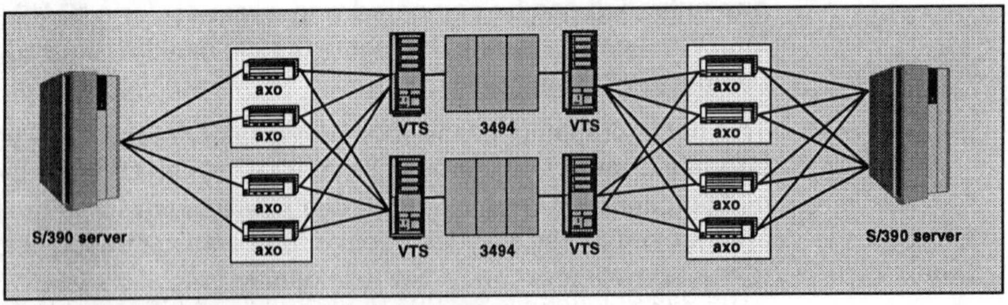

Figure 39. Dual Peer-to-Peer VTS configuration

Availability targets

- The data availability targets for the composite libraries can be different. One library can have a requirement for high data availability in day-to-day operations, while the other composite library has a requirement for high batch throughput.
- From a disaster recovery point of view, both Peer-to-Peer VTSs are the same. Other measures should be put in place for this.

Configuration description

- Both S/390 servers have OS/390 images running. The workload of this images can be different. The images in a single S/390 may share their connected library in a SMSplex or they may partition the library. Images in the other S/390 server are not connected to the same Peer-to-Peer VTS. They can be part of the same SMSplex but they do not share the Peer-to-Peer VTS libraries.
- The S/390 server on the left in the above figure has four channels connected to the Model AX0 controller, thereby limiting the number of ESCON channels required at the server which may be necessary if there is a shortage of channels. Compare this to the S/390 server on the right which has eight channel attachments.
- The Model AX0 controllers can be placed in one Model CX0 frame per composite library. It is possible to split the Model AX0 controllers over the two Model CX0 frames. Each Model CX0 frame has two Model AX0 controllers from one composite library and two Model AX0 controllers from the other.
- There are two 3494 tape libraries. Each has two Model B18 VTSs. Each B18 VTS of a Peer-to-Peer VTS must be attached to a different library.

Configuration considerations

- The use of one ESCON channel connection per Model AX0 controller, as shown for the left S/390 server, limits the requirement for the number of ESCON channels available in the host. However it also limits availability of the Model AX0 controller. If the ESCON connection fails, you lose 16 virtual addresses.
- One of the composite libraries can use the immediate mode of operation while the other can use deferred mode. The 3494 library manager is able to communicate with distributed VTSs running in different modes of operation.
- The use of immediate mode of operation for the composite library ensures that the copy is available at the completion of rewind/unload for the volume, but it increases the duration of a job by the time needed to perform the copy function. Deferred copy mode schedules the copy function asynchronously.
- The best choice is to have all Model AX0 controllers installed with "no-preference". The load is then balanced over the two distributed libraries. Although it is strongly advised not to do so, it may happen that the distributed libraries within a Peer-to-Peer VTS have unequal cache sizes. Configuring AX0 controllers to prefer the Model B18 VTS with the bigger cache size reduces the risk of throttling caused by cache overload.

- One of the distributed libraries from each composite library must be assigned as the UI Distributed Library. It is likely that it will be the 3494 tape library nearest to the operator console bridge.
- A 3494 tape library has some single points of failure. Many of them, but not all, can be removed by installing availability options like the high availability option (HA1), a second accessor and dual grippers. A failure of a 3494 tape library impacts both Peer-to-Peer VTSs.

4.7.1.3 Mixed configuration

In Figure 40, a Peer-to-Peer VTS, a stand-alone Model B18 VTS, and native drives share two 3494 tape libraries in a single location.

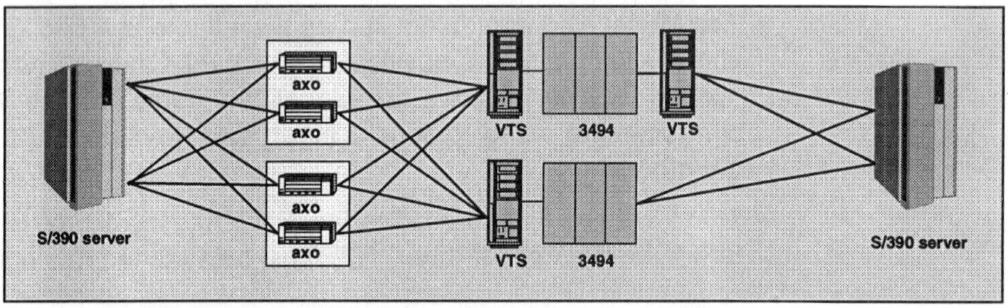

Figure 40. Mixed configuration in a single location

Availability targets

- The data availability targets for Peer-to-Peer VTS are the same as in the previous configuration.
- The data availability targets for the stand-alone Model B18 VTS and for the native drives are not further discussed here.

Configuration description

- Both S/390 servers have OS/390 images running. The images may be part of the same SMSplex but they do not share the logical libraries if they are not running on the same S/390 server.
- For the Model AX0 controllers the same applies as discussed in 4.7.1.1, "Single Peer-to-Peer VTS" on page 79.
- There are three logical libraries: the Peer-to-Peer VTS, the stand-alone Model B18 VTS and the native drives. One 3494 tape library includes a distributed library and the stand-alone library. The other 3494 tape library includes a distributed library and the native drives.

Configuration considerations

- For the Peer-to-Peer VTS, the same considerations apply as described in 4.7.1.1, "Single Peer-to-Peer VTS" on page 79.
- The 3494 tape libraries are not dedicated solely to the Peer-to-Peer VTS. It is possible that the availability of the Peer-to-Peer VTS may be impacted by problems with the other logical libraries.

4.7.2 Dual site configurations

Here, we describe the following scenarios:

- External distributed library
- Remote distributed library
- External distributed library and AX0 controllers
- Mirrored site

4.7.2.1 External distributed library

In Figure 41, one of the distributed libraries is placed in an external location. This library is connected to the Model AX0 controllers with ESCON links.

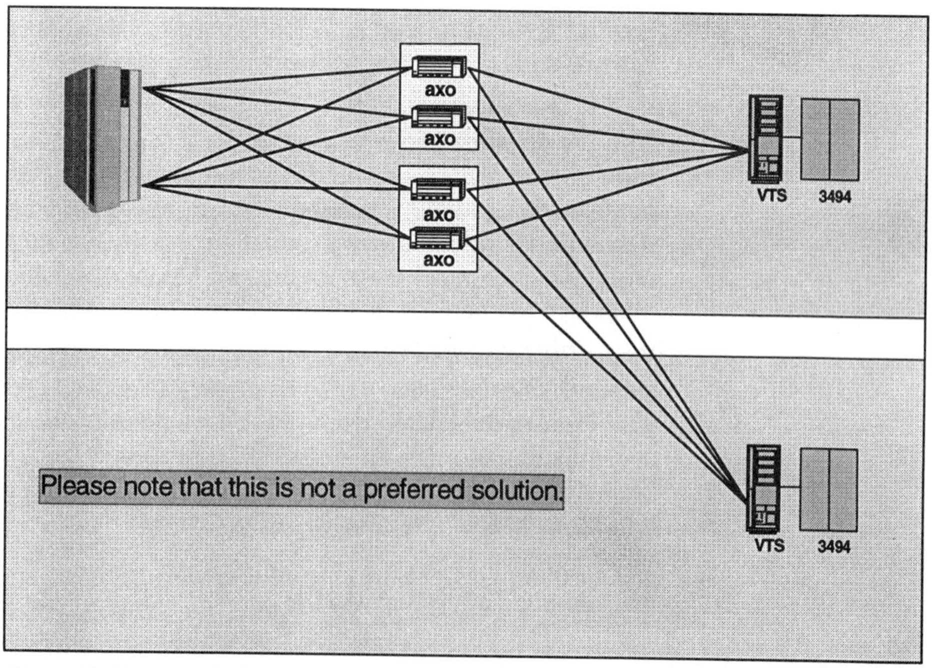

Figure 41. External distributed library

Availability targets

- This configuration addresses the need for having a copy of the tape data available outside the main computer center for disaster recovery reasons. This can be considered as a tier 3 solution for tape data.
- An outage of one of the components of the distributed library in the main location must be handled by the configuration within hours.
- Recover from a full disaster may take from days to one week. There must be arrangements with a recovery service provider like IBM Continuity Services for providing IT facilities in case of a disaster.

Configuration description

- The S/390 servers represents one or more OS/390 images. The images can share in a SMSplex or partition the composite library as is today available on stand-alone Model B18 VTSs.
- All Model AX0 controllers are placed in the main location. There may be several reasons for choosing this configuration.
  - The distance between the two sites requires ESCON channel extenders. When you place two Model AX0 controllers in the remote location there is a need for additional ESCON infrastructure between the two sites. The costs involved for this prohibits this solution.
  - If you place two Model AX0 controllers in the remote location and the ESCON distance between the locations is near its limit, it introduces throughput delays between the host and the remote Model AX0 controllers, and delays between the remote controllers and the distributed library in the main location. This is in addition to the delay already experienced between the two Model AX0 controllers in the main location and the distributed library in the remote location.
  - You may not want to be exposed to the temporary loss of the remote location, given that you would risk being unable to continue writing to your Peer-to-Peer VTS, because you would not have three AX0s available to perform a master switchover. See 7.6.10, “Site failure” on page 187 for details. This could happen if you did not control the remote location.
  - The external location is not owned by you. Placing two controllers at this site adds additional risks to your daily operation.

Configuration considerations

- The availability targets allow the use of either mode of operation for the composite library: immediate copy mode or deferred copy mode. Deferred mode is the option of choice if you are able to continue your workload without tape data which has not been copied to the remote distributed library.

- The choice between balanced I/O and preferred is dependent on the delays expected on the ESCON channels to the remote location. Excessive delays dictates the use of preferred I/O in all Model AX0 controllers for the distributed library in the main location.

  However, if you choose deferred copy mode, it may be advantageous to give the distributed library in the remote location preference. This results in a copy of the tape data in the remote location as early as possible.

- Additional equipment is required in case of a disaster. A distributed library is not able to function without the presence of a pair Model AX0 controllers. These controllers must be installed before you can access the tape data in the remaining Model B18 VTS in the remote location.

4.7.2.2 Remote distributed library

In the configuration presented in Figure 42, the external Model B18 VTS is placed in a remote location requiring the use of channel extenders.

Please remember that you will need to discuss the use of channel extenders in a Peer-to-Peer VTS environment with the vendors to ensure that the channel extenders have been tested and certified for use in this environment.

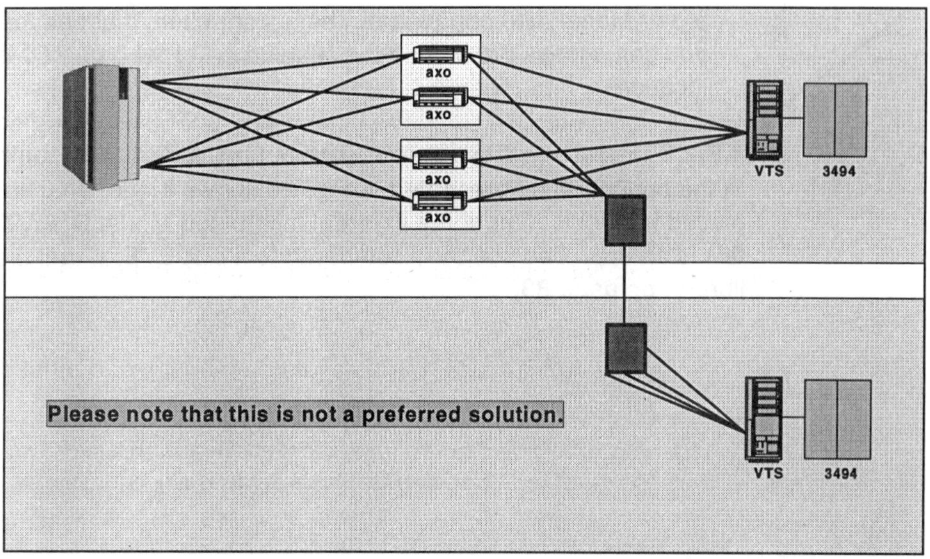

Figure 42. Remote distributed library

Availability targets

- The availability targets for this configuration are the same as in the previous configuration described on "Availability targets" on page 84.

Configuration description

- The main differentiators between this configuration and the previous one is the use of the remote channel extenders. It was calculated that the remote connection was able to handle the load even in peak periods.
- The "Configuration description" on page 84 fully applies to this configuration.

Configuration considerations

- The availability targets allow the use of either mode of operation for the composite library: immediate copy mode and deferred copy mode. Deferred mode is the option of choice here if you are able to continue your workload without tape data that has been produced in the period just before the outage of one of the distributed libraries.
- Current performance measurements for distances up to 25 km show that the choice between non-preferred I/O and preferred is in favor of non-preferred I/O for the distributed library, despite the use of extenders.
- Also in this configuration is additional equipment required in case of a disaster. A distributed library is not able to function without the presence of a pair Model AX0 controllers. These controllers must be installed before you can access the data in the remaining Model B18 VTS in the remote location.

4.7.2.3 External distributed library and AX0 controllers

In the configuration presented in Figure 43, two Model AX0 controllers are placed in the location of the external distributed Model B18 VTS. Basically, this is an improved scenario compared to 4.7.2.1, "External distributed library" on page 83.

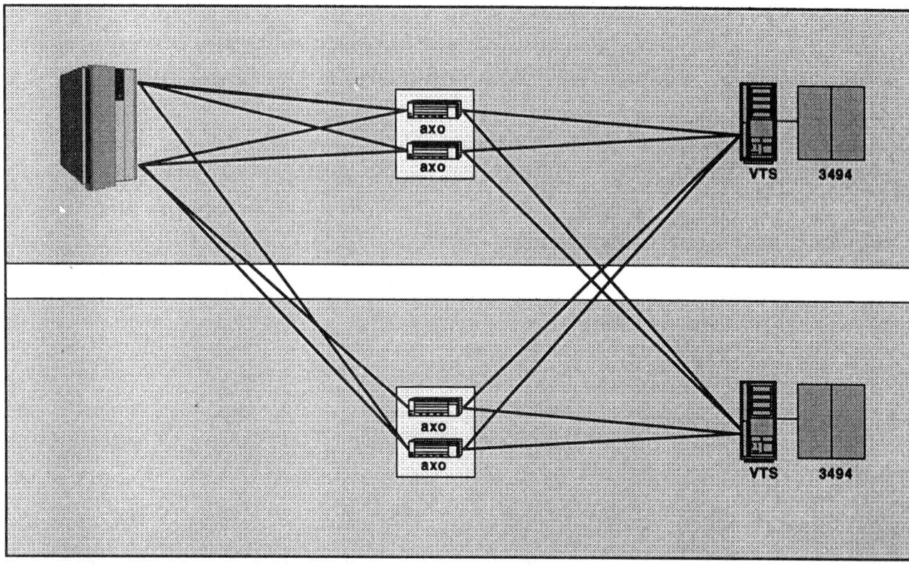

Figure 43. External distributed library and AX0 controllers

Availability targets

- This configuration addresses the need for having a copy of the tape data available outside the main computer center for disaster recovery reasons. This can be considered as a tier 3 solution for tape data.
- A partial disaster with one of the components of the distributed library in the main location must be handled by the configuration within hours.
- Recovery from a full disaster may take from hours to days. There are arrangements made with a recovery service provider like IBM Continuity Services for providing ICT facilities (processing power) in case of a disaster.

Configuration description

- The main differentiator between this configuration and the one described in 4.7.2.1, "External distributed library" on page 83 is the placement of two Model AX0 controllers in a Model CX0 frame in the external site.
- A variation could use channel extenders between the two sites.

Configuration considerations

- The availability targets allow the use of either mode of operation for the composite library: immediate copy mode or deferred copy mode. Deferred mode is the option of choice here if you are able to continue your workload without tape data that has been produced in the period just before the outage of one of the distributed libraries.

- Current performance measurements for distances up to 25 km show that the choice between non-preferred I/O and preferred is in favor of non-preferred I/O for the distributed library, despite the use of extenders.

4.7.2.4 Mirrored site

Figure 44 presents a dual site configuration where all major components are duplicated in both sites. There is no main site because they are mirrors of each other.

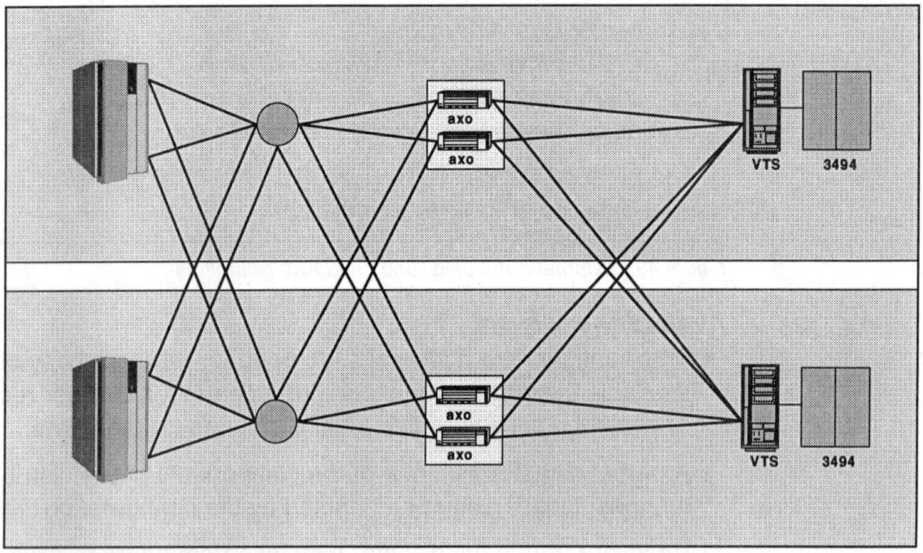

Figure 44. Mirrored external site

The figure shows ESCON directors on the left-hand (host) side of the configuration, as we expect that they will already be present in many installations to allow easy reconfiguration. They could equally well appear on the right of the diagram as well.

This configuration might be included in a Geographically Dispersed Parallel Sysplex (GDPS) configuration. GDPS provide switching capability from one site to another site, for planned and for unplanned outages. It provides the capability to manage the configuration, automates parallel sysplex operational tasks and automates the recovery from a failure through a single point of control. GDPS support all transaction managers (for example CICS and IMS) and database managers (for example DB2, IMS and VSAM). For more information, see Appendix B, “Geographically Dispersed Parallel Sysplex” on page 227.

Availability targets

- This configuration addresses the need for having a high availability data center on a tier 5 or tier 6 level. All data, both DASD and tape data is mirrored in both sites.
- A partial disaster with one of the components of the distributed library in the main location must be recovered immediately.
- Recover from a full disaster may take not more than a couple of hours and probably additional arrangements are made for the critical applications to continue without a service interrupt.

Configuration description

- The S/390 servers represents one or more OS/390 images. The images can share in a SMSplex or partition the composite library as is today available on stand-alone Model B18 VTSs.
- The production OS/390 have at least an active backup system available in the other site. It is likely that the images are part of a parallel sysplex environment.
- Complex data centers usually have ESCON directors in use for connecting the I/O equipment to the hosts.
- There are many ESCON connections between the two sites. They are not only required for DASD and tape mirroring but also needed for channel-to-channel connections, printers and network controllers.
- Each site has two Model AX0 controllers housed in a Model CX0 frame. These frames use the dual power facility.
- The installation of additional ESCON director functionality between the Model AX0 controllers and the Model B18 VTSs improves the configuration flexibility.

Configuration considerations

- The availability targets allow the use of either mode of operation for the composite library: immediate copy mode or deferred copy mode. For your critical workload with a requirement for a tier 6 solution the only option is immediate copy mode. Remember that this mode is set the same in all Model AX0 controllers. If less critical partitions share the Peer-to-Peer VTS, they will also use immediate copy mode. The influence of the load of the less critical partitions, particularly on the batch window of your production partition, may be undesirable. Only a dedicated Peer-to-Peer VTS for your critical workloads prevents this workload from being impacted by other load.

- Most likely you will choose no preference for the I/O VTS if the sites are within ESCON distance. It assures that you exploit the available resources to an optimum level.
- The choice which of the distributed libraries is the UI library is influenced by the location of the operations and support personnel. It influences the initial selection of the Master VTS, but as explained in 2.6.2, "Master VTS switchover" on page 34, the Master function can switchover to the other distributed library after a failure of one of the components of the composite library.

GDPS considerations

- The Peer-to-Peer VTS is not currently supported by GDPS. The FREEZE commands do not apply to tape. A planned cross-site re-configuration does not affect the Peer-to-Peer VTS unless you take action to force a disaster by terminating the Model AX0 controllers.
- If the Peer-to-Peer VTS runs in immediate copy mode and is fully operational, the host control datasets for OAM and for your tape management software are consistent with the data on your logical volumes site-to-site as long as the volumes are copied.
- If a disaster occurs and you are running in immediate copy mode, there is no synchronization for open logical volumes. A rerun of the workload will inform you that you have no valid copy of the data.
- If a disaster takes place and you are in deferred mode, there is no synchronization for closed and open logical volumes. Open logical volumes at time of the disaster become invalidated; for closed logical volumes it depends on which of the distributed libraries is the I/O VTS for that volume. If the I/O VTS is the remaining VTS, then the logical volumes are valid. If the I/O VTS is the damaged VTS and the copy process for a logical volume has not been completed, the logical volume is invalid. Remember that you are not able to have full control of the selection of the I/O VTS.

Chapter 5. Preinstallation planning

In this chapter, we describe many of the preinstallation tasks listed below for a Peer-to-Peer VTS. If you are upgrading an existing VTS subsystem or merging two existing VTS subsystems, some of these tasks may not apply to you. You will find information about the tasks that also apply to a stand-alone VTS in *IBM Magstar Virtual Tape Server: Planning, Implementing and Monitoring*, SG24-2229. The software tasks are described in detail in Chapter 6, “Implementation and migration” on page 117. The tasks that are related only to a Peer-to-Peer VTS are shown in boldface:

- Analyze your tape environment:
  - Determine the workload for the VTS
  - Size the VTS (TVC, storage slots, drives, and more)
  - Determine the number of stacked volumes
  - Determine the number of logical volumes
  - Decide on volser range for stacked volumes and order
  - Decide on volser range for logical volumes
- Complete physical installation planning
- Plan to update or create operations documentation
- Plan for implementation of the StorWatch Peer-to-Peer VTS Specialist and the StorWatch 3494 Tape Library Specialist for monitoring
- Prepare for implementation of the Remote Library Manager Console (if required)[1]
- Prepare for implementation of the SNMP monitoring (if required)[1]
- Arrange telephone line for Remote Support Facility (RSF) connection
- **Select the Copy Mode (Immediate or Deferred)**
- **Select the VTS preference for I/O (non-preferred or prefer one of the distributed VTSs)**
- **Select the UI Distributed Library**
- **Set up the Model AX0 controller LAN connection for the StorWatch Peer-to-Peer Specialist**
- Plan the device address range for I/O configuration definition:
  - IOCP
  - HCD
- Set the correct missing interrupt handler interval

[1] See *VTS: Planning, Implementing and Monitoring*, SG24-2229, for details.

© Copyright IBM Corp. 2000

- Plan the VTS management policies[1]:
  - Fast-ready categories
  - Inhibit reclaim schedule
  - Reclaim threshold percentage
  - Free storage threshold
- Plan the software definition for DFSMS system-managed tape:
  - System parameters
  - SMS CDSs
  - TCDB
  - SMS parameters
  - ACS routine
- Plan to install software support for the Peer-to-Peer VTS
- Plan monitoring from SMF type 94 record enhanced statistics
- Plan the JES3 definitions

There are also some significant tape volume cache hardware changes which can be ordered for stand-alone VTSs as well as Peer-to-Peer VTSs. For completeness, we mention these changes in this chapter.

5.1 Workload analysis and sizing tasks for Peer-to-Peer VTS

The analysis and sizing tasks needed for a Peer-to-Peer VTS are basically the same as those for a stand-alone VTS.

For more information about analysis and sizing a VTS subsystem, please refer to *IBM Magstar Virtual Tape Server: Planning, Implementing, and Monitoring*, SG24-2229.

You should carefully review the need for larger tape volume cache sizes to avoid removal of volumes from the cache before completion of the dual copy during:

- Extended peak periods with deferred copy mode:

  You should have enough cache to prevent removal of volumes from the cache during peak workloads.
- Extended maintenance action:

  You should have enough cache to prevent removal of volumes from the cache during a planned outage so that dual copies can be made efficiently when all the components of the configuration are back in service.

Please refer to 3.1.4, "Deferred Copy Mode considerations" on page 55 for a discussion of the effect of the tape volume cache size and guidance on how large a cache size is needed for different host write rates.

Sizing the number of logical volumes and the number of stacked volumes use the same methods as for a stand-alone VTS. Naturally, you will need to double the number of stacked volumes for a given set of logical volumes.

Similarly, the same considerations apply for your choice of volume serial number ranges for stacked and virtual volumes. See also 5.3.1.2, "Logical volume serial numbers" on page 108.

5.2 Hardware configurations

Both the stand-alone Model B18 VTS and the Peer-to-Peer VTS configuration present themselves to the host as one single logical library containing 64 virtual 3490E tape drives, although the underlying hardware requirements are different. To make it easy to identify the new hardware components and configuration requirements for a Peer-to-Peer configuration, we first summarize those of the stand-alone Model B18 VTS without listing all the feature codes. For a detailed description of the VTS feature codes, please refer to *IBM Magstar Virtual Tape Server: Planning, Implementing, and Monitoring*, SG24-2229 and to the *Magstar IBM 3494 Tape Library Introduction and Planning Guide,* GA32-0279.

Note

Some of the features discussed in this paragraph are not valid for a Peer-to-Peer VTS configuration.

Refer to 5.2.3.8, "Unsupported features" on page 104.

5.2.1 Standalone VTS components and configuration options

A Model B18 VTS that is not part of a Peer-to-Peer configuration consists of the following IBM 3494 tape library hardware components:

- One 3494-D12 frame installed inside an IBM 3494 tape library including the Magstar 3590 tape drives for exclusive use of the VTS.
- One 3494-B18 frame installed up to 14m away from the IBM 3494 tape library. The tape volume cache and the VTS controller are both located in the B18 frame. Host attachment to the VTS is solely through the ESCON channel adapters or SCSI adapters in the B18 frame.

5.2.1.1 Magstar 3590 tape drives

Three to six Magstar 3590 Model B1A or Model E1A tape drives are installed in an IBM 3494 Model D12 frame for the exclusive use of the VTS. All tape drives attached to a single VTS must be of the same model, either all models B1A or all models E1A.

If the Advanced Function feature, which allows exporting and importing of virtual volumes, and/or the Performance Accelerator feature (PAF) are installed in the VTS, a minimum of four Magstar 3590 tape drives are required.

> **Note**
>
> The 3590 Extended High Performance Cartridge Tape is not currently supported in a VTS subsystem.

5.2.1.2 Model B18 VTS features

The Model B18 VTS is available in three forms, depending on the features installed:

- **Base B18:** This model provides 32 virtual devices and attaching through two standard ESCON channel attachments
- **B18 with Extended High Performance Option (EHPO):** EHPO enables compression in the tape volume cache and thus enlarges the usable cache capacity by the compression factor achieved for the data written to the VTS. It also enables addressing of 64 virtual devices in the VTS when the tape volume cache is 144 GB or greater. EHPO is a prerequisite for the Advanced Function feature, and for the Extended Performance ESCON channels.
- **B18 with the Performance Accelerator feature (PAF):** PAF enhances the overall throughput of a VTS by providing a high performance streaming file system, and additional processing power and memory increase of the VTS. It enables new levels of performance for the Model B18 VTS. PAF requires Extended Performance ESCON channels and EHPO to be installed, and a minimum native tape volume cache capacity of 144 GB.

5.2.1.3 Host channel attachment

A stand-alone VTS subsystem attaches to the host systems through ESCON or SCSI channel adapters. You may have up to eight ESCON channels. These may be configured with SCSI attachments; equally, you may have a VTS which only has SCSI host attachments.

The stand-alone Model B18 VTS also attaches to native Fibre Channel host adapters through the SAN Data Gateway IBM 2108 to allow integration of the VTS in a storage area network (SAN).

5.2.1.4 Tape volume cache

The usable size of the tape volume cache (TVC) depends on the disk capacity, on the number of drawers, and the Model B18 VTS features that are installed.

TVC Disk Storage Capacity features

The Disk Storage Capacity feature (feature 3702) provides a single drawer of 72 GB storage capacity using 9 GB disks. The RAID configuration in a single drawer consists of four RAID-5 arrays, logically arranged as two data drives, one parity and one hot spare. Up to four drawers can be installed, allowing a native TVC capacity of 72, 144, 216, or 288 GB with this feature. These TVC configurations apply to older Model B18 VTS installations only. Feature 3702 was withdrawn from marketing as of September 29, 2000.

The most current TVC disk storage features provide native storage capacities ranging from 72 to 1,152 GB for Base B18 and from 216 to 1,728 GB for B18 PAF models. These features use 36 GB disks. Table 2 shows the available TVC features and their corresponding usable TVC capacity in GB. For the Model B18 VTS with EHPO or PAF, a compression ratio of 3:1 is assumed and numbers in brackets show the native storage capacity in GB. Please note that you must have FC 5236 (the Performance Enhancement feature), if you install two or more of the FC 3705 features.

Table 2. Tape volume cache features

Drawers	Features	Base B18	B18 EHPO	B18 PAF (Peer-to-Peer)
1	1 x FC 3703	72	216 (72)	
1	1 x FC 3704	144	432 (144)	648 (216)
1	1 x FC 3705	288	864 (288)	1,296 (432)
2	2 x FC 3705	not applicable	not applicable	2,592 (864)
4	4 x FC 3705	not applicable	not applicable	5,184 (1,728)

The RAID configuration remains the same for the Base Model B18 VTS and Model B18 VTS with EHPO. For the Model B18 VTS with PAF, the RAID configuration in single drawer has been changed to use two arrays, each logically comprising 6 data drives, 1 parity drive, and one hot spare in a

RAID-5 array. This enables an additional increase capacity of 50% for FC 3704 and FC 3705.

The feature codes listed in Table 2 are described below:

- 72 GB Disk Storage (FC 3703):

  FC 3703 provides 72 GB of usable disk storage capacity for TVC. It is available for the entry level VTS system and cannot be installed with the PAF (FC 5236) or used on a Model B18 VTS in a Peer-to-Peer VTS configuration. Therefore, this feature does not support the Peer-to-Peer copy feature FC 4010 as that requires FC 5236. Feature 3703 cannot be installed with any of the other disk storage features (FC 3702, FC 3704, or FC 3705). This feature can be converted to feature FC 3704, or FC 3705.

- 144 GB Disk Storage (FC 3704):

  FC 3704 provides 144 GB of usable disk storage capacity for TVC. If the PAF (FC 5236) is installed, the usable storage capacity for TVC is increased to 216 GB. This feature cannot be installed with any of the other disk storage features (FC 3702, FC 3703, or FC 3705). This feature can be converted to feature FC 3705.

- 288 GB Disk Storage (FC 3705):

  FC 3705 provides 288 GB of usable disk storage capacity for TVC. One, two or four of FC 3705 can be installed. One FC3705 provides a TVC capacity of 288 GB without PAF or 432 GB with PAF. If the PAF is installed, the usable storage capacity for TVC is 432 GB for one drawer, 864 GB for two drawers, or 1,728 GB for three drawers. This feature cannot be installed with any of the other disk storage features (FC 3702, FC 3703, or FC 3704).

Note

FC 3703, FC 3704, and FC 3705 (36 GB disk features) cannot be intermixed within a single Model B18 VTS, and cannot be installed together with FC 3702 (9 GB disk feature).

Each installed FC 3702 can be upgraded to FC 3704 or FC 3705. For upgrade options, refer to the *IBM 3494 Tape Library Introduction and Planning Guide*, GA32-0279.The upgrade includes dual PCC and dual RS/6000 boot disk. If the PAF is installed, the upgrade also includes enhanced SSA adapters, SSA loop reconfiguration (each SSA disk accessible from both SSA adapters for redundant paths), and the new RAID configuration (Figure 45).

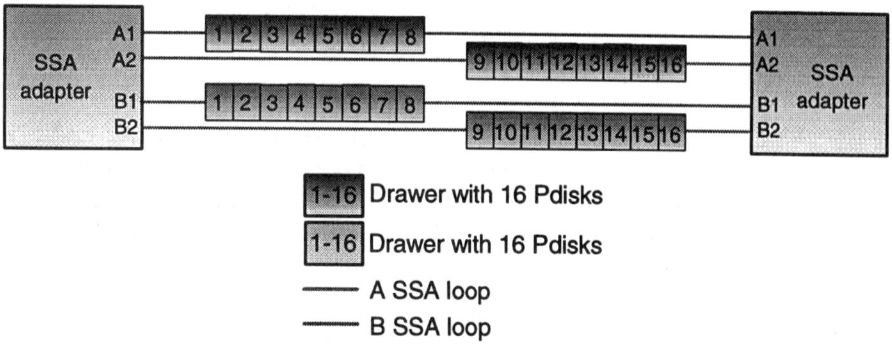

Figure 45. SSA RAID high-availability configuration

File system configuration

All of the FC 3703, FC 3704, and FC 3705 features provide one single drawer with sixteen 36-GB disks. All disks are used to make the system easily upgradable and to provide the higher level of performance. The system is more easily upgraded because no new hardware needs to be installed when going from FC 3703 or FC 3704 to FC 3705. The disk storage capacity is limited by the features ordered.

The Model B18 VTS without the PAF uses the Journal File System (JFS) for the TVC disk storage. When the PAF is installed, it provides the General Parallel File System (GPFS) as the high performance file system for the TVC. JFS and GPFS TVC disk storage capacities are calculated and upgraded differently. Below, we describe details of how the disk storage capacities are calculated and upgraded:

- JFS (without PAF):

  Four [2 data + 1 parity + 1 spare] SSA RAID arrays are created for each single drawer (16 disks). JFS creates one logical disk volume for each of two file systems. When FC 3703 is installed, each logical disk volume is created with 1/4 of the total logical partitions (LPs) available on each SSA RAID array. When FC 3704 is installed, half of the logical partitions are used; when FC 3705 is installed, all of the logical partitions are used.

  For the Disk Storage feature upgrade (via MES), the additional logical partitions are added to each logical disk volume. This can be done while the VTS is *online* if upgrading from FC 3703 to FC 3704, or from FC 3703 to FC 3705, or from FC 3704 to FC 3705. If the upgrade requires new SSA drawers (additional FC 3705s) then the VTS must be *offline* and all data on the TVC must be copied to tape before the upgrade. After new hardware is installed, the file systems are rebuilt, and the data is restored to the TVC.

- GPFS (with PAF) as used in a Peer-to-Peer configuration:

  Two [6 data + 1 parity + 1 spare] SSA RAID arrays are created for single SSA drawer (16 disks). GPFS creates logical disk volumes that each use 1/4 of the total physical partitions available on an SSA RAID array. When FC 3704 is installed, 2 GPFS logical disk volumes are created on each RAID array, for a cache size 1/2 of the total available space. When FC 3705 is installed, 4 GPFS logical disk volumes are created for each RAID array.

  For the disk storage feature upgrade (via MES), the additional GPFS logical disk volumes are created. The upgrade can be done while the VTS is ONLINE if upgrading from FC 3704 to FC 3705 (no new hardware is installed). If additional SSA drawers are installed (additional FC 3705s) then the VTS must be brought offline, but no TVC data copying to tape is needed. After additional hardware installed, the file systems are expanded.

> **Note**
>
> Please remember that you must have feature 5236, the Performance Accelerator feature, for two or more feature 3705 TVC drawers.

Figure 46 shows the logical RAID-5 configuration scheme for the available TVC features of FC 3703, FC 3704, and FC 3705.

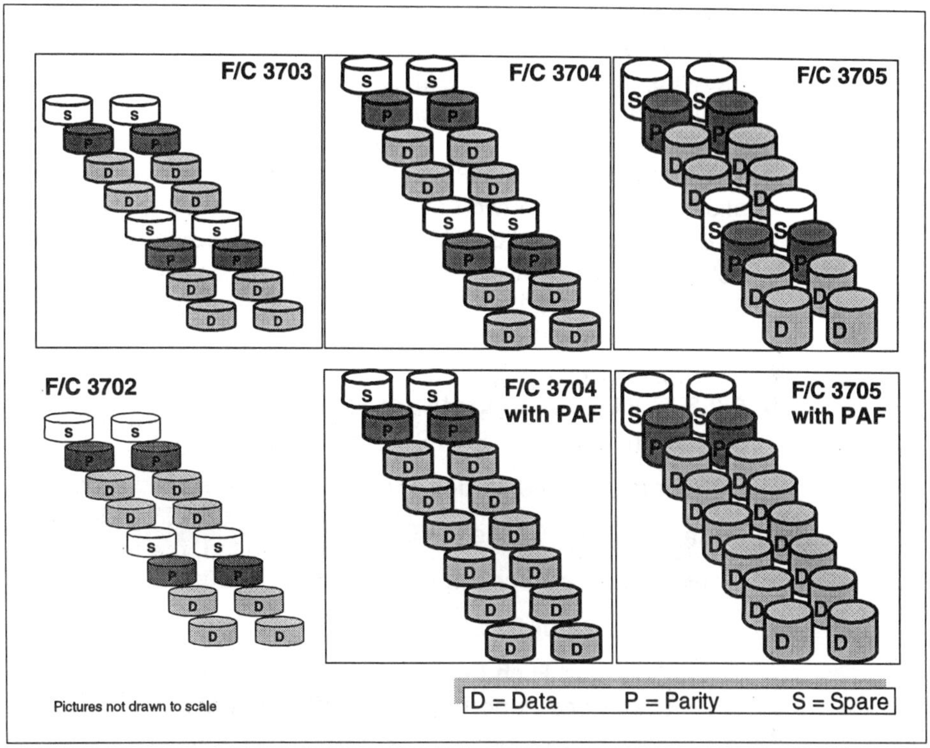

Figure 46. RAID configurations

5.2.2 Peer-to-Peer VTS configuration

The Peer-to-Peer VTS consists of two Model B18 VTSs and four Model AX0 controllers. These two Model B18 VTSs only have ESCON connections to Model AX0 controllers. Each of the Model B18 VTSs is associated with four to six 3590 tape drives that are installed in a Model D12 frame. The Model D12 frames must be installed in separate 3494 tape libraries. The 3494 tape library can have any of the other supported configurations for Model B18 VTS sharing of a 3494 tape library. The Model AX0 controllers are installed in one or two Model CX0 frames. Each Model AX0 controller has two host ESCON connections and an ESCON connection to each Model B18 VTS. We describe each component of a Peer-to-Peer VTS in the following sections.

5.2.3 Model B18 VTS

In this section we describe the specific features of the Model B18 VTS in a Peer-to-Peer VTS. For detailed descriptions of the other Model B18 VTS features, please refer to *IBM Magstar Virtual Tape Server: Planning, Implementing, and Monitoring*, SG24-2229.

The Model B18 VTS has two PCCs, each with its own power cord, which allow connection to two power sources. A model upgrade of a older Model B18 VTS to a Model B18 VTS with Peer-to-Peer Copy feature (FC 4010) does not provide two PCCs and two power cords, however, the TVC upgrades from FC 3702 to FC 3703, FC 3704, FC 3705 provides dual power control compartments (PCC) and two power cords.

5.2.3.1 VTS configuration requirements

Each of the Model B18 VTSs in a Peer-to-Peer VTS requires:

- Four to six 3590 Model B1A or E1A tape drives
- Tape Volume Cache (TVC) must have at least 144 GB capacity
- Performance Accelerator feature (FC 5236)
- Must have four ESCON channels
  - Extended High Performance Option (FC 3400) and two FC 3412 (Extended Performance ESCON channels)
  - ESCON High Performance Option (FC 3200) and one FC 3412
- Must be attached to separate 3494 tape libraries
- Peer-to-Peer Copy base feature (FC 4010) and Peer-to-Peer Copy increments (FC 4011, 4012, 4013) if required (refer to Table 5 on page 103)

Base B18 VTS models, or models with EHPO only, are not supported in a Peer-to-Peer VTS configuration.

5.2.3.2 3590 tape drives

Each Model B18 VTS in a Peer-to-Peer configuration must have a minimum of four Magstar 3590 tape drives installed in the attached Model D12 frame. All tape drives in a frame must be of the same model: either all 3590 Model B1As or all 3590 Model E1As. Using the maximum of six drives per VTS is advisable for maximum throughput.

Although it is not required that both VTS subsystems of the Peer-to-Peer VTS configuration have the same number and type of tape drives installed, we strongly recommend that you install the same number of tape drives in both

Model B18 VTSs in a Peer-to-Peer VTS configuration to avoid disparities in throughput. It is also helpful to have the same model of drive if possible.

> **Note**
>
> In the VTS subsystem, the 3590 Extended High Performance Cartridge Tape currently is not supported.

5.2.3.3 Tape Volume Cache features

Each of the Model B18 VTSs in the Peer-to-Peer VTS must has at least 144 GB TVC with EHPO and PAF. The usable storage capacity of the TVC depends on the number of the VTS cache features installed. Table 3 shows the supported TVC disk storage capacity features for the Model B18 VTS in a Peer-to-Peer VTS configuration.

Important: We strongly recommend that you install the same amount of tape volume cache in both Model B18 VTSs in a Peer-to-Peer VTS configuration.

Table 3. TVC disk storage capacity features

Features	TVC native capacity (GB)	Peer-to-Peer, total usable TVC capacity (GB)
2 x FC 3702 [1]	144	864
4 x FC 3702 [1]	288	1728
1 x FC 3704	216 [2]	1296
1 x FC 3705	432 [2]	2592
2 x FC 3705	864 [3]	5184
4 x FC 3705	1728 [3]	10,368
Note: 1. FC 3702 is withdrawn from marketing with effect from September 29, 2000 2. EHPO and PAF are required feature for Peer-to-Peer Copy feature (FC 4010). With PAF, the disk storage capacities of FC 3704 and FC 3705 are increased by 50% 3. PAF is required for two or more FC3705.		**Note:** The above column shows total capacity for both VTS subsystems in a Peer-to-Peer configuration, assuming 3:1 compression.

For more detailed information about the TVC disk storage features and configuration of the TVC disk storage, please refer to 5.2.1.4, "Tape volume cache" on page 95.

5.2.3.4 Performance Accelerator feature

Each of the Model B18 VTSs must have the Performance Accelerator feature (FC 5236). To enable new levels of performance for the Model B18 VTS, FC 5236 provides a high performance streaming file system, additional processing power and a memory increase. This feature also increases the TVC storage capacity of FC 3704 and FC 3705 by 50%.

5.2.3.5 ESCON channel attachment

Each of the Model B18 VTSs must have four ESCON channel attachments with EHPO option; Extended High Performance Option (FC 3400) or ESCON High Performance Option (FC 3200) for connection to each of four Model AX0 controllers. In the Peer-to-Peer VTS configuration, the Model B18 VTS must not have Activate Additional ESCON Channels feature (FC 3418) and SCSI attachment feature (FC 3422). The Additional Enhanced ESCON Channel Attachment feature (FC 3302) is not supported either. We summarize the channel attachment features in Table 4.

Table 4. Required channel attachment features

Feature combination	Number of ESCON channels
1 x FC 3400 2 x FC 3412	4
1 x FC 3200 1 x FC 3412	4

Each of these connections can use ESCON directors to extend the distance up to 26 km between the Model AX0 controller and the Model B18 VTS.

5.2.3.6 3494 tape library

Each of the Model B18 VTSs must be attached to a separate 3494 tape library. Each of the 3494 tape libraries can have any of the supported configurations for Model B18 VTS and can also be part of a second Peer-to-Peer VTS.

5.2.3.7 Peer-to-Peer Copy features

In this section we describe the feature codes that related the Peer-to-Peer VTS configuration. Table 5 summarizes the feature codes required on the Model B18 VTS in the Peer-to-Peer VTS configuration.

Table 5. Peer-to-Peer Copy features

Feature	Max. Qty.	Prereq	Description
FC 4010	1	-	Peer-to-Peer Copy Base
FC 4011	1	FC 4010	Peer-to-Peer Copy Increment 1
FC 4012	1	FC 4010 FC 4011	Peer-to-Peer Copy Increment 2
FC 4013	1	FC 4010 FC 4011 FC 4012	Peer-to-Peer Copy Increment 3

Details on the feature codes listed in Table 5 are described below.

- Peer-to-Peer Copy Base (FC 4010):

  FC 4010 enables the Model B18 VTS in a Peer-to-Peer VTS. FC 4010 requires Performance Accelerator feature (FC 5236). This feature will disable both Advance Function (Import/Export) feature (FC 4000), and ESCON Channel Activation feature (FC 3418) if installed. SCSI Host Attachment feature (FC 3422) must not be installed on the Model B18 VTS with this feature.

- Peer-to-Peer Copy Increment 1 (FC 4011):

  FC 4011 extends the Model B18 VTS in a Peer-to-Peer VTS configuration when greater than 250 GB of usable Tape Volume Cache (TVC) disk capacity is installed. This feature is required on a Model B18 VTS when FC 4010 is installed and four of Disk Storage Capacity feature (FC 3702) or one or more of 288 GB Disk Storage feature (FC 3705) are installed.

- Peer-to-Peer Copy Increment 2 (FC 4012):

  FC 4012 extends the Model B18 VTS in a Peer-to-Peer VTS configuration when greater than 500 GB of usable TVC capacity is installed. This feature is required on a Model B18 VTS when FC 4010 and FC 4011 is installed and two or more of 288 GB Disk Storage feature (FC 3705) are installed.

- Peer-to-Peer Copy Increment 3 (FC 4013):

  FC 4013 extends the Model B18 VTS in a Peer-to-Peer VTS configuration when greater than 1 TB of usable TVC capacity is installed. This feature is required on the Model B18 VTS when FC 4010, FC 4011 and FC 4012 is installed and four of 288 GB Disk Storage feature (FC 3705) are installed.

Table 6 shows the supported combinations of the Peer-to-Peer Copy features and the Disk Storage features.

Table 6. Supported feature combinations

Disk storage feature	TVC native capacity (GB)	Peer-to-Peer Copy feature
2 x FC 3702 [1]	144	FC 4010
4 x FC 3702 [1]	288	FC 4010 FC 4011
1 x FC 3704	216 [2]	FC 4010
1 x FC 3705	432 [2]	FC 4010 FC 4011
2 x FC 3705	864 [2]	FC 4010 FC 4011 FC 4012
4 x FC 3705	1728 [2]	FC 4010 FC 4011 FC 4012 FC 4013

Note:
1. FC 3702 is withdrawn from marketing with effect from September 29, 2000.
2. The Performance Accelerator feature (FC 5236) is a required feature for the Peer-to-Peer Copy feature (FC 4010). With FC 5236, the disk storage capacities of FC 3704 and FC 3705 are increased by 50%.

5.2.3.8 Unsupported features

With the Peer-to-Peer Copy feature (FC 4010), the following features are not supported. If any of these features is installed in an existing Model B18 VTS, it will be disabled or removed during the model upgrade of the Model B18 VTS to the Model B18 VTS with FC 4010 in a Peer-to-Peer VTS configuration.

- Advanced Function (FC 4000) Import/Export:

  FC 4000 provides the Import/Export function for VTS logical volumes and VTS tape volume cache management. Import/Export must be disabled as part of a Peer-to-Peer upgrade. Tape volume cache management is still supported.

- Activate Additional ESCON Channels (FC 3418):

  FC 3418 provides two additional Extended Performance ESCON Channel attachments for the Model B18 VTS.

- SCSI Host Attachment (FC 3422):

  FC 3422 provides two SCSI bus host attachments for the Model B18 VTS. This feature must actually be removed, because the physical card slots are needed for the ESCON host attachment cards.

5.2.4 Model AX0 controller

The Model AX0 controller is one of the new components of the Peer-to-Peer VTS configuration. The Model AX0 controller is an RS/6000 that is used to connect the two Model B18 VTSs in the Peer-to-Peer VTS configuration with the host system. Figure 47 shows the Model AX0 controllers.

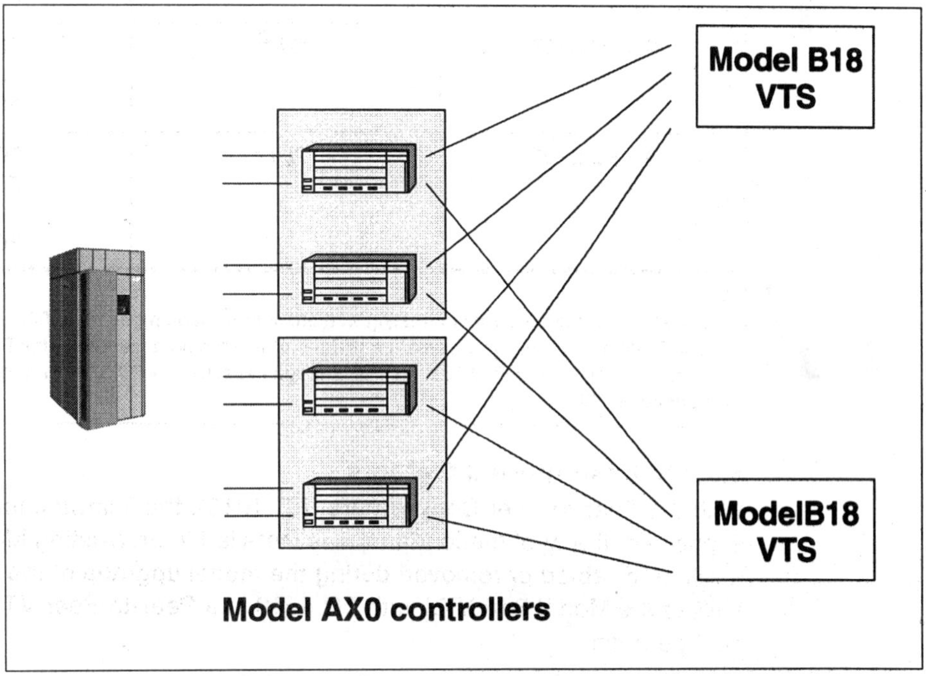

Figure 47. Model AX0 controllers

5.2.4.1 Remote Support Facility for AX0 controllers

The Remote Support Facility (RSF) features and connections are the same as for the 3494 tape library and the Model B18 VTS. The modem and switch can be shared with other 3494 tape libraries, 3590 model Axx ESCON controllers and the Model B18 VTS. Table 7 shows the RSF features.

For more detailed information about the RSF features, please refer to *IBM Magstar Virtual Tape Server: Planning, Implementing, and Monitoring,*

SG24-2229 and to the *Magstar IBM 3494 Tape Library Introduction and Planning Guide*, GA32-0279.

Table 7. RSF features

Features	Description
FC 2710	Remote Support Facility
FC 2711	Remote Support Switch
FC 2712	Remote Support Attachment

5.2.4.2 Model AX0 LAN connection

Each Model AX0 controller provides an Ethernet connection for the customer LAN. When this connection is used, each of the Model AX0 controllers provides the StorWatch Specialist Web interface that is a Web Page for monitoring the status of the Peer-to-Peer VTS. This is the only interface to monitor the Peer-to-Peer VTS except the SMF type 94 record. The use of this connection and Web access is optional. However, we recommend that you use the StorWatch Peer-to-Peer Specialist to monitor the state of the Peer-to-Peer VTS.

Note

The Model AX0 controller does not support a Token-Ring LAN connection for providing the StorWatch specialist Web interface.

5.2.5 Model CX0 frame

The Model CX0 frame is one of the new components in a Peer-to-Peer VTS configuration. It provides the housing and power for two or four Model AX0 controllers. Two Model AX0 controllers in a Model CX0 frame must be within the same Peer-to-Peer VTS. An additional two Model AX0 controllers in the Model CX0 frame can be used for another Peer-to-Peer VTS, or all four Model AX0 controllers in a Model CX0 frame can be for the same Peer-to-Peer VTS.

Model CX0 frame contains two power control compartments (PCC), each with its own power cord, which allows connection to two power sources. Figure 48 shows the Model CX0 frame.

The position numbers for the AX0s are 0, 1, 2, and 3 (see Figure 48). Position 0 is the lowermost position and position 3 is the uppermost position. When only two Model AX0s are in the Model CX0, they are in position 0 and 1. The lower PCC powers AX0s in position 0 and 2. The upper PCC powers Model AX0s in position 1 and 3.

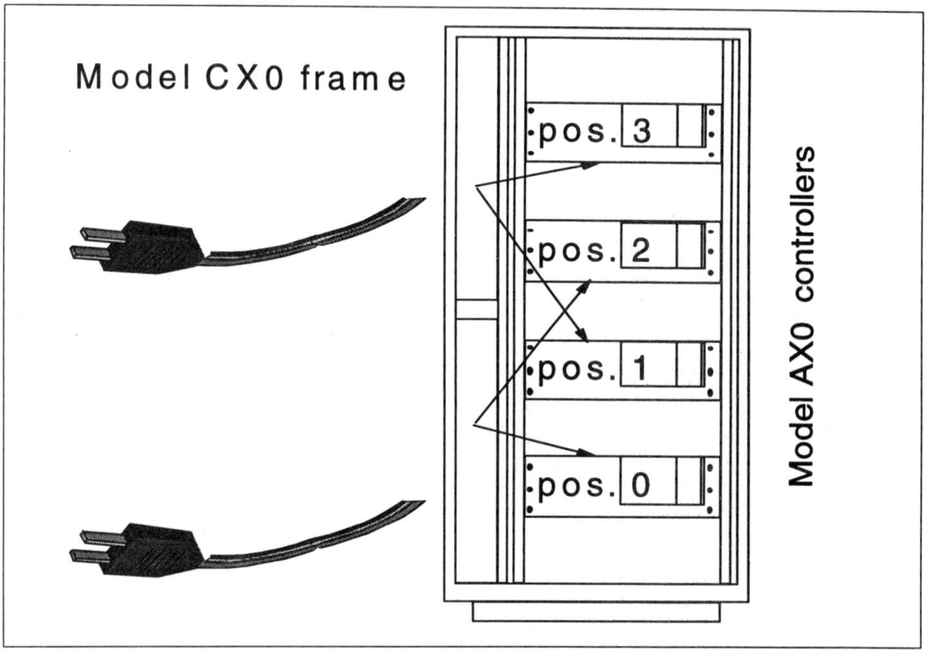

Figure 48. Model CX0 frame and power scheme

5.3 Configuration considerations

In this section, we describe specific configuration considerations for a Peer-to-Peer VTS. For more information about configuration considerations for a stand-alone VTS subsystem, please refer to *IBM Magstar Virtual Tape Server: Planning, Implementing, and Monitoring*, SG24-2229.

5.3.1 Configuration recommendations

In this section, we describe the configuration recommendations for a Peer-to-Peer VTS.

5.3.1.1 Model B18 VTS configuration

We strongly recommend that both Model B18 VTSs should have the same TVC capacity as well as the same number and, ideally, model of 3590 tape drives. If one of the Model B18 VTS has less TVC capacity or fewer 3590 tape drives, its sustained throughput will be less than that of the other VTS. The Model AX0 controllers balance the work load between the Model B18

VTSs so the less capable VTS will tend to do less work than the more capable VTS, thereby reducing the combined throughput.

5.3.1.2 Logical volume serial numbers

The logical volumes are defined for the composite library to be used by the host system. Each distributed library will contain the logical volumes defined for the composite library. However, as with a stand-alone VTS, system-managed tape requires that the logical volume serial numbers must not duplicate other volume serial numbers in your systems.

5.3.1.3 Stacked volume serial numbers

We recommend that the stacked volume serial numbers must be unique, to clearly distinguish each set of the two distributed library's stacked volumes.

5.3.1.4 Sharing and partitioning with multiple hosts

A Peer-to-Peer VTS can be shared by multiple OS/390 (MVS) systems in the same way that a stand-alone VTS and a physical tape library can be shared. For details on sharing and partitioning a library, refer to *IBM Magstar Virtual Tape Server: Planning, Implementing, and Monitoring*, SG24-2229 and *Guide to Sharing and Partitioning IBM Automated Tape Library Dataservers*, SG24-4409.

In a stand-alone VTS, all logical devices and logical control units are associated with one VTS controller. Therefore, the bandwidth available and ESCON channel activities of the VTS do not depend on which logical devices and logical control units are in use.

In a Peer-to-Peer VTS, however, the logical devices and logical control units are associated with four Model AX0 controllers. Each Model AX0 controller provides one quarter of the Peer-to-Peer VTS addresses, that is, one logical control unit with 16 logical devices, and two ESCON channels. The total bandwidth of the Peer-to-Peer VTS is divided among the four Model AX0 controllers.

Therefore, if you want to use the full bandwidth of the Peer-to-Peer VTS when sharing and partitioning a Peer-to-Peer VTS between multiple hosts, each host should attach to all Model AX0 controllers. In any case, each host should attach to at least two Model AX0 controllers to provide additional paths in the event of failure. For the purposes of balancing the workload of each Model AX0 controller, each host should be assigned logical drives equally from each of the four Model AX0 controllers. Figure 49 shows a sample drive assignment when partitioning a Peer-to-Peer VTS between four host systems.

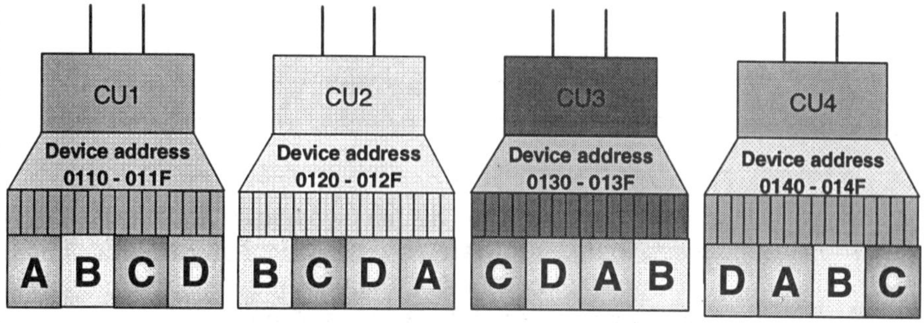

	Host A	Host B	Host C	Host D
CU1	0110-0113	0114-0117	0118-011B	011C-011F
CU2	012C-012F	0120-0123	0124-0124	0127-012B
CU3	0138-013B	013C-013F	0130-0133	0134-0137
CU4	0144-0147	0148-014B	014C-014F	0140-0143

Figure 49. Sample drive assignment in a partitioned Peer-to-Peer VTS

5.3.2 Configuration options

When configuring a Peer-to-Peer VTS, you must provide the following information to the service representative:

1. Library name and library sequence number (also known as library ID) for the composite library and both distributed libraries
2. Selection of the User Interface (UI) Distributed library
3. Selection of the copy mode
4. For each AX0, the switch address for each interface routed dynamically through an ESCON director
5. Selection of VTS preferencing for each Model AX0 controller
6. Local LAN information to set up the StorWatch Peer-to-Peer Specialist for each Model AX0 controller and the StorWatch 3494 Library Specialist for each of the 3494 tape libraries as described in 5.3.3, “StorWatch Specialist configuration” on page 113.

Details of each item are described below:

1. Library name and library sequence number (library ID) for the composite library and the two distributed libraries

- Library name:

  Each of the libraries in the Peer-to-Peer VTS configuration must have a name that you specify. We recommend you should use the same library names as in the SMS tape library definition to let you recognize each library easily.

- Library ID (Library sequence number):

  Each of the libraries has its own library ID. Usually, the convention has been to use hardware serial numbers of the library frames or VTSs as library IDs. For a Peer-to-Peer configuration, you could use the serial number of the local CX0 frame. These would be provided by your service representatives.

  However, we would recommend that you move away from this approach as it becomes misleading if hardware is replaced as part of an upgrade. You may prefer to use a more descriptive library ID such as a name or a number that you assign.

2. Selection of the UI distributed library:

   One of the distributed libraries in a Peer-to-Peer VTS has to be selected as the UI distributed library. The UI distributed library controls inserting logical volumes. The insert logical volume operation can only be performed on this UI distributed library and the other non-UI Distributed library cannot perform the operation. In addition, the selection of the UI distributed library influences the selection of the master VTS at start-up time. All of the AX0s get the clock time from the UI distributed library.

   We recommend that you use the distributed library that allows easiest access as the UI distributed library.

   This designation is static and can only be changed by taking the entire Peer-to-Peer VTS offline and performing CE reconfiguration.

3. Selection of a copy mode:

   A Peer-to-Peer VTS has two modes of copy operation for creating dual logical volume copies, either *Immediate Copy* mode or *Deferred Copy* mode. The default mode is Deferred Copy mode. For detailed information on the copy mode operations, please refer to Section 2.4, “Creating the secondary copy of a virtual volume” on page 19.

   The mode of the operation that is specified affects the peak performance of the Peer-to-Peer VTS.

   In Immediate Copy mode, while both Model B18 VTSs are active, a Model AX0 controller will initiate the creation of a dual copy when a rewind/unload is received and will signal completion when the dual copy operation is complete. This mode provides the highest level of data protection.

In Deferred Copy mode, a Model AX0 controller will schedule creation of the dual copy operation when a rewind/unload is received and will signal completion immediately. The time needed to complete the dual copy operation will depend on the activity of the Model B18 VTSs.

In Deferred Copy mode, you also need to specify a Deferred Copy Priority Threshold. This is a time parameter which determines when the deferred copy will be processed with a priority for processing bandwidth equal to host I/O activity. The time has a range of 0-24 hours in one hour increments. The default Deferred Copy Priority Threshold is 8 hours.

In Deferred Copy mode, when a longer Deferred Copy Priority Threshold is specified, the Peer-to-Peer VTS can maintain a high level of performance for a longer time without the dual copy operation overhead. However, each of the Model B18 VTS in the Peer-to-Peer VTS **must** have enough TVC capacity to keep in cache the logical volumes that do not yet have a dual copy or have not been copied to a stacked volume. If their TVCs do not have enough capacity, the VTS subsystems may reach a state where the logical volumes created that have not been copied to the other VTS must be copied to a stacked volume and removed from the TVC to make room for newly created or recalled logical volumes by the host. Then, when their dual copy operation is to be performed, the logical volumes would have to be recalled back into the TVC.

In a remote Peer-to-Peer VTS configuration, based on the distance of the connections, the data transfer rate between the Model B18 VTSs may be slower than would be the case for a local configuration. It may take more time to complete the dual copy operation. In Immediate Copy mode, every write may take a longer time to complete the dual copy operation. In Deferred Copy mode, it is not necessary to wait for the completion of the copy operation.

This choice is a trade-off between the level of the data protection and the performance in a Peer-to-Peer VTS configuration.

The mode of operation is specified in each of the Model AX0 controllers. All four Model AX0 controllers in the Peer-to-Peer VTS configuration must use the same mode of operation.

4. ESCON director link address:

   This address must be provided for each AX0 attached through an ESCON director that is using dynamic switching.

5. Selection of VTS preferencing:

   Each Model AX0 controller can be specified to send I/O activity to a specific Model B18 VTS if it is available. The selections that you are allowed are *VTS0*, *VTS1*, and *no-preference*. VTS0 and VTS1 indicate which one of the two Model B18 VTSs. There is no default selection; you must set the desired mode at installation time.

   If no-preference is selected, a Model AX0 controller will try to balance the workload between the two Model B18 VTSs. Therefore, no-preference is recommended for a local Peer-to-Peer configuration. Figure 50 shows the work load balanced by all four Model AX0 controllers.

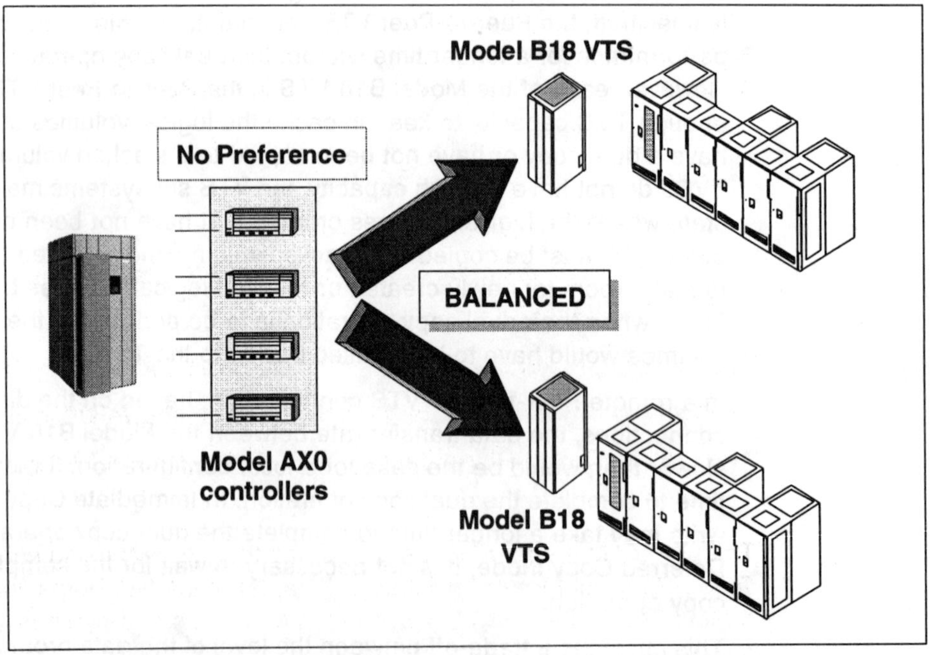

Figure 50. Balanced work load

   In a remote Peer-to-Peer configuration, you can choose to have the Model AX0 controllers local to each VTS prefer that VTS as the I/O VTS. However, current measurements show that this provides worse performance than the no-preference case because of the imbalance between VTSs.

5.3.3 StorWatch Specialist configuration

There are two StorWatch Specialists for the 3494 tape library: the 3494 Tape Library Specialist and the Magstar 3494 Peer-to-Peer VTS Specialist. The 3494 Tape Library Specialist is a Web-based interface to the 3494 Library Manager which lets you monitor the Library Manager and VTSs remotely. The Magstar 3494 Peer-to-Peer VTS Specialist is the Web-based user interface used to view the current status and configuration of the Peer-to-Peer VTS.

You can access the StorWatch Specialists using a Web browser. The StorWatch Specialists have been tested with Microsoft Internet Explorer 5 and Netscape Navigator 4.7, both with Java and JavaScript enabled.

5.3.3.1 3494 Tape Library Specialist

The 3494 Tape Library Specialist functions are read-only. You can monitor the status of the library, but there is no capability to make configuration changes or issue commands. The 3494 Tape Library Specialist has:

- A home page
- A set of Library Manager pages
- A set of VTS pages (if a VTS is installed)
- Links to the Magstar 3494 Peer-to-Peer VTS Specialist (if a Peer-to-Peer VTS is installed)

The following features are required for the 3494 Tape Library Specialist:

- FC 5045 (Enhanced Library Manager) or an equivalent is installed.
- FC 5219 (Token-Ring Adapter) or FC 5220 (Ethernet Adapter) for connection to the LAN

The Library Manager must be connected to your LAN using either a Token-Ring Adapter or an Ethernet Adapter. If the 3494 tape library is part of a Model HA1 high availability configuration, the stand-by Library Manager also must be connected to the LAN.

During the installation process, the service representative will set up TCP/IP on the Library Manager to use your assigned TCP/IP host name and TCP/IP address (and router information, if necessary). You must provide the following information before the installation starts (items marked * are optional):

- TCP/IP host name for the library manager
- TCP/IP address for the library manager
- Subnet mask (or network mask)
- Router address (or Gateway address)*
- Domain name*

- Name server address*

5.3.3.2 Peer-to-Peer VTS Specialist

The Model AX0 Virtual Tape Controller provides an optional Web server for the display of status on your Web browser by way of your intranet. In a Peer-to-Peer VTS, there are four Model AX0 Virtual Tape Controllers, each of which can be configured to provide the Web server function. The Peer-to-Peer VTS Specialist only provides monitoring functions. There is no capability to make changes or issue commands. Refer to 8.2.1, "StorWatch Specialists" on page 196.

> **Note**
>
> The Peer-to-Peer VTS Specialist does not allow any access to user data contained in the logical volumes.

You must provide the following hardware and information to the service representative before the installation:

- An Ethernet/twisted pair cable (category 5, 4-pair stranded, PVC, RJ45 connector) for connection to a 100/10 Base T connector on each Model AX0 controller
- Standard Ethernet Network Interface (en0)
- Network names and addresses are required for each Model AX0 controller (items marked * are optional):
  - Host name for each Model AX0 controller
  - Internet address of each Model AX0 controller
  - Network mask
  - Name server Internet address *
  - Name server domain name *
  - Default Gateway address*

5.4 Software requirements

For OS/390, the Peer-to-Peer VTS is supported only in a DFSMS/MVS system-managed tape environment. The software levels required to support the Peer-to-Peer VTS are DFSMS/MVS 1.4, 1.5, and DFSMS 2.10.

The levels of DFSMS/MVS that do not fully support the Peer-to-Peer VTS (DFSMS/MVS 1.2, or 1.3), or support the Peer-to-Peer VTS but do not have the supporting PTFs installed on the system (DFSMS/MVS 1.4 or 1.5) are able to use the Peer-to-Peer VTS; however, toleration PTFs are required.

Toleration PTFs are available for DFSMS/MVS 1.2 and above. DFSMS/MVS 1.1 does **not** support the Peer-to-Peer VTS.

For adequate usability and error reporting capabilities, at least one host attached the Peer-to-Peer VTS must have the full support Peer-to-Peer VTS PTFs installed. Table 8 shows the Peer-to-Peer VTS support APAR numbers.

Table 8. Peer-to-Peer VTS support APARs

Component	Toleration support	Full support
OAM	OW42068	OW42069
Device Services	OW42070	OW42071, OW42073
DFSMSrmm	OW42910	OW42074

There are no associated PTFs required for OS/390 support.

We are not aware of any maintenance needed or available for vendor tape management systems that is unique to a Peer-to-Peer configuration.

A Peer-to-Peer VTS may be attached to hosts running either VM/ESA or VSE/ESA as a VM/ESA guest as long as the Peer-to-Peer VTS is also attached to an OS/390 host with the full support installed. The levels of VM/ESA and VSE/ESA supported are the same as for a stand-alone VTS.

Note:

Support for the Peer-to-Peer VTS is not available for BTLS.

Chapter 6. Implementation and migration

In this chapter we describe the steps and tasks to implement a Peer-to-Peer VTS. Again, we assume that the reader is familiar with basic VTS concepts and thus we concentrate specifically on information for a Peer-to-Peer VTS.

6.1 Hardware I/O configuration definition

From a host perspective, a Peer-to-Peer VTS looks like four IBM 3490E tape control units, each with 16 devices attached through ESCON channels.

In a stand-alone VTS, all logical devices and logical control units are associated with one VTS controller. To define a stand-alone VTS, it is necessary to define four tape control units using logical unit address (CUADD) = 0 to 3, and four strings, 16 drives each. Table 9 shows the differences regarding logical tape control unit definition between a Peer-to-Peer VTS and a stand-alone VTS.

In a Peer-to-Peer VTS, the logical devices and logical control units are associated with four independent Model AX0 controllers. Each Model AX0 controller provides one quarter of the Peer-to-Peer VTS, that is, one logical control unit with 16 logical devices, and two ESCON channels. To define a Peer-to-Peer VTS, it is necessary to specify logical unit address (CUADD) = 0 for all four independent tape control unit definitions.

Table 9. Difference between Peer-to-Peer VTS and stand-alone VTS

VTSs	Logical tape control unit definition	
	# of ESCON path	**CUADD**
Stand-alone VTS	2, 4 or 8	0 - 3
Peer-to-Peer VTS	2	0

The logical 3490E tape drives are defined just like a physical IBM 3490-A10 controller with 16 addresses through the HCD. You must define them through the HCD dialog, specifying LIBRARY=YES. Before you can use the VTS, you need to define it to the MVS system and processor through HCD.

You may need to update missing interrupt handler (MIH) values as well. In this section we discuss the steps required to configure a Peer-to-Peer VTS.

© Copyright IBM Corp. 2000

6.1.1 Defining devices through IOCP

This example and Figure 51 show a typical Peer-to-Peer VTS configuration that has eight ESCON channel paths and four logical tape control units. Each logical control unit definition is specified with CUADD = 0. Although you cannot use IOCP to define a Peer-to-Peer VTS (you must use HCD), you may find the IOCP statements helpful in understanding how the Peer-to-Peer VTS has to be defined in HCD.

```
CHPID PATH = 10,TYPE=CNC
CHPID PATH = 20,TYPE=CNC
CHPID PATH = 30,TYPE=CNC
CHPID PATH = 40,TYPE=CNC
CHPID PATH = 50,TYPE=CNC
CHPID PATH = 60,TYPE=CNC
CHPID PATH = 70,TYPE=CNC
CHPID PATH = 80,TYPE=CNC
:
CNTLUNIT  CUNUMBR=410,PATH=(10,20),UNIT=3490,UNITADD=((00,16)),CUADD=0
IODEVICE  ADDRESS=(A10,16),UNIT=3490,CUNUMBR=(410),UNITADD=00
CNTLUNIT  CUNUMBR=420,PATH=(30,40),UNIT=3490,UNITADD=((00,16)),CUADD=0
IODEVICE  ADDRESS=(A20,16),UNIT=3490,CUNUMBR=(420),UNITADD=00
CNTLUNIT  CUNUMBR=430,PATH=(50,60),UNIT=3490,UNITADD=((00,16)),CUADD=0
IODEVICE  ADDRESS=(A30,16),UNIT=3490,CUNUMBR=(430),UNITADD=00
CNTLUNIT  CUNUMBR=440,PATH=(70,80),UNIT=3490,UNITADD=((00,16)),CUADD=0
IODEVICE  ADDRESS=(A40,16),UNIT=3490,CUNUMBR=(440),UNITADD=00
```

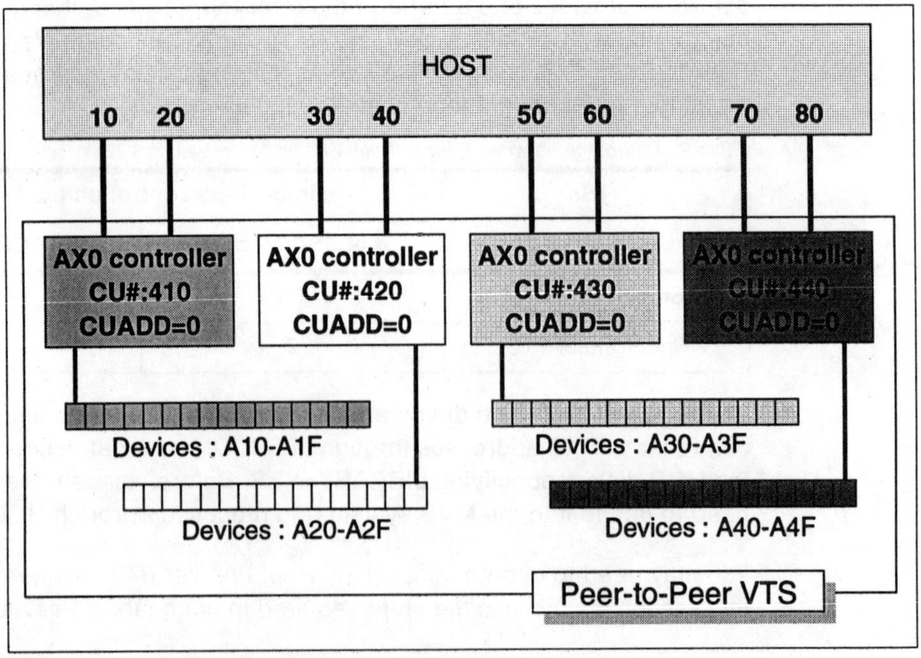

Figure 51. Peer-to-Peer VTS definition

Note

In the CNTLUNIT macro for each of the four logical control units, you must specify CUADD=0 because, in a Peer-to-Peer VTS configuration, each logical control unit is associated with one independent Model AX0 controller.

6.1.2 Defining devices through HCD panels

In this section we describe the process of defining the Peer-to-Peer VTS through HCD panels. The most important points to observe are:

- HCD definitions are required for SMS tape.
- Four 3490 tape control units have to be defined, with 16 3490E drives each.
- Keep the link address blank when no ESCON director is used.
- Specify LIBRARY=YES when using system-managed tape.

Remember, when defining a Peer-to-Peer VTS it is necessary to define four independent tape control units with CUADD=0, and four strings, 16 drives each. In a stand-alone VTS, the definitions of the four tape control units use a logical unit address of CUADD = 0 to 3. In a Peer-to-Peer VTS, however, the definition must be specified as CUADD = 0 for each of the four tape control units.

The following two screens show the important panels for specifying one tape control unit.

```
          ------------------------ Add Control Unit --------------------
CBDPCU10
Specify or revise the following values.
Control unit number . . . . 0410 +

Control unit type . . . . . 3490       +

Serial number . . . . . . . __________
Description . . . . . . . . ________________________________
Connected to switches . . . __ __ __ __ __ __ __ __ +
Ports . . . . . . . . . . . __ __ __ __ __ __ __ __ +
If connected to a switch, select whether to have CHPIDs/link
addresses, and unit address range proposed.

Auto-assign . . . . . . . . . 2  1. Yes
                                 2. No

 F1=Help   F2=Split   F3=Exit   F4=Prompt   F5=Reset   F9=Swap
F12=Cancel
```

After you have specified the control unit number and the type (here, 3490) in the first panel, then choose the processor to which the control unit is connected, as shown in the following panel.

```
-------------------------- Add Control Unit ------------------------
CBDPCU12
Specify or revise the following values.
Control unit number  . : 0410      Type . . . . . . : 3490
Processor ID . . . . . : PROC1     This is the main processor
Channel path IDs . . . . 10 20 __ __ __ __ __ __ +
Link address . . . . . . __ __ __ __ __ __ __ __ +

Unit address   . . . . . 00 __ __ __ __ __ __ __ +
Number of units  . . . . 16 ___ ___ ___ ___ ___ ___ ___
Logical address   . . . . 0 + (same as CUADD)
Protocol . . . . . . . . . __ + (D,S or S4)
I/O concurrency level   . 2 + (1, 2 or 3)

F1=Help   F2=Split   F4=Prompt   F5=Reset   F9=Swap   F12=Cancel
```

Note that, if the VTS is attached through ESCON directors, the link address fields would specify the ESCON director's port number. You should define the second to fourth VTS tape control units, specifying the logical unit address CUADD = 0 as same as the first tape control unit definition in the CBDPCU12 panel. The number of drives to be specified for a Peer-to-Peer VTS control unit is always 64, but you must specify these in two or four strings, with each string associated with one of the previously defined control units. To define the IBM 3490E virtual drives, you need to go to the Device List Panel either from the Main Panel by entering 1 and then 5, or by means of the Control Unit List Panel by using action **s**. To add the VTS virtual drives, press PF11. The screen is shown below.

```
------------------------------ Add Device ---------------------------
CBDPDV10
Specify or revise the following values.
Device number . . . . . . . . 0A10 (0000 - FFFF)
Number of devices . . . . . . 16__
Device type . . . . . . . . . 3490________ +

Serial number . . . . . . . . __________
Description . . . . . . . . . ________________________________

Connected to CUs . . 0410 ____ ____ ____ ____ ____ ____ ____ +

 F1=Help   F2=Split   F3=Exit   F4=Prompt   F5=Reset   F9=Swap
F12=Cancel
```

After entering the required information and specifying to which processors and operating systems the devices are connected, you can update the device parameters using the following screen.

```
      CBDPDV13 Define Device Parameters / Features Row 1 of 6
Command ===> __________________________________________ Scroll ===> PAGE
Specify or revise the values below.
Configuration ID . : AB        MVS operating system
Device number  . . : 0A10      Number of devices :16
Device type  . . . : 3490

Parameter /
Feature      Value  P Req.  Description
OFFLINE      Yes            Device considered online or offline at IPL
DYNAMIC      Yes            Device supports dynamic configuration
LOCANY       No             UCB can reside in 31 bit storage
LIBRARY      Yes            Device supports auto tape library
AUTOSWITCH   No             Device is automatically switchable
LIBRARY-ID   12345          5 digit library serial number
LIBPORT-ID   01             2 digit library string ID (port number)
ALTCTRL      No             Separate physical control unit path
SHARABLE     No             Device is Sharable between systems
COMPACT      Yes            Compaction
**************************** Bottom of data ****************************
 F1=Help        F2=Split      F4=Prompt       F5=Reset        F7=Backward
 F8=Forward     F9=Swap      F12=Cancel      F22=Command
```

Notes

1. You must specify LIBRARY=YES
2. You must specify the composite library ID in LIBRARY-ID field
3. LIBPORT-ID is dependent on the device number that was assigned to the logical drive. The first 16 devices that have lowest device numbers must be specified LIBPORT-ID = 1, the second 16 devices must be specified LIBPORT-ID = 2, the third 16 devices must be specified LIBPORT-ID = 3, and the fourth 16 devices must be specified LIBPORT-ID = 4
4. If more than one MVS system will be sharing the virtual drives in the VTS, specify SHARABLE=YES. This will force OFFLINE to YES. It is up to the installation to ensure proper serialization from all attached hosts.

To define the next 16 VTS 3490E virtual drives, you need to go back to the Device List Panel from the Main Panel by entering 1 and then 5. To add the VTS virtual drives, press PF11. The CBDPDV10 screen is displayed again.

6.1.3 Set value for Missing Interrupt Handler (MIH)

An MIH time of 45 minutes is recommended for the all logical devices in the Peer-to-Peer VTS. You must specify the MIH time-out values for the Peer-to-Peer VTS devices. MIH time-out values can be specified only by class (for example, all tapes) or on an individual device basis. You can specify the MIH values either in PARMLIB member IECIOSxx or through the MVS operator command, SETIOS.

The following shows a sample MIH value specified in the PARMLIB member IECIOSxx with Peer-to-Peer VTS device addresses from 0A10 to 0A4F.

```
MIH DEV=(0A10-0A4F),TIME=45:00
```

The following is an example of the operator command used to specify the MIH value on a device basis.

```
SETIOS MIH,DEV=(0A10-0A4F),TIME=45:00
```

6.2 VTS definition from the library manager

After the hardware installation of a Peer-to-Peer VTS, you must define the environment for each of two distributed libraries. The VTS definitions for both distributed VTSs are performed from the respective library manager console except for the define (insert) logical volumes operation. The insert logical volumes operation can only be performed on the UI distributed library.

Table 10 shows operations that must be performed at the library managers.

Table 10. Library manager operations

Operations	Distributed libraries	
	VTS 0 (UI library)	**VTS 1**
Define stacked volume ranges	X	X
Define (insert) logical volumes [1]	X	-
Define fast ready categories	X	X
Define VTS management policies • Inhibit reclaim schedule • Reclaim threshold percentage • Free storage threshold	X	X
Make sure the "Send Interventions to Host Console" button is activated on both library manager operator intervention screens	X	X

Note:
1. The insert logical volumes operation is allowed only on the UI distributed library.

For details on VTS definition and operating a library manager, please refer to *IBM Magstar Virtual Tape Server: Planning, Implementing, and Monitoring*, SG24-2229 and *Magstar 3494 Tape Library Operator Guide*, GA32-0280.

6.3 Software setup

In this section, we describe the software setup for a Peer-to-Peer VTS. We provide specific information about the definition of a Peer-to-Peer VTS for each of DFSMS/MVS SMS-managed tape, JES3, and tape management systems. For more information about the software definitions for implementing a VTS subsystem, please refer to *IBM Magstar Virtual Tape Server: Planning, Implementing, and Monitoring*, SG24-2229.

6.3.1 DFSMS/MVS SMS-managed tape

In this section we describe the DFSMS definitions for the Peer-to-Peer VTS. To define the Peer-to-Peer VTS, you use the ISMF panels to create a new definition of the VTS logical tape library to be recognized from the host. This definition is done in the same way as for a new installation of a stand-alone VTS except for making definitions for **three** tape libraries: one composite library and two distributed libraries. To use the Peer-to-Peer VTS, a storage group should be created to allow the VTS logical tape library virtual drives to be allocated by the ACS routine. Since all of the logical drives and volumes are associated with the composite library, **only the composite library should be defined in the storage group**. The distributed libraries must not be defined in the storage group. Refer to *IBM Magstar Tape Products Family: A Practical Guide*, SG24-4632, and to *DFSMS/MVS OAM Planning Guide for Tape Libraries*, SC26-3051 for a complete discussion of the host software implementation tasks for IBM tape libraries.

The following is a summary of the basic definition procedures for a tape library installation:

1. Modify SYS1.PARMLIB member (such as IEFSSNxx, SCHEDxx, IGDSMSxx, LOADxx, DEVSUPxx, and COMMANDxx)
2. Create VOLCAT

   IDCAMS IMPORT CONNECT to the other system is required when tape library sharing capability is used.
3. Add the procedure to start the OAM address space.
4. Define the tape library as a DFSMS resource

   Define the composite library and two distributed libraries.

This example shows the definition of a composite library:

```
 Panel   Utilities   Scroll    Help
------------------------------------------------------------------------------
                             TAPE LIBRARY DEFINE                 Page 1 of 2
Command ===>_

SCDS Name . : SCDS.TEMP.PRIMARY
Library Name : P2PLIB1

To Define Library, Specify:
  Description ===> Peer-to-Peer VTS Composite library
              ===>
  Library ID . . . . . . . . . . .1234C       (00001 to FFFFF)
  Console Name . . . . . . . . . .LIB1CON
  Entry Default Data Class . . . .DCATLDS
  Entry Default Use Attribute . . S           (P=PRIVATE or S=SCRATCH)
  Eject Default . . . . . . . . . K           (P=PURGE or K=KEEP)

  Media Type:          Scratch Threshold
    Media1 . . . . 100           Media3 . . . . 0    (0 to 999999)
    Media2 . . . . 400           Media4 . . . . 0    (0 to 999999)
 .
Use ENTER to Perform Verification; Use DOWN Command to View Next Panel;
Use HELP Command for Help; Use END Command to Save and Exit; CANCEL to Exit.
```

And here is a sample panel to define one of the distributed libraries:

```
 Panel   Utilities   Scroll    Help
------------------------------------------------------------------------------
                               TAPE LIBRARY DEFINE              Page 1 of 2
Command ===>_

SCDS Name . : SCDS.TEMP.PRIMARY
Library Name : P2PLIBA

To Define Library, Specify:
  Description ===> Peer-to-Peer VTS Distributed library A
              ===>
  Library ID . . . . . . . . . . .12349       (00001 to FFFFF)
  Console Name . . . . . . . . . .
  Entry Default Data Class . . . .
  Entry Default Use Attribute . .             (P=PRIVATE or S=SCRATCH)
  Eject Default . . . . . . . . .             (P=PURGE or K=KEEP)

  Media Type:         Scratch Threshold
    Media1 . . . . 0           Media3 . . . . 0    (0 to 999999)
    Media2 . . . . 0           Media4 . . . . 0    (0 to 999999)

Use ENTER to Perform Verification; Use DOWN Command to View Next Panel;
Use HELP Command for Help; Use END Command to Save and Exit; CANCEL to Exit.
```

Note

Library ID is the only field that applies for the distributed libraries; all other fields can be blank or left to default.

5. Create or update the data class (DC), storage class (SC), and management class (MC) for the Peer-to-Peer VTS.
6. Create the storage group (SG) for the Peer-to-Peer VTS.

   The composite library must be defined in the storage group. Do **not** define the distributed libraries in the storage group.

Note

At OAM address space initialization, if a distributed library is defined to a storage group, warning message CBR3017I is issued indicating that the distributed library is incorrectly defined to the storage group.

7. Create ACS to assign VTS storage class.

   Translate, test, and validate ACS routines.

8. Activate new SCDS.
9. Bring the composite library and distributed libraries online.
10. Bring the VTS virtual drives online.

For more detailed information about defining a VTS subsystem in a DFSMS environment, please refer to *IBM Magstar Virtual Tape Server: Planning, Implementing, and Monitoring*, SG24-2229.

6.3.2 JES3 initialization deck definition

In this section we provide an example of a JES3 initialization deck for a Peer-to-Peer VTS configuration. The INISH deck is comparable to the definition of a single IBM 3494 tape library containing four IBM 3490E tape control units, each of them with 16 device addresses. For a detailed description about JES3 in a SMS managed tape environment, please refer to *IBM Magstar Virtual Tape Server: Planning, Implementing, and Monitoring*, SG24-2229.

To balance the workload across all Model AX0 controllers, the tape drives must be specified in a certain order without allowing JES3 to sort them. Therefore it is required that you specify `ADDRSORT=NO`. This specification should not cause any problems in your JES3 environment. For DASD devices, if they are still defined in the JES3 INISH deck, ADDRSORT does not matter at all. Even without DEVICE statements, the JES3-Data Set Awareness support will be kept, so most installations do not have DEVICE statements for DASD devices defined any more.

The following example is based on the Peer-to-Peer VTS outline shown in Figure 15 on page 28. The device addresses in this example range from 0110 to 014F. The library ID for the Peer-to-Peer VTS is 70299.

You must specify the library ID of the composite library.

```
/*
/*SPECIFY ADDRSORT=NO
/*
ADDRSORT=NO
/*
/* Devices (Peer-to-Peer VTS virtual 3490E) 0110 to 014F
/*
DEVICE,XTYPE=(PTPVTS,CA),XUNIT=(0110,SY1,,ON)
DEVICE,XTYPE=(PTPVTS,CA),XUNIT=(0120,SY1,,ON)
DEVICE,XTYPE=(PTPVTS,CA),XUNIT=(0130,SY1,,ON)
DEVICE,XTYPE=(PTPVTS,CA),XUNIT=(0140,SY1,,ON)
```

```
DEVICE,XTYPE=(PTPVTS,CA),XUNIT=(0111,SY1,,ON)
DEVICE,XTYPE=(PTPVTS,CA),XUNIT=(0121,SY1,,ON)
DEVICE,XTYPE=(PTPVTS,CA),XUNIT=(0131,SY1,,ON)
DEVICE,XTYPE=(PTPVTS,CA),XUNIT=(0141,SY1,,ON)
DEVICE,XTYPE=(PTPVTS,CA),XUNIT=(0112,SY1,,ON)
                                      :
DEVICE,XTYPE=(PTPVTS,CA),XUNIT=(013F,SY1,,ON)
DEVICE,XTYPE=(PTPVTS,CA),XUNIT=(014F,SY1,,ON)
/*
/* This SETNAME is for Peer-to-Peer VTS virtual 3490E drives
/*
SETNAME,XTYPE=PTPVTS,NAMES=(LDGW3495,LDG70299,LDG3490E,LDE70299)
/*
/* Sysplex Wide Library Name
/*
HWSNAME,TYPE=(LDGW3495,LDG70299,LDG3490E,LDE70299
/*
/*
/* Library Specific Library Name
/*
HWSNAME,TYPE=(LDG70299,LDG3490E,LDE70299,LDGW3495
/*
/*
/* Sysplex Wide Device Name
/*
HWSNAME,TYPE=(LDG3490E,LDE70299,LDGW3495,LDG70299)
/*
/*
/* Library Specific Device Name
/*
HWSNAME,TYPE=(LDE70299,LDGW3495,LDG70299,LDG3490E)
/*
```

If you use the definition scheme as strongly recommended for Peer-to-Peer VTS, you will not be able to benefit from the enhancements in JES3 R9 allowing simpler DEVICE definitions. With JES3 R9, ascending device addresses (max. 0001 - FFFF, usually 64 addresses on one statement) can be defined. However, you will still be able to benefit from much more important R9 enhancements, such as activation of new definitions per HOTSTART/REFRESH without IPL.

6.3.3 Tape management systems

For the host perspective, a Peer-to-Peer VTS is a single VTS subsystem. There is no difference from the tape management system's point of view between a Peer-to-Peer VTS and a stand-alone VTS. Therefore, there is no special setup for the Peer-to-Peer VTS. For basic considerations for tape management systems, please refer to *IBM Magstar Virtual Tape Server: Planning, Implementing, and Monitoring*, SG24-2229.

6.4 Setup of StorWatch Specialists

Both the 3494 Tape Library Specialist and the Peer-to-Peer VTS Specialist are configured by the service representative using information about the network configuration that you provide.

To monitor the information provided by the 3494 Tape Library Specialist and the Peer-to-Peer VTS Specialist, your system must be LAN-attached to the Library Manager and to at least one of the four Model AX0 controllers using TCP/IP protocols, and you must have a Web browser. For example, Microsoft Internet Explorer version 5.0 or Netscape Navigator version 4.7 with Javascript and Java enabled provide the ability to access the StorWatch Peer-to-Peer Specialist. Text-based Web browsers are not supported.

See 5.3.3, "StorWatch Specialist configuration" on page 113 for more detail on what you need to supply.

6.5 Peer-to-Peer VTS migration

Whenever one or more IBM VTSs are already installed and functional, if the existing hardware has to be reused to build a Peer-to-Peer VTS configuration, you will need to consider a **migration** approach to move to a Peer-to-Peer environment.

This means that, based on the hardware installed, some or all the components that are part of your 3494 and VTS configuration, needs to be upgraded and therefore temporarily stopped.

Note

It is very important to understand that, once data has been committed to a Peer-to-Peer VTS, a reconfiguration of the Model B18 VTSs to stand-alone VTSs is **not** reversible back to a Peer-to-Peer configuration unless you discard the data. This is because the token data on the files would be out of sync. This process is explained in 2.6.3, "Token processing" on page 35.

This migration section is divided into two main topics:

- Planning for migration
- Upgrading an existing VTS

The first topic, planning for migration, describes general migration considerations. The second topic has a detailed task list for the upgrade of an existing VTS.

At the time of writing, a process for merging two existing 3494-VTS libraries in a Peer-to-Peer configuration had not been tested, and so we do not provide details.

6.6 Planning for migration

In this section we describe general migration considerations.

6.6.1 The Peer-to-Peer VTS hardware configuration

You need to consider the difference in the data processing capability between stand-alone existing VTSs and a Peer-to-Peer VTS with the copy processing overhead. The performance of the Peer-to-Peer VTS depends on selection of the copy mode and the I/O preference setting. You may need to add TVC capacity and 3590 tape drives.

For more information, please refer to Chapter 2, “Peer-to-Peer VTS concepts” on page 7 and Chapter 5, “Preinstallation planning” on page 91.

6.6.2 The existing VTS subsystem configuration

To upgrade the existing VTS subsystem, there are prerequisite features for the Model B18 VTS configured in a Peer-to-Peer environment. You have to check the existing VTS subsystem configuration and add the features, if required.

For more information about the prerequisite features, please refer to Section 5.2.3, “Model B18 VTS” on page 100.

6.6.3 Stacked volumes

Additional stacked volumes are required to hold the duplex copies of logical volumes. Each distributed library must have enough stacked cartridges to hold all the logical volumes.

6.6.4 Software implementation

You need to install the required PTFs on your system to use a Peer-to-Peer VTS. For more information about the software requirements of a Peer-to-Peer VTS, please refer to 5.4, “Software requirements” on page 114

6.6.4.1 I/O definition

You need to modify the I/O definition in IOCDS and HCD for the four independent logical tape subsystem with 16 drives configured in a Peer-to-Peer VTS.

For more information about the I/O definition of a Peer-to-Peer VTS, please refer to 6.1, “Hardware I/O configuration definition” on page 117.

6.6.4.2 SMS tape library definition

The library name of the existing VTS is used for the composite library, therefore, the existing tape library definition can be used for the composite library. This causes all logical volumes in the existing VTS subsystem to be associated with the composite library.

In addition, you need to add two tape library definitions for the distributed libraries. One of the two distributed libraries is the existing VTS subsystem with a new library name. Figure 52 shows a sample modification of the SMS tape library definition.

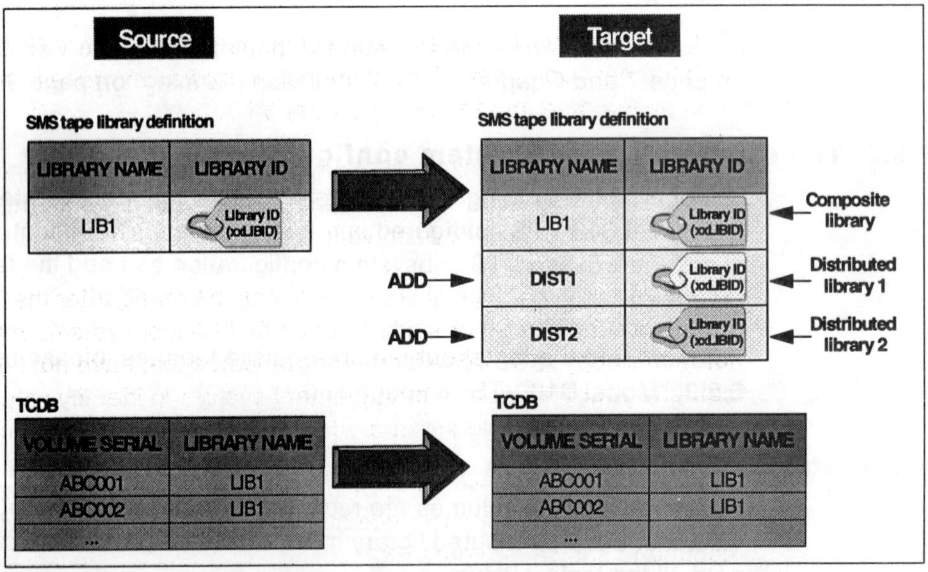

Figure 52. SMS tape library definition

For more information about the SMS tape library definition of a Peer-to-Peer VTS, please refer to 6.3.1, “DFSMS/MVS SMS-managed tape” on page 125.

6.6.4.3 JES3 environments

In a JES3 system environments, you need to modify the INISH deck to provide load balancing across the four Model AX0 controllers.

For more information about the JES3 definition of a Peer-to-Peer VTS, please refer to 6.3.2, "JES3 initialization deck definition" on page 128.

6.6.5 Application changes

In a Peer-to-Peer VTS, the hardware automatically creates dual copies of all logical volumes. Therefore, you may no longer need to use software functions like DFSMShsm TAPECOPY or DFSMSdss duplexing to create dual backup copies.

6.6.6 Volumes and data migration

Migrating from a stand-alone VTS configuration to a Peer-to-Peer VTS does not imply data movement; this differs from the migration process for a physical tape library to a VTS. You do not need to use a tape copy tool to move data from the stand-alone VTS to the Peer-to-Peer library.

The logical volumes already present in the stand-alone VTS are associated with the new Composite library during the migration process without the need to copy the data into the Peer-to-Peer VTS.

Remember that you will need to provide an additional quantity of scratch stacked volumes equal to the original number used before the upgrade to hold the second copy of each volume.

The dual copy of a logical volume will only be made after the volume has been accessed (read or written) again by the host system. You may wish to force this copy to be done by reading volumes that have not been copied. You can use your tape library management system to identify volumes with a last reference date prior to the upgrade and build jobs to read from them.

For example, if you are using DFSMSrmm, you can get a list of volumes that have not been referenced since a Peer-to-Peer upgrade by issuing the command shown in Figure 53.

```
RMM SEARCHVOLUME VOLUME(*) -
    LOCATION(library name) -
    STATUS(NOTSCRATCH) -
    LIMIT(*) -
    TYPE(LOGICAL)
    OWNER(*) -
    CLIST
```

Figure 53. Finding volumes without a copy — step 1

This command gives you a list of volumes that are not in scratch status. We now need to issue another command, as shown in Figure 54, to find out which volumes have not been copied:

```
RMM LISTVOLUME VOLUME(volser) -
    STATS -
    LIMIT(*) -
    OWNER(*) -
    CLIST
```

Figure 54. Finding volumes without a copy — step 2

This command will tell you the date last read and the date last written. If either of these is earlier than the date of the upgrade to a Peer-to-Peer configuration, there is no second copy.

Warning!

Do **not** try to copy every volume that does not have a second copy.

The upgrade process does not include a step to copy these uncopied volumes, because the performance impact would be severe. The process of creating a second copy will require a specific mount for a recall to cache, cache space, and a write to a stacked volume. This will take resources away from normal activity and would impact performance.

This technique should **only** be used to identify a small number of volumes for which you must have copies.

Once you have decided whether you need to copy any of these volumes, you could build jobs (such as IEBGENER to read the volume label, requiring BLP authority) or issue mount commands.

Please note that it is much better to allow the Peer-to-Peer VTS to create copies as volumes are accessed as part of your normal workload. The technique discussed in this section should only be used for very small numbers of volumes because of the performance impact.

6.6.7 Unsupported features

With the Peer-to-Peer Copy base feature (FC 4010), the following features are not supported. If these features are installed in existing Model B18 VTS, they will be disabled during upgrade of the Model B18 VTS to the Model B18 VTS with FC 4010 in a Peer-to-Peer VTS configuration.

6.6.7.1 Advanced Function (FC 4000)

FC 4000 provides an Import/Export logical volume function for the VTS subsystem. This function must be disabled during an upgrade. The VTS tape volume cache management function (also part of the Advanced Function feature) is unaffected by the upgrade.

6.6.7.2 Activate Additional ESCON Channels (FC 3418)

FC 3418 provides two additional Extended Performance ESCON Channel attachments for the Model B18 VTS.

- The Peer-to-Peer VTS also has eight ESCON paths.
- There are differences in the channel configurations between a stand-alone VTS and a Peer-to-Peer VTS. Refer to 6.1, "Hardware I/O configuration definition" on page 117.

6.6.7.3 SCSI Host Attachment (FC 3422)

FC 3422 provides two SCSI bus host attachments for the Model B18 VTS. This feature must be physically removed from the B18 VTS controller.

- Plan to use other devices.
- Data movement is required from the existing VTS subsystem to others.

6.7 Upgrading an existing VTS to a Peer-to-Peer configuration

In this section we give you a step-by-step approach to upgrade an existing Magstar 3494 with VTS to a Peer-to-Peer VTS configuration.

This phased procedure is intended to minimize the impact of the migration, reusing the previous VTS attributes and the definitions as much as possible to reduce migration outages and impact on your operations.

Migration of the existing VTS subsystem is performed by your service representatives. It involves the physical replacement of essential parts of your 3494 tape library and VTS subsystem so you must plan for the appropriate outage of your tape library and the VTS.

The hardware upgrade consists of the addition of:

- Additional Magstar 3590 cartridges to hold the logical volume copies
- A Magstar 3494 tape library
- A new VTS with the copy feature
- The CX0 auxiliary frame or frames
- The four AX0 virtual tape controllers

The existing VTS must be upgraded with the copy features, and, if not already present, EHPO and PAF features must be installed, together with any appropriate cache upgrade. Much of this work can and should be done as preparation work in advance of the Peer-to-Peer feature installation. The tasks that you can do and test early are shown in 6.7.2.1, "Update existing 3494-B18" on page 137.

The hardware MES can be completed in two parts. First, we have the installation of the new hardware components: 3494, VTS, CX0 frame, and AX0s. This can be done without affecting the operations of the existing VTS. These tasks are shown in 6.7.2.2, "Install new hardware" on page 137.

The second part requires that the existing VTS is down, because we need to install the Copy base feature. These tasks are shown in 6.7.2.3, "Install Peer-to-Peer upgrade" on page 137.

6.7.1 Prepare for migration

The preparation steps can and should be done well in advance of the delivery of the new hardware. You should decide upon the configuration and collect data for the installation of the StorWatch Specialists. The 3494 Installation and Planning Guide contains some worksheets that you may find helpful in documenting what will be done. After you have completed these worksheets, review them with your service representative.

See 5.3.2, "Configuration options" on page 109 and 5.3.3, "StorWatch Specialist configuration" on page 113 to see what information you will need.

6.7.2 Hardware migration steps

The hardware migration is performed by your service representatives, who will complete the following sets of tasks.

6.7.2.1 Update existing 3494-B18

1. Move any logical volumes accessed by SCSI hosts to another library.
2. Vary existing VTS offline.
3. Add EHPO channels if not already installed.
4. Add Performance Accelerator feature if not already installed.
5. Remove SCSI host attachment feature if installed.
6. Increase cache size if necessary.
7. Install LAN card in Library Manager if not already installed.
8. Install additional 3590 drives if needed.
9. Install Library Manager licensed internal code supporting Peer-to-Peer.
10. Install the VTS licensed internal code supporting Peer-to-Peer.
11. Vary VTS online.
12. Configure and enable Web access to the library manager.
13. Install the DFSMS/MVS support and toleration code for Peer-to-Peer.

6.7.2.2 Install new hardware

1. Install CX0 frame or frames.
2. Install four AX0s.
3. Configure the AX0s.
4. Install new 3494 tape library, 3590 drives, and new stacked volumes.
5. Install new B18 VTS including the copy features.
6. Configure the new library manager for Peer-to-Peer.
7. Install new ESCON directors if required.
8. Connect ESCON links from the new B18 to the AX0s.
9. Install and configure RSF for the new B18 and AX0s.
10. Configure and enable Web access to the AX0s.
11. Configure and enable Web access to the new library manager.

6.7.2.3 Install Peer-to-Peer upgrade

1. Vary original 3494 virtual devices and VTS offline.
2. Install the Peer-to-Peer features on the original VTS:
    a. This disables Advanced Function feature (#4000) and Additional ESCON Channels feature (#3418).

b. Installation creates the token database.
3. Confirm that the code levels on both library managers and VTSs match.
4. Connect ESCON links from original (now upgraded) B18 to AX0s.
5. Connect host ESCON channels to AX0s.
6. Back up the VTS partition of the original library manager data base.
7. Restore the library manager database to the new library manager.
8. Configure the original library manager for Peer-to-Peer.
9. Designate one library as the User Interface library.
10. Bring each VTS and the AX0s online.
11. Initiate the creation of tokens in the new VTS.
    The Peer-to-Peer VTS will initialize as available.
12. Vary online virtual devices at host.

6.7.3 Software migration steps

These are the steps that you must perform to define the Peer-to-Peer VTS and make the appropriate SMS changes:

1. Use HCD to delete the drive addresses for the existing VTS[1].
2. Use HCD to define 64 device addresses for the Peer-to-Peer VTS as four strings of 16 devices each.
3. Use the ISMF library definition of the existing library as the definition for the composite library to avoid TCDB changes.
4. Use ISMF to define each of the distributed libraries.
5. Activate the IODF with the device address for the Peer-to-Peer VTS.
6. Activate the SCDS to use changed SMS definitions.
7. Verify that the composite library and both distributed libraries come online.

We will discuss these steps in this section.

Let us assume that the existing VTS is configured as in Figure 55, installed and active, using 64 virtual drives with:

- Virtual drive addresses ranging from 100 to 13F
- A library name of LIBVTS1
- A library sequence number (LIBID) of 11111

[1] You could also use HCD to alter the definitions for the existing VTS; for completeness, we will show this approach in the section that describes merging two existing VTSs in 6.8, "Merging two existing 3494-VTS in a Peer-to-Peer configuration" on page 142.

The TCDB contains thousands of volumes in the range from V00001 to V99999. These virtual volumes have LIBVTS1 as the library name in the volume record, as shown in Figure 55.

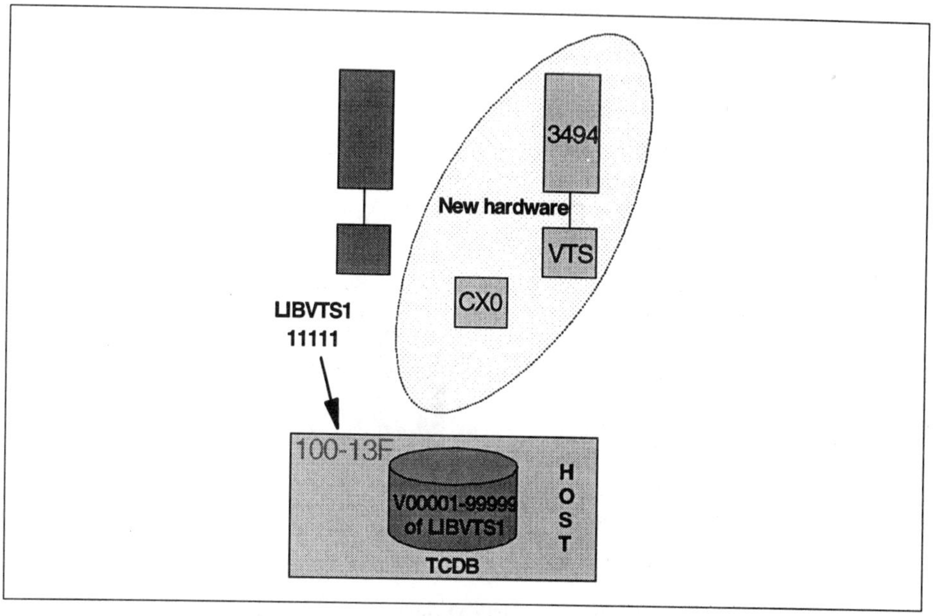

Figure 55. Upgrading an existing VTS: MES installation adding new hardware

Once the hardware installation is completed, you can start the software implementation as detailed in the following steps.

6.7.3.1 Delete old device addresses

Using HCD, delete the range of 64 addresses used by the original VTS, 100 to 13F.

The new Peer-to-Peer VTS will use the 64 virtual devices of the Composite Library.

6.7.3.2 HCD define of new Composite library devices

Using HCD, define a new range of 64 devices (addresses 200-23F) as documented in 6.1.2, "Defining devices through HCD panels" on page 119. These will be the new 64 virtual devices of the Composite library.

6.7.3.3 Composite library definition

We will reuse the library name, LIBVTS1, of the original VTS so that we do not need to make any TCDB changes. The LIBPORT ids will be 1, 2, 3 or 4 respectively for the four emulated 3490 CUs. The device address range is 200-23F in this example. See the panels on page 122.

We will use ISMF to alter LIBVTS1 to point to library ID 33333, which we will assume is the library ID of the composite library. If you do not supply a library ID, the convention is to use the last five digits of the CX0 frame.

6.7.3.4 ISMF define of distributed libraries

Use ISMF to define the distributed libraries. In this example, we use the B18 serial number as the Library ID, for example, 11111 and 22222; and put in a name for the Distributed VTSs, for example, DISTLIB1 and DISTLIB2, as you can see in Figure 56.

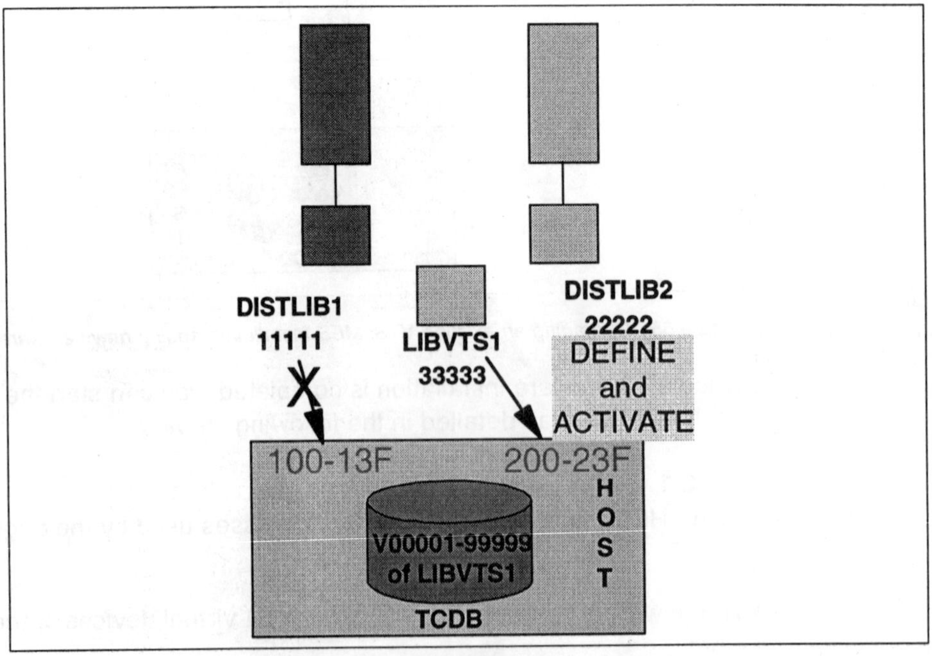

Figure 56. HCD and ISMF definitions for the newly installed hardware

6.7.3.5 Activate the HCD definitions

Activate the new definitions: using the ACTIVATE IODF command from the MVS console for the HCD definitions, and using the SETSMS SCDS command for the SMS definitions.

After activating the IODF, the new 3490 addresses should be available and can be varied online.

6.7.3.6 Activate the SMS definitions

Activating the SCDS should bring online the Composite library (LIBVTS1) and the two Distributed libraries (DISTLIB1 and DISTLIB2). If OAM is not automatically restarted upon SCDS activation (RESTART=NO is specified in the OAM started procedure), you need to restart it manually, using the F OAM,RESTART command.

Then you can submit jobs to LIBVTS1 as you did before the upgrade, because the TCDB records remain the same.

6.7.3.7 Verify the definitions

If the new libraries go online, this means that the Distributed VTSs and the AX0s are successfully communicating with host. The final Peer-to-Peer VTS configuration is shown in Figure 57.

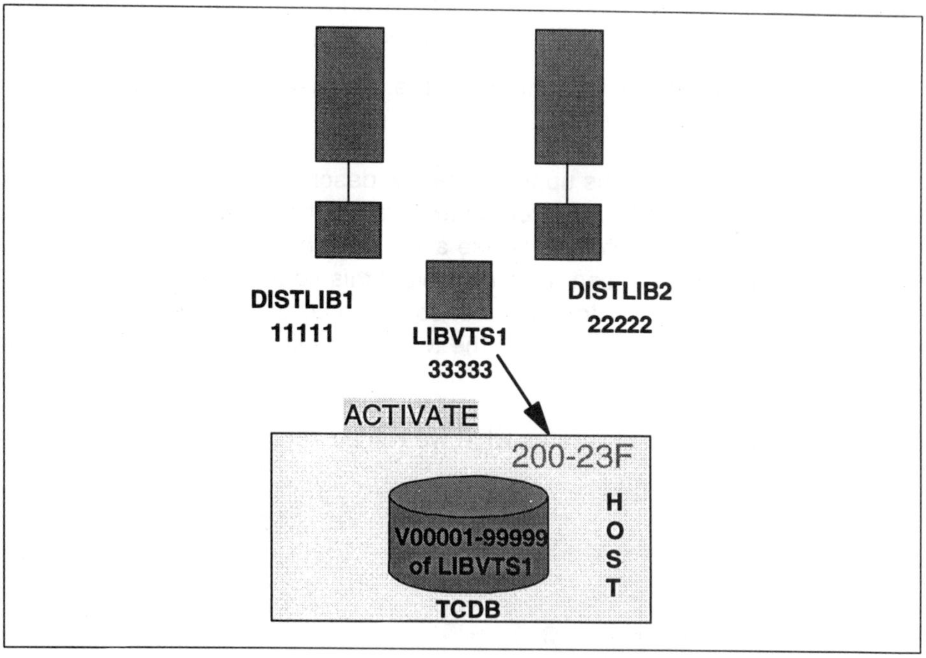

Figure 57. Peer-to-Peer VTS configuration after the MES is completed

From a host perspective, both the original VTS subsystem and the Peer-to-Peer VTS can be seen as a single VTS. Therefore, after the migration process, the host system still sees the VTS image as originally defined, even though it is now a Peer-to-Peer VTS.

6.8 Merging two existing 3494-VTS in a Peer-to-Peer configuration

From a host system point of view, merging two existing stand-alone VTS systems into one Peer-to-Peer configuration means that you are consolidating two libraries into one. This means that you should consider these points:

- You must make sure that there are no duplicate volume serial numbers for the logical volumes across the two source VTSs.
- A Peer-to-Peer VTS may have up to 250,000 logical volumes as may one stand-alone VTS; so, the combined total of logical volumes in the two source stand-alone VTSs must be less than 250,000.
- Each stand-alone VTS can have 64 device addresses for a total of 128 addresses; a Peer-to-Peer configuration has 64 addresses.
- Two existing VTSs may be used for different workloads which would have to be combined for the Peer-to-Peer configuration.
- If the two existing VTSs are attached to the same 3494 library, one must be moved to a different library.

In the previous upgrade that we described, where we added a new VTS to an existing VTS, we were able to reuse the library name of the original VTS for the composite and hence avoid any changes to TCDB and DFSMSrmm entries. We can no longer avoid this so there will be additional tasks to reconcile library names in control records. However, it is still wise to use the library name of one of the two source libraries as the library name for the composite library.

Figure 58 illustrates what we will be changing.

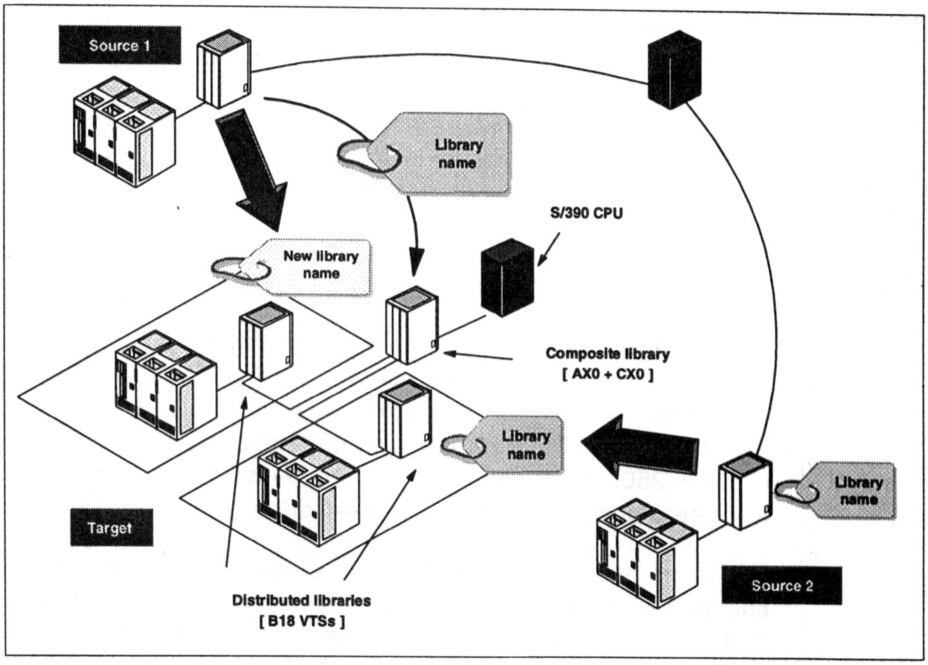

Figure 58. Merging two existing VTSs into a Peer-to-Peer VTS

6.8.1 Migration overview

The new hardware consists of:

- Any necessary upgrades to the existing VTSs so that they have all the prerequisites to be able to install the copy features on each,
- The AX0 virtual tape controllers and CX0 frames, and
- The copy features on each VTS.

The migration can and should be broken down into separate stages to minimize outages:

- Planning
- Hardware and software preparation
- System definitions
- Merge
- Reconciliation

We will describe each of these steps in more detail.

6.8.2 Planning

The preparation steps can and should be done well in advance of the delivery of the new hardware. You should decide upon the configuration and collect data for the installation of the StorWatch Specialists. The 3494 Installation and Planning Guide contains some worksheets that you may find helpful in documenting what will be done. After you have completed these worksheets, review them with your service representative.

See 5.3.2, “Configuration options” on page 109 and 5.3.3, “StorWatch Specialist configuration” on page 113 to see what information you will need.

At this stage, you should also estimate how many logical volumes are defined across the two VTSs that you will be merging. If the total is less than 250,000, you need take no action. If the total exceeds 250,000, you must remove logical volumes. Once you are sure that the combined total of logical volumes is below 250,000, it would be wise not to insert further logical volumes until the merge has been completed to avoid the need to repeat the check.

As the merged Peer-to-Peer VTS will create copies of logical volumes changed after the merge, you should review the number of scratch stacked 3590 volumes and order sufficient extra volumes to insert into the libraries to hold the copies.

You should also check the volume serial number ranges defined to the two VTSs and resolve any volume serial number duplication.

6.8.3 Hardware and software preparation

The hardware preparation is performed by your service representatives who will complete the following set of tasks.

6.8.3.1 Update existing 3494-B18s and prepare for merge

The service representative will complete these tasks:

1. Vary existing VTS offline.
2. Add EHPO channels if not already installed.
3. Add Performance Accelerator feature if not already installed.
4. Remove SCSI host attachment feature if installed.
5. Increase cache size if necessary.
6. Install LAN card in Library Manager if not already installed.
7. Install additional 3590 drives if needed.

8. Install the Library Manager licensed internal code supporting Peer-to-Peer.
9. Install the VTS licensed internal code supporting Peer-to-Peer.
10. Vary VTS online.
11. Check for duplicate volume serial numbers.
12. Configure and enable Web access to the library manager.
13. If both VTSs are attached to the same 3494 tape library, you must move one of them to a different 3494 library.
14. Build a REXX exec, DFSORT job or similar to assist in the TCDB updates.

The level of licensed internal code that supports Peer-to-Peer configurations includes tools that your service representative should use to check for duplicate volume serial numbers.

In addition to the tasks done by your service representative, you need to:

1. Move any volumes accessed by SCSI hosts to another library.
2. Plan system definition changes (see 6.8.4, "System definitions" on page 145).
3. Install the DFSMS/MVS support and toleration code for Peer-to-Peer.
4. Insert additional scratch stacked 3590 volumes.

6.8.3.2 Install new hardware

The virtual tape controllers should be installed and configured before the VTSs are merged.

1. Install CX0 frame or frames.
2. Install four AX0s.
3. Configure the AX0s.
4. Install new ESCON directors if required.
5. Configure and enable Web access to the AX0s.
6. Configure and enable RSF for the AX0s.

6.8.4 System definitions

Changes are needed to the device addresses and to the SMS definitions. You should prepare the changes before you merge the VTSs by taking copies of your existing definitions and making the changes to the copies. You cannot change the SMS definitions, TCDB records, or DFSMSrmm volume records at this stage; this is best done during the physical merge. However, you can build the jobs to do the changes in preparation for running them during the merge.

6.8.4.1 Device addresses

The HCD definitions must be changed. The definitions for one of the libraries should be changed to reflect a configuration of four independent control units, each with 16 addresses, for use as the definitions for the composite library. The other set of addresses can be deleted.

6.8.4.2 SMS definitions

The library name of one of the source VTSs will be used for the composite library so we can reuse one set of library definitions within ISMF. We can reuse the ISMF library definition of the other source library for one of the distributed libraries, and we will need to provide a new set of definitions for the second distributed library. Figure 59 shows an example of how the SMS library definitions would be changed.

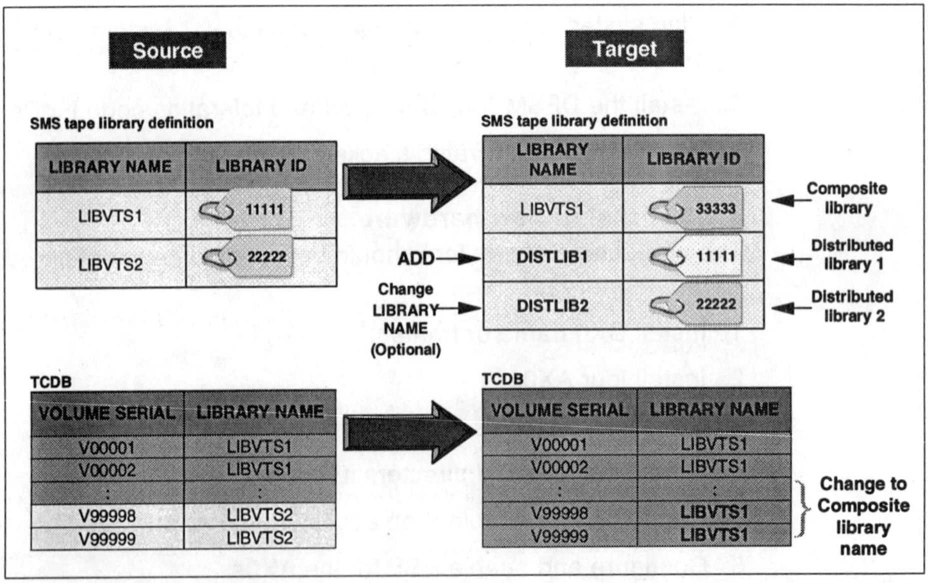

Figure 59. Changing definitions for merge

6.8.4.3 ACS routines

You start with two independent stand-alone VTSs and SMStape uses tape storage groups to direct allocations. You should review the tape storage groups and decide whether you want to keep them all, but just use the new composite library as the allocation target, or whether you might want to redirect some of the work to other VTSs that you might have.

After reviewing tape storage group assignment to VTSs, you may need to prepare and test changes to your ACS routines that you will activate following the completion of the merge.

6.8.4.4 JES3 definitions

In a JES3 environment, you should modify the INISH deck to balance the load across the virtual tape controllers. You should also remove the device definitions of the library whose name is not becoming the composite library name.

6.8.4.5 Definition changes

We assume that your existing VTSs are configured as shown in Table 11. They are installed and in production, defined as follows:

Table 11. Definitions before merge

VTS	Library ID	Volser range	Device addresses
LIBVTS1	11111	V00001-V49999	100-13F
LIBVTS2	22222	V50000-V99999	200-23F

The TCDB contains thousands of volumes in the range V00001 to V99999. Volumes V00001 to V49999 are in LIBVTS1 while V50000 to V99999 are in LIBVTS2 as shown in Table 11.

We will choose to reuse LIBVTS1 as the composite library name. LIBVTS2 will disappear.

Table 12 shows the target configuration.

Table 12. Target definitions after merge

VTS	Library ID	Volser range	Device addresses
LIBVTS1	333333	V00000-V99999	100-13F
DISTLIB1	111111	not applicable	not applicable
DISTLIB2	222222	not applicable	not applicable

We must change the HCD definitions for addresses 100-13F so that we have four control units with LIBPORT IDs from 1 to 4 for the four emulated control units and that each logical control unit has a control unit address of 0. We need a new library ID, and we will use 33333.

In ISMF, we alter the library definition for LIBVTS1 by changing the library ID from 11111 to 33333.

By doing this, LIBVTS1 will be the composite library. This means that virtual volume entries in the TCDB and DFSMSrmm control data set which referred to that stand-alone library LIBVTS1 now refer to the composite library and do not need to be changed.

Define a new library (called DISTLIB1 in this example) and use the existing library ID of 11111. As the library ID is unchanged, there is no need for a hardware teach.

We also need a definition for the second distributed library. In this case, we define a new library, DISTLIB2, with a library ID of 22222. Again, by keeping the same library ID we avoid a hardware teach. To summarize the changes:

1. Using the HCD panels, change the definitions for addresses 100-13F.
2. Using ISMF, alter the definition of LIBVTS1 to have a new library ID of 33333.
3. Using ISMF, delete the definition for LIBVTS2.
4. In ISMF, define the distributed library DISTLIB1 with library ID 11111.
5. Define the distributed library DISTLIB2 with library ID 22222.

Figure 60 shows the effect of the HCD and ISMF changes.

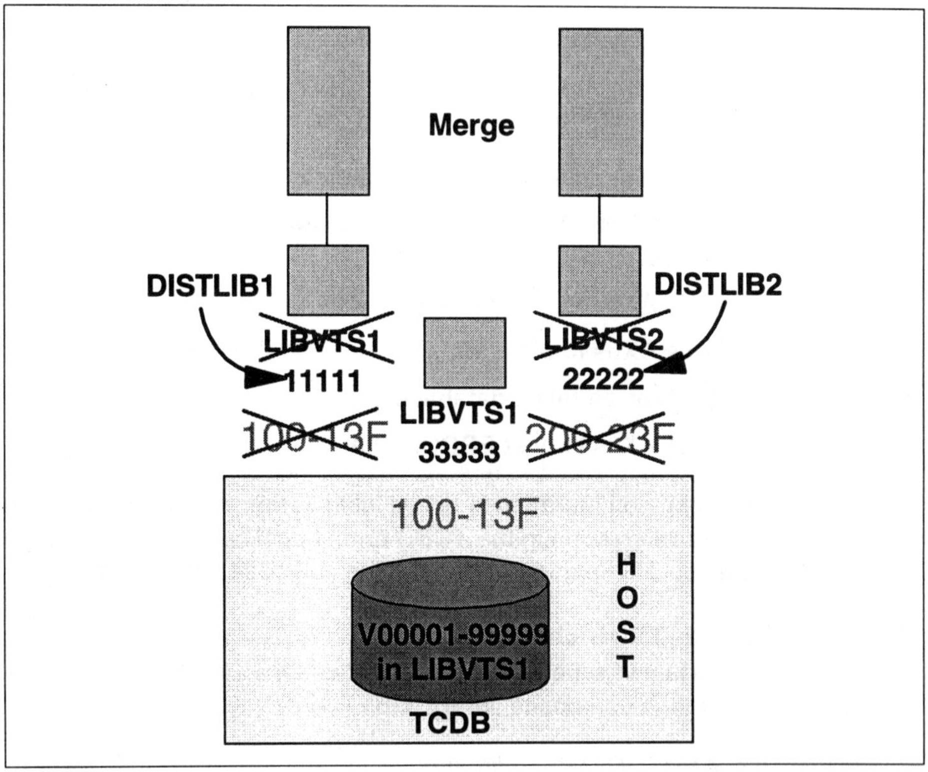

Figure 60. Summary of definition changes for merge

6.8.5 Merge the VTSs

The steps shown below will result in a Peer-to-Peer configuration. You should plan for an outage of about eight hours.

6.8.5.1 Install copy features and merge

For each B18:

1. Vary VTS offline
2. Remove host ESCON cables
3. Establish the VTS as a Peer-to-Peer distributed VTS
4. Select the UI library
5. Define the composite library name
6. Vary the VTS online

7. Backup database
8. Install copy feature
9. Merge database records from the other VTS being upgraded[2]

   This step will also confirm that there are no duplicate volume serial numbers. If there are, the merge cannot be completed.

Complete the physical merge by completing these tasks:

1. Verify that both library managers have the same category attributes defined.
2. Cable AX0s to VTS in UI library.
3. Cable AX0s to other VTS.
4. Synchronize token databases.
5. Cable AX0s to host ESCON channels.

While the configuration is unavailable during the merge, you can correct volume references in the TCDB and, if applicable, the DFSMSrmm control data set. These must all refer to the composite library name.

6.8.5.2 TCDB changes

The virtual volume TCDB entries for volumes in LIBVTS2 must be changed to refer to the composite library, LIBVTS1.

Issue the IDCAMS command:

```
LISTC VOLUMEENTRIES(V*) LIBRARY(LIBVTS2)
```

This will list all the TCDB volume entries referring to the old library name, LIBVTS2. At this stage, ensure that you have a valid backup of your TCDB in the event of any problems with the updates that you will do next.

For each volume, issue this IDCAMS command to correct the library name to refer to the composite library:

```
ALTER Vvolser VOLUMEENTRY LIBRARYNAME(LIBVTS1)
```

You may choose to use a REXX exec or DFSORT to build a list of commands that you can review before submitting. A sample REXX exec is included in Appendix F, “Altering TCDB entries after merging VTSs” on page 269.

[2] If the VTSs are physically remote, consider how to exchange the database backups quickly.

6.8.5.3 Tape library management systems

We are not aware of any tape management systems other than DFSMSrmm that holds library names in control data set records.

For DFSMSrmm, you will need to update the DFSMSrmm volume entries.

Issue the command:

```
RMM SEARCHVOLUME VOLUME(*)
   OWNER(*) LIMIT(*) -
   LOCATION(LIBVTS2) -
   CLIST('RMM CHANGEVOLUME ',' LOCATION(LIBVTS1) HOME(LIBVTS1)')
```

This will build a data set containing a list of DFSMSrmm `changevolume` commands. After ensuring that you have a valid backup of the DFSMSrmm control data set, you can execute this list of commands by issuing:

```
EXEC EXEC.RMM.CLIST
```

This will change both the location and the home location name in the DFSMSrmm volume records to refer to the composite library.

6.8.6 Activate the definitions

When the upgrade has been completed, you can activate the new definitions.

Use the ACTIVATE IODF operator command to change the IOCDS and use the SETSMS SCDS operator command to activate the SMS definitions.

Chapter 7. Operating and using the Peer-to-Peer VTS

In this chapter we describe operational considerations and usage guidelines unique to the IBM Peer-to-Peer VTS. For general guidance on how to operate a Magstar 3494 tape library and an IBM 3494 Virtual Tape Server, refer to the *Magstar 3494 Tape Library Operators guide*, GA32-0280, *IBM Magstar Tape Products Family: A Practical Guide*, SG24-4632, and *IBM Magstar Virtual Tape Server: Planning, Implementing, and Monitoring*, SG24-2229.

7.1 Overview

For successful operation of your Peer-to-Peer VTS, it is important that you understand its concepts and its components. They are described in detail in Chapter 2, “Peer-to-Peer VTS concepts” on page 7. In this chapter, we combine the components and functions of the Peer-to-Peer VTS in two groups: the logical view and the physical view. Each component and each function belongs to only one view.

The logical view is also the host view. From the host allocation point of view, there is only one library to deal with — the composite library. A composite library has 64 virtual addresses for tape mounts. A composite library can run in immediate copy mode or in deferred copy mode. The host view is aware of the existence of the physical libraries. The term distributed library is used to denote the physical libraries which are part of the Peer-to-Peer VTS.

The physical view is directly related to the hardware components and their functions. The hardware is clearly part of the physical view: The Model AX0 controllers, the ESCON links, the Model B18 VTSs and the 3494 tape library. Also, the Master VTS and the I/O VTS can be considered as elements of the physical view. The preferred VTS for I/O is in this view too.

The UI distributed library is part of the physical view. The host view currently does not know about the UI library, which is the library you must go to when defining new logical volumes.

When you operate the Peer-to-Peer VTS, you deal with one view at a time. There are three operator interfaces for providing information about the Peer-to-Peer VTS.

- The library manager panels deals with information in the Library Manager database. This is part of the physical view. There is limited information available on the Model B18 VTSs in the 3494 tape library. You can directly display them on the library manager console, or you can use the

© Copyright IBM Corp. 2000

Distributed Console Access Facility (DCAF) for remote operations of the library manager console. For more information, see *Magstar 3494 Tape Library Operator Guide*, GA32-0280.

- OAM commands are available from the host operator console for information regarding the Peer-to-Peer composite and distributed libraries. This information represents the host view of the components within the Peer-to-Peer VTS. Other OS/390 commands can be used against the virtual addresses. These commands are not aware that the 3490E addresses are part of a Peer-to-Peer VTS configuration.
- StorWatch Specialist functions are available via a Web-based user interface. There are two new StorWatch Specialists available for the 3494 tape library. The Magstar 3494 Tape Library Specialist enables you to monitor the Library Manager and the VTSs. The Magstar 3494 Peer-to-Peer VTS Specialist is used for the Peer-to-Peer VTS. Because a Web interface is provided, they can be used from any suitable Web browser allowed to use the IP addresses. StorWatch panels display information related to the physical view. For StorWatch installation requirements, see 6.4, "Setup of StorWatch Specialists" on page 130.

7.2 Hardware

The Model AX0 controller and the Model CX0 frame are new hardware components in a Peer-to-Peer VTS.

7.2.1 Model AX0 control and indicators

The only controls directly accessible on a Model AX0 controller are the power switch under the media bay cover and the warm boot button. These affect only the operation of a particular Model AX0 controller and will not impact the other controllers. They are for service personnel use only.

Service access to each Model AX0 controller is provided by modem or ASCII terminal connection to the communication port of the controller. This function is available only for the service representative.

7.2.2 Model CX0 control and indicators

The operator panel is mounted on the rear door of the Model CX0 frame. It has one unit emergency switch, which removes power only to the Model CX0 frame and installed Model AX0 controllers. The switch should be set in the *OFF* (**O**) position only in an emergency, and must be set to the *ON* (**I**) position to allow the installed Model AX0 controllers to be powered manually by service personnel.

The power of the Model CX0 frame is not remotely controlled by the IBM 3494 tape library or the Model B18 VTSs in the Peer-to-Peer VTS.

7.3 Monitoring the Peer-to-Peer VTS

As explained in the introduction, there are three interfaces for querying information on the Peer-to-Peer VTS.

- The library manager panels deal with information about the library manager, the 3494 tape library, and attached VTSs.
- OAM commands are available from the host operator console for information regarding the Peer-to-Peer composite and distributed libraries.
- StorWatch Specialist display functions are available via a Web-based user interface.

7.3.1 StorWatch Specialists

There are two new StorWatch Specialists now available for the 3494 tape library. The Magstar 3494 Tape Library Specialist enables you to monitor the Library Manager and the VTSs from a remote location. The Magstar 3494 Peer-to-Peer VTS Specialist is used for the Peer-to-Peer VTS. You activate StorWatch for your Peer-to-Peer VTS by entering the correct IP address on your Web browser.

The Magstar 3494 Tape Library Specialist home panel directs you to all the Specialists panels available for the 3494 tape library. From the home panel, you can select one of the following items.

- Library Manager
- VTS
- Virtual Tape Controller (the Model AX0 controllers); this leads you to the Peer-to-Peer VTS panels

From each main panel, you are directed to panels with more detailed information. A sample of the library manager main panel is shown in Figure 61.

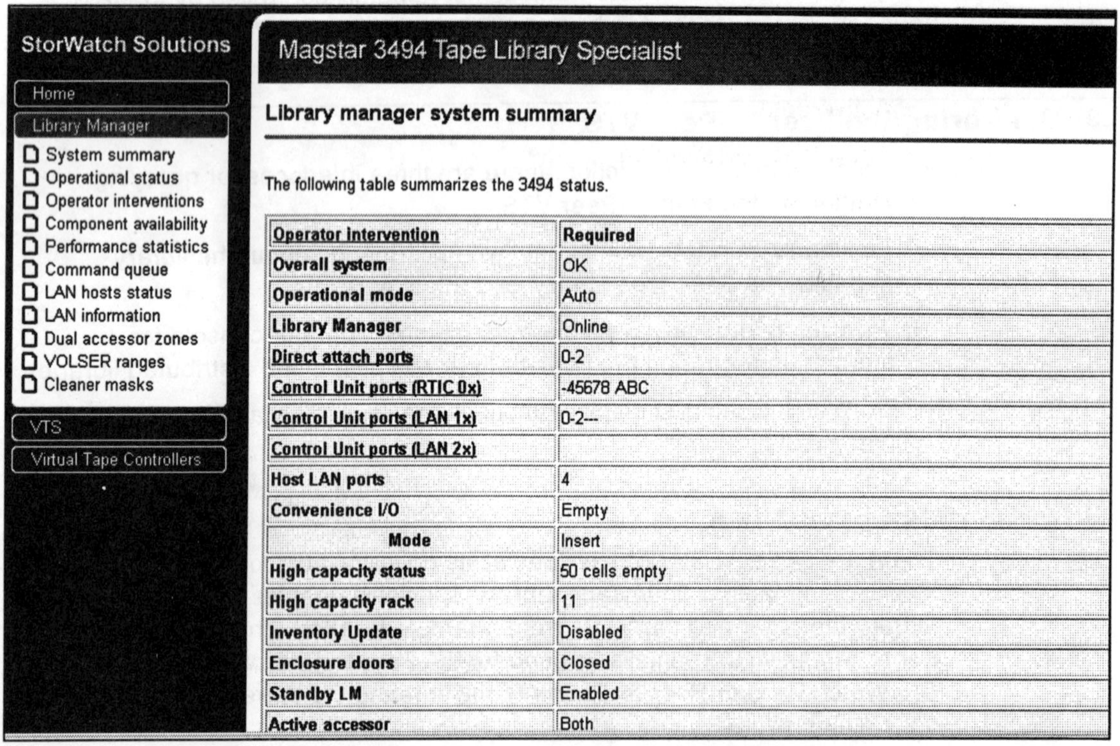

Figure 61. Library manager main panel

Library Manager

The following detailed panels are available for the library manager:

- System summary
- Operational status
- Operator interventions
- Component availability
- Performance characteristics
- Command queue
- LAN hosts status
- LAN information
- Dual accessor zones
- Volser ranges
- Cleaner mask

VTS

The following detailed panels are available for each VTS in your configuration:

- Active data
- Active data distribution
- Data flow
- Logical mounts per hour
- Mount hit rate
- Physical device mount history
- Category attributes
- Management policies
- Status
- VOLSER ranges
- Real time statistics

Virtual Tape Controllers

These panels deal with the physical view of the Peer-to-Peer VTS. First you must select the Peer-to-Peer VTS by name, which is the name of the composite library as defined to DFSMS/MVS using ISMF. The initial panel shows a list of the Model AX0 controllers. You can then select one of them. They all present you the same information because each controller maintains the complete view of the composite library. So, if a Model AX0 controller is down or is in service mode, you can select one of the remaining model AX0 controllers.

The following detailed panels are available for the Peer-to-Peer VTS:

- Home page
- System status
- System configuration
- Current device activity
- Logical volume status
- Current copy workload

7.3.2 Peer-to-Peer VTS configuration

Information on the configuration details is available on a number of panels.

7.3.2.1 Library manager

On the VTS Status panel of the library manager, information is added to show you if a Model B18 in the 3494 tape library is part of a Peer-to-Peer VTS. A model B18 VTS is Peer-to-Peer capable if it is part of a Peer-to-Peer VTS configuration; the VTS name and number are presented on the panel.

7.3.2.2 Host commands

From the host operator console, the following commands are enhanced to present information related to the Peer-to-Peer VTS:

```
DISPLAY SMS,OAM
```

The console message from `D SMS,OAM` now displays the number of composite and distributed libraries.

```
DISPLAY SMS,LIBRARY(libname),DETAIL
```

The messages produced by `D SMS,LIBRARY` have changed as follows:

- For a VTS composite library, *VCL* is displayed in the LIB TYP field.
- For a VTS distributed library, *VDL* is displayed in the LIB TYP field.
- Peer-to-Peer VTS library association is displayed. The display of the composite library provides the names of the distributed libraries, and the display of the distributed library provides the name of the related composite library.
- The display of the distributed library provides information on the private stacked volume count in addition to the already provided scratch stacked volume count.
- The following new operational states are displayed:
  - Copy operations disabled.
  - VTS operations degraded.
  - Immediate mode copy operations deferred.
  - Service preparation occurring.

An example of the display for a composite library follows. The library type is a VCL. There are logical volumes, but no stacked volumes and no slots are associated with the composite library. Note the distributed libraries information line and the status line.

```
TAPE      LIB  DEVICE    TOT  ONL  AVL  TOTAL  EMPTY SCRTCH  ON OP
LIBRARY   TYP  TYPE      DRV  DRV  DRV  SLOTS  SLOTS   VOLS
ATLBA041  VCL  3494-L10   64   16    4      0      0    969  Y  Y
--------------------------------------------------------------------
MEDIA         SCRATCH       SCRATCH
TYPE            COUNT     THRESHOLD
MEDIA1              0            10
MEDIA2            969            10
--------------------------------------------------------------------
DISTRIBUTED LIBRARIES:  ATL70680 ATL70677
--------------------------------------------------------------------
OPERATIONAL STATE:  AUTOMATED
ERROR CATEGORY SCRATCH COUNT:                        0
--------------------------------------------------------------------
Immediate Mode Copy operations deferred.
VTS operations degraded.
Bulk input/output not configured.
```

An example of a display of a distributed library follows. The library type is a VTS distributed library (VDL). There are no drives or logical scratch volumes associated with a distributed library, but the display does show stacked volumes and cartridge slots.

```
TAPE      LIB  DEVICE    TOT  ONL  AVL  TOTAL  EMPTY SCRTCH  ON OP
LIBRARY   TYP  TYPE      DRV  DRV  DRV  SLOTS  SLOTS   VOLS
ATL70680  VDL  3494-L10    0    0    0    413    236      0  Y  Y
--------------------------------------------------------------------
COMPOSITE LIBRARY:       ATLBA041
--------------------------------------------------------------------
OPERATIONAL STATE:  AUTOMATED
SCRATCH STACKED VOLUME COUNT:                 95
PRIVATE STACKED VOLUME COUNT:                 81
--------------------------------------------------------------------
Bulk input/output not configured.
```

7.3.2.3 StorWatch Specialists

A number of Specialist pages contain configuration information. The most important panels containing configuration information are the following.

- ***Library manager:*** System summary (see example on Page 155), Component availability.
- ***VTS:*** Status (see example below).
- ***Virtual Tape Controllers:*** System status (see example on Page 162), System configuration.

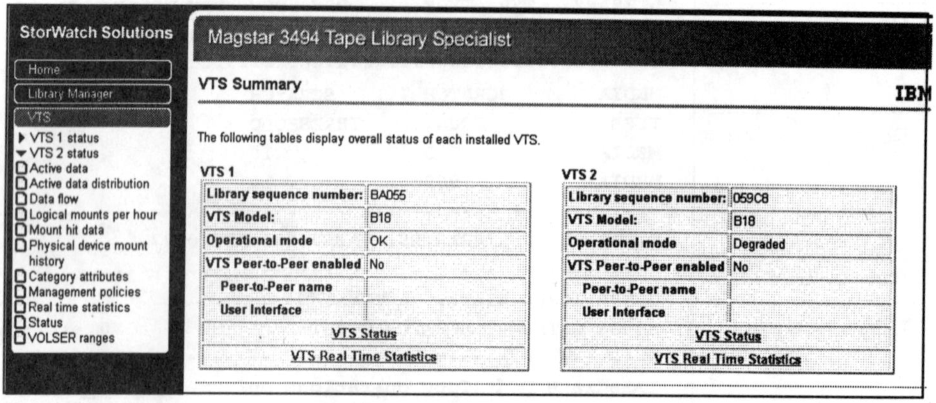

7.3.3 Composite library

The composite library reflects the overall state of the Peer-to-Peer VTS. For some information it combines the states of the distributed libraries to generate the state of the composite library.

7.3.3.1 State condition

If the composite library is in a certain state that is based on the state of the distributed libraries, you must look at the status of the underlying distributed library to determine which 3494 tape library caused the composite library state condition.

Table 13 shows the relationship between the composite and the distributed states.

Table 13. Relationship between composite and distributed states

Condition	Composite value	Comments
Automated mode	If *any* distributed library is in that mode	
Paused mode	If *all* distributed libraries are in that mode	
Manual mode	If *all* distributed libraries are in that mode or if one is in manual mode and the rest are in paused mode.	
Degraded operation	If *any* distributed library is in this state.	This indicates that some part of the Peer-to-Peer VTS is not functioning properly.
Vision system non-operational	If *any* distributed libraries are in this state.	The barcode scanner has failed.
Offline	If *all* distributed libraries are in this state.	The library is offline.
Library manager check 1 condition	If *all* distributed libraries are in this state.	The library manager has entered the check 1 recovery state.
All storage cells full	If *all* distributed libraries are in this state.	All storage cells have a volume assigned to it. No more physical inserts are allowed.
Out of cleaner volume	If *all* distributed libraries are in this state.	There are no cleaner cartridges available.
Dual write disabled	If *all* distributed libraries are in this state.	The library manager with the 2nd hard drive feature or an HA1 configuration is not keeping the secondary database synchronized.
Environmental alert	Composite library is never in this state.	Smoke is detected in the library enclosure.
Insufficient resources for mounts	If *all* distributed libraries are in this state.	The Peer-to-Peer VTS is out of usable physical drives.
Library manager switchover in progress	If *all* distributed libraries are in this state.	The library managers in an HA1 environment are in process of switching states.
Out of empty stack volume	If *all* distributed libraries are in this state.	The Peer-to-Peer VTS has no more available physical stacked volumes to be used to copy data to (operations are halted).

The following panel shows an example of the detailed system status of the Peer-to-Peer VTS. A number of the Peer-to-Peer VTS conditions are presented in the library part of the panel.

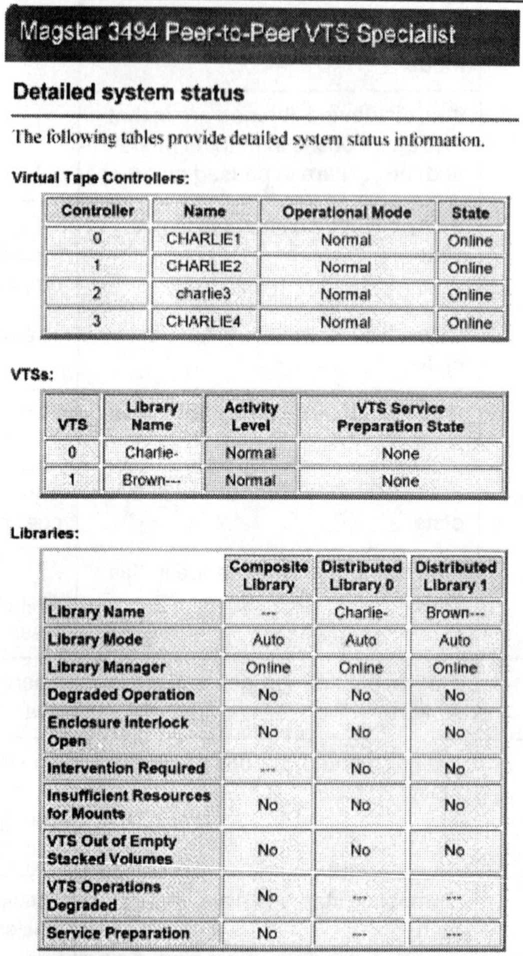

Magstar 3494 Peer-to-Peer VTS Specialist

Detailed system status

The following tables provide detailed system status information.

Virtual Tape Controllers:

Controller	Name	Operational Mode	State
0	CHARLIE1	Normal	Online
1	CHARLIE2	Normal	Online
2	charlie3	Normal	Online
3	CHARLIE4	Normal	Online

VTSs:

VTS	Library Name	Activity Level	VTS Service Preparation State
0	Charlie-	Normal	None
1	Brown---	Normal	None

Libraries:

	Composite Library	Distributed Library 0	Distributed Library 1
Library Name	---	Charlie-	Brown---
Library Mode	Auto	Auto	Auto
Library Manager	Online	Online	Online
Degraded Operation	No	No	No
Enclosure Interlock Open	No	No	No
Intervention Required	---	No	No
Insufficient Resources for Mounts	No	No	No
VTS Out of Empty Stacked Volumes	No	No	No
VTS Operations Degraded	No	---	---
Service Preparation	No	---	---

7.3.3.2 Copy mode

The copy mode is set at Peer-to-Peer VTS installation time by the service representative. In immediate copy mode, component failures may result in a temporary deferral of copies. The copy mode at installation time can be found on the system summary panel of the Magstar Peer-to-Peer VTS Specialist. The deferred copy workload is indicated on the Current copy workload panel.

7.3.4 Distributed library

You can display the status of a distributed library just as you can today with stand-alone libraries. As described in 7.3.3, "Composite library" on page 160, the status of the distributed libraries determines the status of the composite library.

If, for instance, one of the distributed libraries is in paused mode and the other is in automated mode, the overall status of the Peer-to-Peer VTS will be in automated mode with messages to the host indicating which of the distributed libraries is paused. Also, if one of the distributed libraries is taken offline at the library, the state of the composite library will remain online and operational as long as one of the distributed libraries is operational.

Since all of the drives and volumes are defined to and associated with the composite library, the display of the distributed library will show that, from a host perspective, there are no drives associated with that library. The distributed libraries should be displayed for an accurate picture of the total slot count and empty slot counts.

The Peer-to-Peer VTS selects at initialization time which of the distributed VTS becomes the Master VTS. But failures of some components of the Peer-to-Peer VTS afterwards may cause a master switchover.

The designation of a distributed library as User Interface (UI) distributed library is a Peer-to-Peer VTS installation task. It can be verified in the VTS summary panel of the Magstar 3494 Tape Library Specialist or in the VTS status window of the 3494 library manager.

7.3.5 Library manager database

Each of the library managers of the 3494 tape library associated with the distributed libraries have their own library management databases. The information on the logical volumes in these databases is equal because synchronization of the status and the contents of the logical volumes is a primary task of the Model AX0 controllers. The Model AX0 controller communicates with both VTSs and they communicate with the library manager before a status change (for instance, a change from scratch to private) takes place.

The Peer-to-Peer VTS is designed to continue operation with the remaining configuration in case of failure of a component of one of the distributed libraries. This will result in temporary differences between the library manager databases of the two 3494 tape libraries. As soon as the Peer-to-Peer VTS is recovered, a synchronization process starts from the Model AX0 controllers that results in synchronized distributed libraries, and as a consequence, also synchronized library manager databases.

7.3.6 Virtual drives

OS/390 commands providing information on the status of your Peer-to-Peer virtual addresses returns information from the Model AX0 controllers. In addition to the D U,,,*address* command and the LIBRARY DISPDRV,*libname* command you have the ability to display the current device activity panel from the 3494 Peer-to-Peer VTS Specialist.

When the host is not able to process logical volumes, it may be useful to investigate if communication is possible between your host and the AX0 controller. If you are not able to communicate with the controller, your ESCON links may be broken. This can be investigated by issuing the following command:

```
DEVSERV QTAPE,(address),1,{RDC/DLD}
```

You will get information from the Model AX0 controller in return. If you have completely lost the connection, the command cannot get the data from the controller and is not able to fill in all the fields of the command output. It is an indication that the ESCON link may be causing problems and not your Peer-to-Peer VTS configuration. Normally the command displays fields specific for the Peer-to-Peer VTS.

Below, we show an example of DEVSERV command output, highlighting the changes for a Peer-to-Peer VTS. The first thing to look for is model type=41 in the RDC data. The second thing to check is DLD data (this is a new Distributed Library Data information provided). In the example below, composite library BA071 includes distributed libraries BA71A (library 0001) and BA71B (library 0002). The number marked in the rectangle (0002) is the number of distributed libraries in this configuration. If any of the marked items are incorrect, the library will not work properly.

```
DS QT,2724,,,,RDC
IEE459I 08.29.58 DEVSERV QTAPE 237
UNIT DTYPE  DSTATUS CUTYPE  DEVTYPE  CU-SERIAL  DEV-SERIAL ACL LIBID
2724 3490L  OFFLINE 3494C2A 3590B1A* 0113-78007 0113-78007 I   BA071
  READ DEVICE CHARACTERISTIC
34905434905400E0 1FD8808004000000 0000000000000000 3494413590100002
0BA0710100000000 4281000000000000 0000000000000000 0000000000000000

DS QT,2724,,,,DLD
IEE459I 08.28.33 DEVSERV QTAPE 114
UNIT DTYPE  DSTATUS CUTYPE  DEVTYPE  CU-SERIAL  DEV-SERIAL ACL LIBID
2724 3490L  OFFLINE 3494C2A 3590B1A* 0113-78007 0113-78007 I   BA071
  DISTRIBUTED LIBRARY DATA
010A101F0000405A 000200BA71A0001 3494000000000000 0000000BA71B0002
3494000000000000 0000000000000000 392C026B00000000 0000000000000000
```

A Peer-to-Peer VTS (and, at suitable microcode levels, a stand-alone VTS) has a virtual device recovery function. If a virtual device is boxed, a *reset allegiance* channel command will allow a functioning alternate path to the boxed device to be used. The allegiance of the boxed device over the failed path is reset so that the alternate path can be used.

VTS virtual drive recovery enables the automatic recovery of virtual devices from boxed conditions that may be caused by link failures, ESCON director failures, or channel adapter failures.

No software support is needed for virtual device recovery.

7.3.7 Logical volume status

Information on logical volumes is available in the library manager database of both 3494 tape libraries, in the Peer-to-Peer VTS, in the Tape Configuration DataBase (TCDB), and in the database of your tape management system in use.

A Peer-to-Peer VTS is transparent to your tape management system and to the TCDB. They deal with the logical view of your data.

The logical volume information details in the library manager database are the same as today for a stand-alone VTS. The information for a Peer-to-Peer VTS logical volume is, however, available in two library manager databases. This information is the same in a fully operational Peer-to-Peer VTS. If there is a component failure in the Peer-to-Peer VTS, you may see temporary differences.

Information on the dual copy status of your logical volume is available on the logical volume status result panel. You can submit the logical volume serial number on the logical volume status panel. You get back a panel as shown below. It summarizes all important information related to the logical volume.

Magstar 3494 Peer-to-Peer VTS Specialist

Logical volume status results

The following table provides data for the requested logical volume.

Logical Volume: JQ1018

	VTS 0	VTS 1
Library Name	Charlie-	Brown---
Stacked (Physical) Volume	PHX365	PHX378
Data Level	Current	Current
Category	0002	0002
Category Level	Current	Current
Volume in Cache	Yes	Yes
Compressed File Size	4 KB	4 KB
Last Modified Time	Wed 08/16/2000 14:03:37	Wed 08/16/2000 14:08:13
Last Access Time	Wed 08/16/2000 14:03:37	Wed 08/16/2000 14:11:18

7.4 Peer-to-Peer VTS basic operations

In the next few paragraphs, we explain some of the basic tasks that may be needed during the operation of a Peer-to-Peer VTS.

7.4.1 Power on/off

An IML of the complete Peer-to-Peer VTS requires that at least one Model AX0 controller and both Model B18 VTSs to be functional prior to completing the logical subsystem IML. The individual Model AX0 controllers and Model B18 VTSs may be IML'd without all components being operational.

In these scenarios, the IML of a Model AX0 is seen as an IML of a control unit, but the rest of the system remains the same. The IML of the Model B18 VTS does not affect the online status of the Peer-to-Peer VTS, but may temporarily limit access to certain volumes. Only after a successful IML of the

Peer-to-Peer VTS can failures be tolerated. Upgrades and service action can be performed on individual components without making the whole Peer-to-Peer VTS unavailable.

A scheduled power-off of one the components requires a Service preparation to be performed in advance. For further details see 2.7, "Service considerations" on page 40.

7.4.2 Clock setting

The Peer-to-Peer VTS adds some complexity to clock setting of your configuration. In a standalone VTS the clock of the VTS is synchronized with the clock of the library manager at VTS initialization time. As consequence, you have to vary your VTS offline and change the 3494 tape library to pause mode before you are allowed to change the clock. A service representative is responsible for performing this task.

With the Peer-to-Peer VTS, the clocks of the Model AX0 controllers are synchronized with the clock of the UI distributed library. If this library is not available, the clock of the other distributed library will be used. Clock synchronization will take place at initialization time of the Model AX0 controllers. Changing the clock to daylight saving time requires that you power off your Peer-to-Peer VTS.

The VTS clock time plays no role in the exchange of information between the host and the Peer-to-Peer VTS. Messages and SMF records related to the Peer-to-Peer VTS contain the time stamps of the host. Messages and statistics in the 3494 tape library contain time stamp originated from the library manager clock. In case of problems with hardware components, it may be possible that Service Information Messages (SIMs) are sent to the host containing the time stamp based on the library manager clock.

Recommendation

We recommend that, for a VTS, you should not change your clocks twice a year, but rather, use your winter time or use GMT throughout the year.

You should realize that the time difference can be important in communication with your service representative in case of problems with a hardware component. Problem records normally contain the host time or the real time of the occurrence of the problem. Your service representative must be aware of the clock time difference when performing the problem determination using information generated from the Peer-to-Peer VTS.

7.4.3 Vary online/offline

A composite VTS library can be varied online and offline like a stand-alone VTS. You are also able to use the VARY command for a distributed library, but VARYing a distributed library offline from the host really has no meaning, because it does not prevent the usage of the library as part of the Peer-to-Peer VTS. Warning message CBR3016I will be used when a distributed library is initialized or VARYed offline. A Model AX0 controller can be taken offline by varying the associated addresses offline.

7.4.4 Library in pause mode

A distributed library can enter the pause mode as is possible today with a stand-alone VTS. Reasons for the pause can include an enclosure door being opened for clearing a device after a load/unload failure or removing cartridges from the high capacity I/O station.

With the Peer-to-Peer VTS support, a new functional enhancement allows logical mounts for scratch volumes, logical mounts for private volumes where the volume is resident in the tape volume cache, demounts, and ejects, to be executed while in pause mode. These mounts will use the active distributed library as I/O VTS.

Other mounts will be started, but will be held up by the resulting physical mounts needed to execute a recall. Those mounts will be queued by the library manager for later processing when the library leaves the pause mode.

Since both scratch mounts and private mounts with data in the cache are allowed to execute but not physical mounts, no more data can be moved out of the cache after the currently mounted stacked volumes are completely filled. The cache is filling up with data which has not been copied to stacked volumes. This results in significant throttling and finally in stopping any mount activity on the distributed library.

Although the Peer-to-Peer VTS has enhanced support for library pause mode it is for performance reasons very important that you minimize the library in pause mode condition.

7.4.5 Add and delete logical volumes

You must use the library manager console of the 3494 tape library where the UI distributed library resides for defining new logical volumes to the Peer-to-Peer VTS. This function is restricted on the other library manager for your Peer-to-Peer VTS. Insert processing by a host of new logical volumes requires that both distributed libraries must be online.

When you have defined the new logical volumes, the host is notified and can request the library manager to change the status of the logical volumes to private or scratch. OAM communicates with your tape management software if available for determining the category for the logical volume. In response to the request, the Peer-to-Peer VTS synchronizes the logical volume information in both library manager databases and distributed libraries. When one of the distributed libraries fails during this process, the synchronization will be suspended and resumed after the failing distributed library becomes available.

Removing logical volumes from a library must be performed by executing an eject command against the logical volume. The Peer-to-Peer VTS ensures that the logical volumes are deleted in both tape libraries. The maximum number of ejects in progress is limited to 1000. Both distributed libraries must be online for the eject to complete successfully.

7.4.6 Add stacked volumes

Stacked volumes must be inserted for both distributed libraries in a Peer-to-Peer VTS as today in a stand-alone Model B18 VTS. It is recommended that both distributed libraries have about the same number of stacked volumes.

When one of the distributed libraries runs out of stacked volumes, many of the operations of that library cannot continue. To prevent the tape volume cache from reaching an overflow state and throttling, all logical mount processing is suspended as soon as the number of available scratch physical volumes in the distributed library is zero. The library enters the "VTS out of stacked volumes" state. The actions taken by the Peer-to-Peer VTS are similar to those described in 7.4.4, "Library in pause mode" on page 168. As soon as new stacked volumes are entered, normal processing resumes.

7.4.7 Deferred/immediate copy mode

As stated in 2.4, "Creating the secondary copy of a virtual volume" on page 19, the copy mode, deferred or immediate, which the Peer-to-Peer VTS is using is determined at installation time. This state can change when failures of components of the Peer-to-Peer VTS enforce it. You are able to display it (on the system configuration panel of the Peer-to-Peer VTS Specialist); however, there is no way to change it dynamically. The Peer-to-Peer VTS will use the initial copy mode as soon as the availability of the components allows it.

7.4.8 Distributed library aspects

The VTS management policies definitions for a distributed library must be entered on the library manager console and can dynamically be changed. These definitions apply only to the distributed library associated with the 3494 library manager and are not propagated to the other distributed library. See 6.2, "VTS definition from the library manager" on page 124 for further details.

As described in 2.6.1, "Initializing the Peer-to-Peer VTS configuration" on page 33, the Peer-to-Peer VTS selects the Master VTS associated with one of the distributed libraries based on a number of selection criteria. If a master switchover has taken place because of a failure of a component of the Peer-to-Peer VTS, you are not able to reassign the Master VTS to the originally chosen VTS to be the master. The service representative may reassign the master after completion of repairs.

7.4.9 Prepare for service

When an element of the Peer-to-Peer VTS needs to be serviced, it must be prepared prior to taking the element away; otherwise continued host access to data may not be possible. The service preparation task is a service representative responsibility, together with operations when needed to vary the virtual addresses offline. More details on service preparation can be found in 2.7, "Service considerations" on page 40.

Preparing a Model B18 VTS for service:
When an operational Model B18 VTS needs to be taken offline for service, the Peer-to-Peer VTS must first prepare for loss of the resources involved, in order to provide continued access to customer data. The controls to prepare a Model B18 VTS to be taken offline for service are provided through the service menu on an Model AX0 controller.

Preparing a 3494 tape library for service:
If a 3494 tape library in a Peer-to-Peer VTS requires service, the Model B18 VTS associated with it must first be prepared for service. Once the Model B18 VTS has completed service preparation, then the normal procedures for servicing of the 3494 tape library can continue.

Preparing a Model AX0 controller for service:
Preparing a Model AX0 controller for service is the same as preparing any tape control unit for service. All tape devices addressable by the control unit must be varied offline, and all jobs in process must be completed or stopped.

7.5 Maintain Peer-to-Peer VTS availability

With a stand-alone VTS, when a failure occurs which causes the VTS subsystem to become unavailable, all the data stored in the VTS is unavailable until the repair is complete.

The Peer-to-Peer VTS is a solution for this problem. Its major design criterion is improving the data availability and recoverability characteristics of the VTS by duplicating all components of the VTS and by maintaining a dual copy of the data in the subsystem. It is also a solution for disaster recovery and electronic tape vaulting with transparent failover and fail back.

The availability, recoverability, and performance characteristics will depend on the mode of operation selected. A performance enhancement is gained in the deferred copy mode of operation by scheduling the creation of the dual copy as Peer-to-Peer VTS activity permits. This, however, creates the risk that access to a successfully written volume may not be possible when there is a failure in one VTS. In this mode, the system as a whole continues to operate and provide access to most of the previous written virtual volumes. The amount of data that is inaccessible will depend on the particular workload and how much delay has occurred for the deferred copy operations.

It is, therefore, important that you understand the characteristics of the Peer-to-Peer VTS, and in particular, the consequences of the mode of operations prior to a failure. This section describes various availability scenarios. For each scenario, it summarizes what the failing component is, what happens in your system if a failure occurs, and how to regain normal operations. The theoretical number of failure scenarios, particularly with multiple component failures, is too great for us to address all of them. If you understand the consequences of a failure of a single component, you will be able to deal with multiple component failures.

But first, we will first address the failure mode principles of the Peer-to-Peer VTS, which provides the availability service characteristics in case of a failure.

It is important that you check from time to time that your Peer-to-Peer VTS is in a fully operational state. This is not unique for the Peer-to-Peer VTS; it is good practice for all the equipment in your data center. Experience shows that you can avoid problems with your equipment if you verify your configuration at regular intervals. We identify the major items to verify in 7.5.2, “Verification procedure” on page 173. Some of the items can by automated if you use OS/390 system automation and monitoring software.

As stated earlier, disaster recovery is a major reason for having a Peer-to-Peer VTS. The disaster recovery procedures, as performed by your service representative, are globally described together with changes in mount processing and disaster recovery alternatives.

The message support is enhanced for the Peer-to-Peer VTS. This includes new messages as well as improvements to the current message support, and is described in C.1, "Enhanced message support" on page 233.

7.5.1 Component availability principles

The Peer-to-Peer VTS provides the flexibility to separate hardware components for remote backup and recovery which can improve data availability. Interconnected VTSs can also enable remote copy operations for remote vaulting applications. Each component in a Peer-to-Peer VTS is replicated one or more times to maximize data access and eliminate single points of failure. Access to volumes can then be maintained after component failures. In addition, service of one component of the Peer-to-Peer VTS can occur concurrently with operation of the rest of the Peer-to-Peer VTS. The Peer-to-Peer VTS provides the following availability and service characteristics:

- As long as one of the four Model AX0 controllers remains online, only one of the Model B18 VTSs needs to be operational for the Peer-to-Peer VTS system to be operational. Data access when only one VTS is operational depends on the mode of operation prior to the failure.
  - **Immediate copy mode:** Access to data written by completed jobs (successful rewind/unload) prior to the failure is maintained. Access to data is lost for jobs that were in process at the time of the failure.
  - **Deferred copy mode:** In addition to the loss of access to data as in immediate copy mode, access to logical volumes written by previously completed jobs may not be possible until the failed Model B18 VTS is returned to service.
- When only one Model AX0 controller is operational, a second controller must be brought online before the first controller may be taken down for service.
- If all four Model AX0 controllers fail at the same time, both Model B18 VTSs must be operational to bring one of the Model AX0 controllers online and restore Peer-to-Peer VTS operation.
- If both Model B18 VTSs fail at the same time, both must be brought up to restore normal Peer-to-Peer VTS operation.

- Changing logical volumes from the insert category to another category requires both Model B18 VTSs to be operational.
- A failure of either a Model AX0 controller or a Model B18 VTS may cause jobs to abend. The jobs must be restarted.
- Failure of a Model B18 VTS which is the Master VTS and failure of AX0 controllers will result in failure of a master switchover. The other VTS will be able to *read* logical volumes which have previously been closed after service representative action to enable the remaining VTS for read-only operation.
- Failure of a Model B18 VTS which is not a Master VTS will allow the Master VTS to continue writing logical volumes and reading logical volumes which have previously been closed.
- In the event of a failure in the Peer-to-Peer VTS where one of the Model AX0 controllers can no longer communicate with the Master VTS, the other VTS will become the Master VTS. The process to change the Master VTS is called switchover.
- A Master switchover fails if:
  - There are less than three operational Model AX0 controllers remaining in the Peer-to-Peer VTS.
  - The current Master VTS and more than one AX0 controller fails.
- If the current Master VTS and more than one AX0 controller fails, data operations with the Peer-to-Peer VTS cannot continue until action is taken by an IBM support specialist to put the AX0 controllers in either read/write disconnected mode or read-only mode with the remaining VTS. For more details, see 2.6.7, “Special AX0 operational modes” on page 40.
- If in immediate copy mode, copy operations are deferred if:
  - One of the Model B18 VTSs is not operational.
  - All links to a B18 are lost.
  - The tape library associated with a distributed VTS is not operational.

7.5.2 Verification procedure

Here is a list of some helpful console commands to verify the status of a Peer-to-Peer VTS:

- D SMS,LIBRARY(ALL),DETAIL (check distributed and composite library; check state messages)
- D M=DEV (verify channel path)

- LI DD (verify virtual drives)
- D R,L,KEY=OAM (list outstanding replies)

7.6 Failure scenarios

We will discuss the impact and recovery procedures for failures in each of the Peer-to-Peer VTS components.

7.6.1 Stacked volume media errors

The Peer-to-Peer VTS has improved capability to read a logical volume:

- If a permanent media read error occurs when a logical volume is recalled from a stacked volume
- If incorrect data is detected when being transferred to the host

Recovery is achieved either transparently within the Peer-to-Peer configuration or through use of DDR by the host.

7.6.1.1 Unreadable recall from stacked volume

Recovery for a logical volume which has a stacked volume media error is provided by the Model B18 VTS and the AX0 controller. The following actions are taken:

- If a recall fails due to a permanent media read error on a 3590 tape drive, the VTS will retry the recall on another tape drive. Failure on the second 3590 results in the stacked volume being placed in 'read-only' status. This action is the same as for a standalone B18 VTS.
- The AX0 controller detects when a VTS has not been able to recall a logical volume due to a 3590 media error and changes the I/O VTS for this logical volume to the other VTS. Recall of the dual copy into the tape volume cache of the second VTS makes the logical volume available.
- In the unlikely event of another media error on the second stacked volume, an equipment check error will occur on the first I/O operation after the mount completion and the job will fail.

7.6.1.2 Read-only status volume recovery enhancement

Once an hour, a VTS checks for stacked volumes which are in read-only status and recalls the logical volumes into the tape volume cache, thus removing the logical volumes from the damaged stacked volume. The Peer-to-Peer VTS enhances this process by copying logical volumes which cannot be read from the other VTS in a transparent manner, thus restoring two available copies.

If a dual copy of the unreadable logical volume has not yet been created in the second VTS at the time of the read-only status volume recovery, the intervention required message *Logical volume xxxxxx was not fully recovered from damaged stacked volume yyyyyy* is posted to the attached hosts. An IBM service representative can initiate action for logical volumes which must be recovered.

7.6.1.3 Tape Volume Cache and ESCON adapter errors

Data from the Tape Volume Cache is checked for errors as read commands are being processed through the ESCON adapters which provide host attachment.

The recovery process proceeds as follows:

- A read command failure causes MVS hosts to initiate the DDR process.
- When the logical volume is remounted and positioned, and the read command that failed is reissued, the Peer-to-Peer AX0 controller being used will access the copy of the logical volume in the other VTS.
- A successful completion of a rewind/unload command causes the Peer-to-Peer VTS configuration to make a new copy of the logical volume in the VTS which originally had the failure, thereby replacing the erroneous copy and ensuring that two copies remain accessible.
- Continuing failures to read the logical volume with use of the DDR process must be reported to the service representative.

7.6.2 Failure of Host to AX0 controller link

Figure 62 shows the failing component.

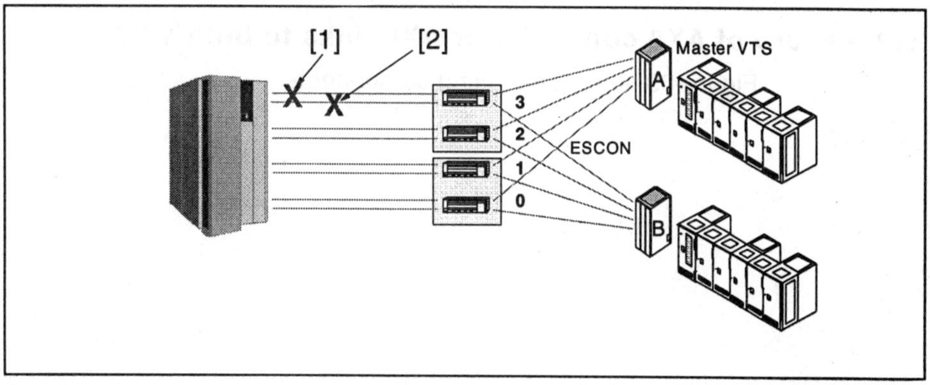

Figure 62. Host to Model AX0 controller link failure

What fails

One or more ESCON links between the host and the Model AX0 controller fail. It may be that the intermediate ESCON directors, ESCON channel extenders, or remote channel extenders fail.

What happens *([1] fails — one link to AX0 number 3)*

- All Peer-to-Peer VTS components continue to operate.
- Copied data remains available.
- All channel activity on the failing link is stopped.
- Channel errors are reported or error information becomes available from the intermediate equipment.
- Jobs which were using the 16 virtual drives on AX0 number 3 may fail.

What happens *([1] fails and [2] fails — both links to AX0 number 3)*

- All Peer-to-Peer VTS components continue to operate.
- Copied data remains available.
- The16 virtual addresses from AX0 number 3 are no longer available.
- Jobs which were using AX0 number 3 will fail.
- Logical volumes in use on AX0 number 3 are made available for subsequent use on other AX0s.

How to recover

- Normal error recovery procedures and repair will apply for the ESCON channel and the intermediate equipment.
- Rerun the failed workload.

7.6.3 Failure of AX0 controller or AX0 links to both VTSs

Figure 63 shows the failing components.

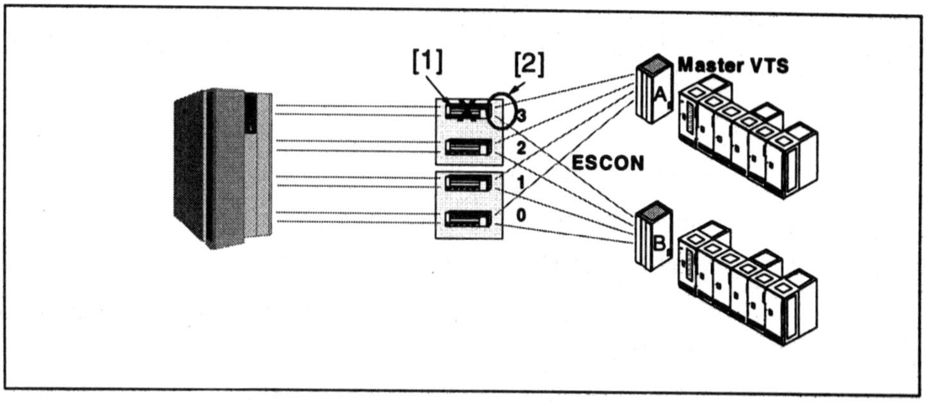

Figure 63. Model AX0 controller failure

What fails

One or more of the model AX0 controllers stops processing or both links from one AX0 to the VTSs fail. No communication is possible on the ESCON links to the host, nor on the ESCON links to the distributed VTSs.

What happens *([1] AX0 #3 fails; or [2] both VTS links fail from AX0 #3)*

- All remaining Peer-to-Peer VTS components continue to operate.
- The 16 virtual drive addresses provided by AX0 number 3 are unavailable.
- Copied data remains available.
- The virtual addresses for the failing AX0 may be boxed.
- Jobs using the virtual drives on the failing controller will fail.
- Call home support may be invoked by the AX0.
- Logical volumes in use by the failing Model AX0 controller are made available for subsequent use by the other controllers.
- Performance degradation is possible because the remaining controllers must handle the total workload.

How to recover

- Contact your service representative for the repair of the failing Model AX0 controller or links.
- Rerun the failed workload.

7.6.4 Failure of AX0 controller link to non-Master VTS

Figure 64 shows the failing components.

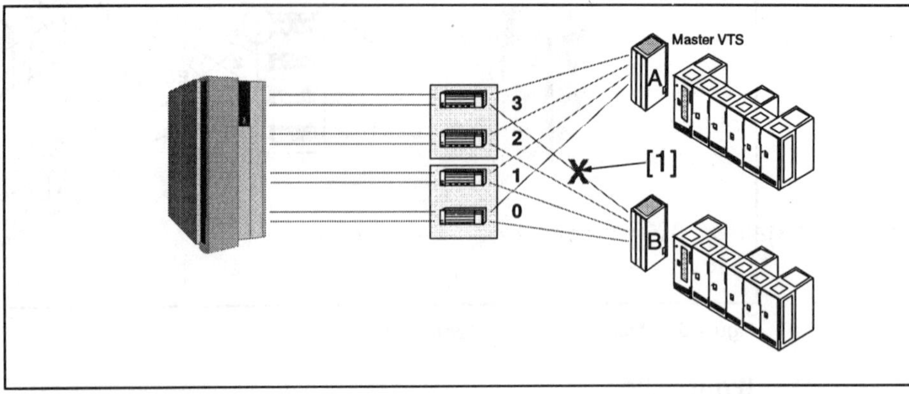

Figure 64. Model AX0 controller to VTS link failure

What fails

One ESCON link between an AX0 controller and VTS B fails. VTS A is the master.

What happens *(connection [1] with VTS B fails)*

- All Peer-to-Peer VTS components continue to operate.
- Copied data remains available.
- DDR is performed for the tape drive addresses for the AX0 with the failed link if they were reading logical volumes with VTS B as the I/O VTS. When DDR is performed and a tape drive address of another AX0 is used, the job continues. If a tape drive address for the AX0 with the failed link is used, the job continues if a copy of the logical volume is available in the connected Model B18 VTS A.
- Any jobs writing logical volumes with the tape drive addresses for the AX0 with the failed link with VTS-B as the I/O VTS will fail and must be rerun.
- In Immediate Copy Mode, any dual copy of a logical volume in process at the time of the failure will be processed by other AX0s in the configuration as if it were a deferred copy (as workload permits).
- Logical volumes which had failure of I/O operations in process due to the failed link are made available for subsequent use by other controllers. Any workload writing logical volumes fails.
- Performance degradation is possible because the remaining controllers must handle the total workload.

- Call home support is invoked.

How to recover

- Rerun the failed workload.
- Contact your service representative for repair of the failed connection.

Note: After the failed link is repaired, immediate copy mode operation is automatically resumed by the AX0 which had the failed link, if it was the copy mode before the failure.

7.6.5 Failure of AX0 controller link to Master VTS

Figure 65 shows the failing components.

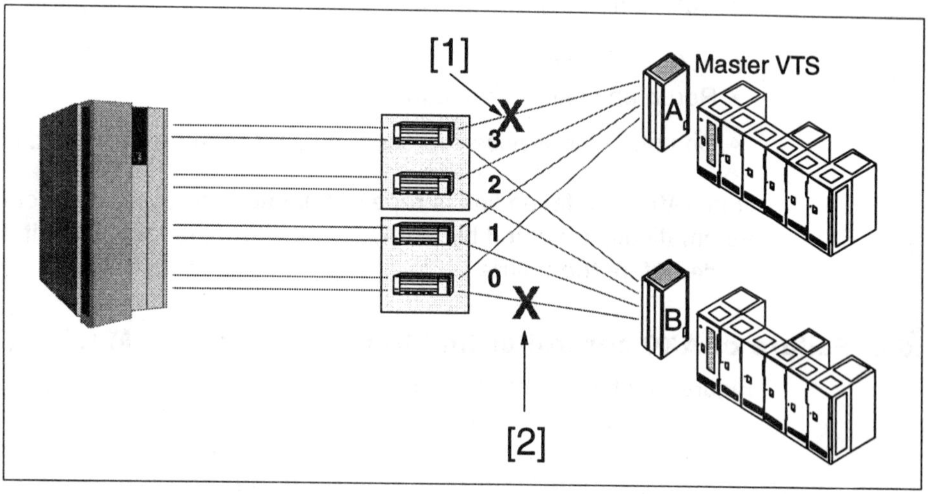

Figure 65. Model AX0 to master VTS link failure

What fails

One ESCON link between a Model AX0 controller and the Model B18 VTS-A fails. VTS-A is the Master VTS.

***What happens** (connection [1] with VTS-A fails)*

- All Peer-to-Peer VTS components continue to operate.
- Copied data remains available.
- Master VTS switchover occurs.
- DDR is performed for the tape drive addresses for the AX0 with the failed link if they were reading logical volumes with VTS-A as the I/O VTS. When DDR is performed and a tape drive address of another AX0 is used, the job continues. If a tape drive address for the AX0 with the failed link is

used, the job continues if a copy of the logical volume is available in the connected Model B18 VTS-B.

- Any jobs writing logical volumes with the tape drive addresses for the AX0 with the failed link with VTS-A as the I/O VTS will fail and must be rerun.
- In Immediate Copy Mode, any dual copy of a logical volume in process at the time of the failure will be processed by other AX0s in the configuration as if it were a deferred copy (as workload permits).
- Logical volumes which had failure of I/O operations in process due to the failed link are made available for subsequent use by other controllers.
- Performance degradation is possible because the remaining controllers must handle all workload.
- Call home support is invoked.

How to recover

- Rerun any failed workload.
- Contact your service representative for repair of the failed connection.

Note: After the failed link is repaired, immediate copy mode operation is automatically resumed by the AX0 which had the failed link, if it was the copy mode before the failure.

7.6.6 Failure of AX0 controller link to Master and non-Master VTSs

Figure 66 shows what has failed.

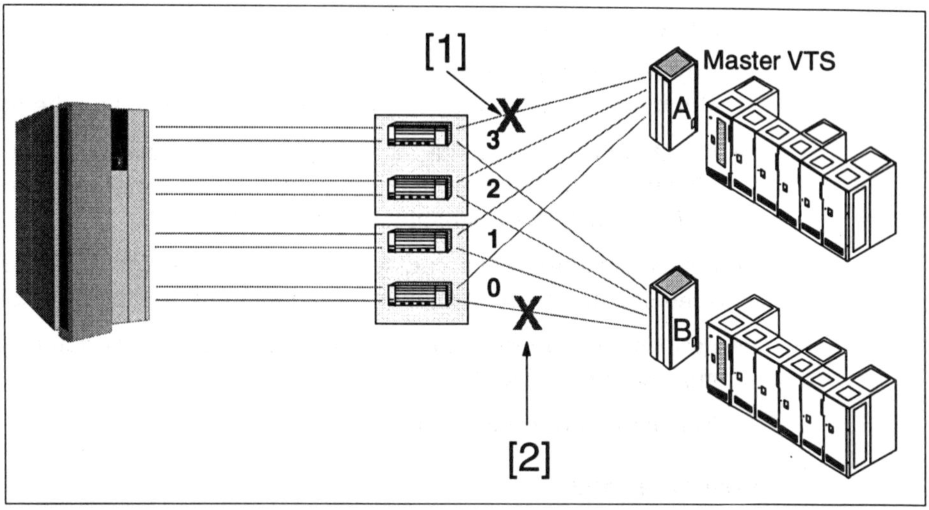

Figure 66. Model AX0 to master VTS link failure

What fails

One ESCON link between an AX0 controller and the Master VTS and one ESCON link between another AX0 controller and the non-Master VTS fail. VTS-A is the Master VTS.

What happens *(connections [1] and [2] with the VTSs fail)*

- All Peer-to-Peer components continue to operate.
- Copied data remains available.
- AX0 number 3 will become *Master Disabled* and its virtual tape drives addresses will be varied off.
- Master VTS switchover fails.
- DDR is performed for the tape drive addresses for AX0 number 3 if they were reading logical volumes with VTS-A as the I/O VTS. When DDR is performed, a tape drive address of another AX0 is used and the job continues.
- DDR is performed for the tape drive addresses for AX0 number 0 if they were reading logical volumes with VTS-B as the I/O VTS. When DDR is performed and a tape drive address for another AX0 is used, the job continues. If a tape drive address for AX0 number 0 is used, the job continues if a copy of the logical volume is available in the connected Model B18 VTS-A.

- Any jobs writing logical volumes with the tape drive addresses for AX0 number 3 with VTS-A as the I/O VTS will fail and must be rerun.
- Any jobs writing logical volumes with the tape drive addresses for AX0 number 0 with VTS-B as the I/O VTS will fail and must be rerun.
- In Immediate Copy Mode, any dual copy of a logical volume in process at the time of the failure will be processed by other AX0s in the configuration as if it were a deferred copy (as workload permits).
- Logical volumes which had failure of I/O operations in process due to the failed link are made available for subsequent use by other controllers.
- Performance degradation is possible because the remaining controllers must handle all workload.
- Call home support is invoked.

How to recover

- Rerun all failed workload
- Contact your service representative for repair of the failing connections.
- After the failed link for AX0 number 3 link is repaired, vary on its virtual tape drives addresses.

Note: After the failed links are repaired, immediate copy mode operation is automatically resumed by the AX0s which had a failed link, if it was the copy mode before the failure.

7.6.7 Failure of all links to a VTS

Figure 67 shows what fails.

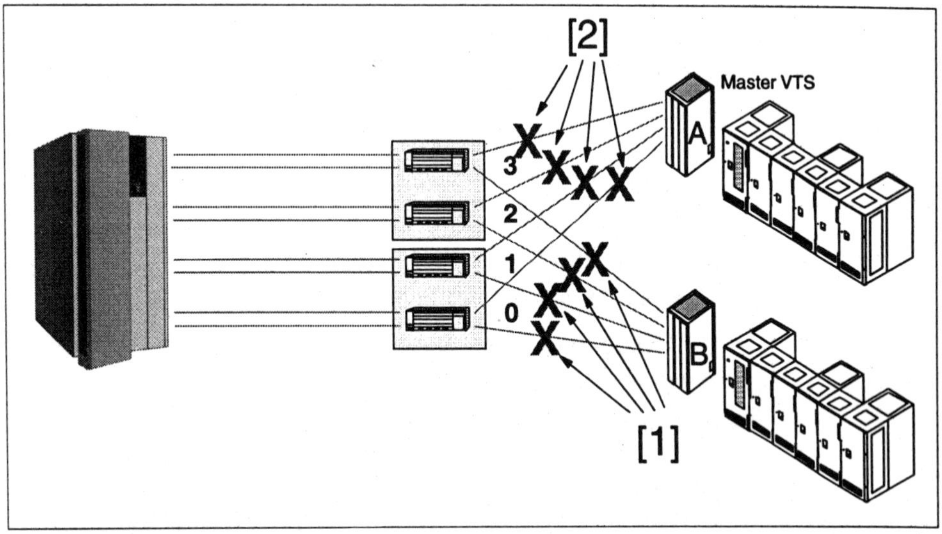

Figure 67. Failure of all links to a VTS

What fails

All ESCON links between Model AX0 controllers and a Model B18 VTS fail. VTS-A is the Master VTS.

What happens (connections [1] with VTS-B fail)

- All Peer-to-Peer components continue to operate.
- Copied data remains available.
- Logical volumes in VTS-B which have not been copied will not be available.
- If in Immediate Copy Mode, the dual copy of logical volumes will be deferred.
- DDR is performed for tape drive addresses which were reading logical volumes with VTS-B as the I/O VTS. When DDR is performed, the job will continue if a copy of the logical volume is available in the connected Model B18 VTS-A.
- Any jobs writing logical volumes with VTS-B as the I/O VTS will fail and must be rerun.
- Logical volumes which had failure of I/O operations in process due to the failed links are made available for subsequent use by other controllers.
- Performance degradation is possible because only one VTS must handle the total workload.

- Insert or eject of logical volumes is not possible.
- Preferencing is bypassed for Model AX0 controllers which were preferencing VTS-B.
- Call home support is invoked.

What happens *(connections [2] with VTS-A fail)*

- All Peer-to-Peer components continue to operate.
- Copied data remains available.
- Master VTS switchover occurs.
- Logical volumes in VTS-A which have not been copied will not be available.
- If in Immediate Copy Mode, the dual copy of logical volumes will not be made before completion of a Rewind/Unload command.
- DDR is performed for tape drive addresses which were reading logical volumes with VTS-A as the I/O VTS. When DDR is performed, the job will continue if a copy of the logical volume is available in the connected Model B18 VTS-B.
- Any jobs writing logical volumes with VTS-A as the I/O VTS will fail and must be rerun.
- Logical volumes which had failure of I/O operations in process due to the failed links are made available for subsequent use by other controllers.
- Performance degradation is possible because only one VTS must handle the total workload.
- Insert of new logical volumes is not possible.
- Preferencing is bypassed for Model AX0 controllers which were preferencing VTS-A.
- Call home support is invoked.

How to recover

- Rerun any failed workload.
- Contact your service representative for repair of the failed links.

Note: After the failed links are repaired, immediate copy mode operation is automatically resumed by all AX0s, if it was the copy mode before the failure. This starts the copy operations for the deferred copies and will impact the bandwidth for data between the host and the Peer-to-Peer VTS if there is a large backlog of copies to be made.

7.6.8 Model B18 VTS failure

Figure 68 shows the failing components.

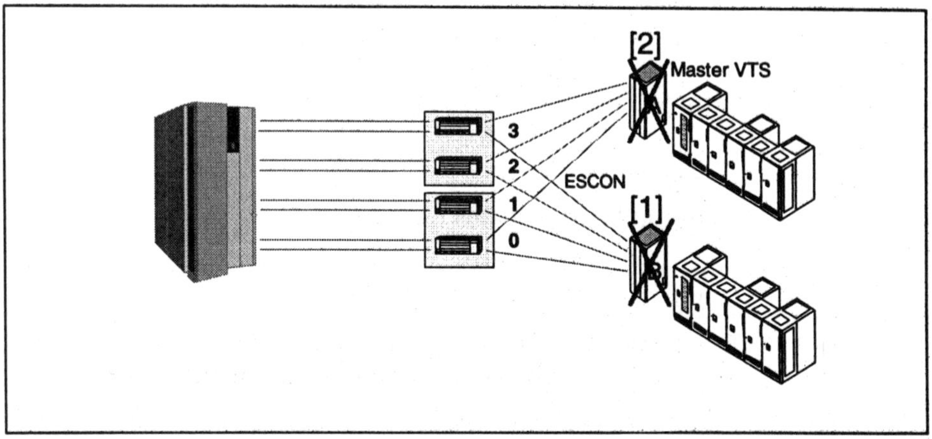

Figure 68. Model B18 VTS failure

What fails

One Model B18 VTS fails. VTS-A is the Master VTS.

***What happens** (VTS-B [1] fails)*

- All remaining Peer-to-Peer VTS components continue to operate.
- Copied data remains available.
- Logical volumes in the failed VTS which have not been copied will not be available.
- DDR is performed for tape drive addresses which were reading logical volumes with the failed VTS as the I/O VTS. When DDR is performed, the job will continue if a copy of the logical volume is available in the connected Model B18 VTS which has not failed.
- Any jobs writing logical volumes with the failed VTS as the I/O VTS will fail and must be rerun.
- Logical volumes which had failure of I/O operations in process due to the failed VTS are made available for subsequent use by other controllers.
- Performance degradation is possible because only one VTS must handle the total workload.
- Insert or eject of logical volumes is not possible.
- Preferencing is bypassed for Model AX0 controllers which were preferencing the failed VTS.

- Call home support is invoked.

What happens *(Master VTS [2] fails)*
- The same as for failing VTS [1].
- VTS-B [1] becomes the Master VTS.

How to recover
- Contact your service representative for the activation of the failing Model B18 VTS.
- Rerun the failed workload.

Note: After the failed VTS is repaired, immediate copy mode operation is automatically resumed by all AX0s if it was the copy mode before the failure. This starts the copy operations for the deferred copies and will impact the bandwidth for data between the host and the Peer-to-Peer VTS if there is a large backlog of copies to be made.

7.6.9 3494 tape library failure

Figure 69 shows the failing components.

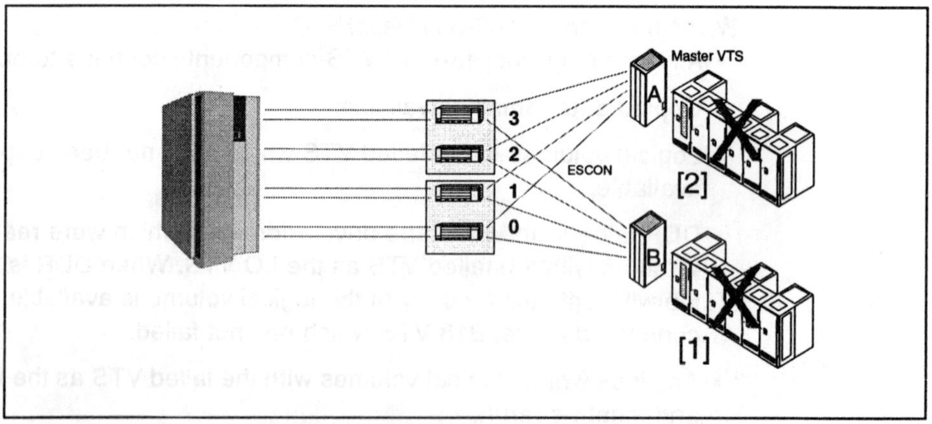

Figure 69. 3494 tape library failure

What fails

A 3494 tape library housing one of the Model B18 VTSs of the Peer-to-Peer VTS fails. The Master VTS, VTS-A, is associated with library [2].

What happens *(3494 tape library [1] with VTS-B fails)*
- All remaining Peer-to-Peer VTS components continue to operate.
- Copied data remains available.

- The mount of a logical volume requiring recall from a stacked volume in the failed tape library will fail.
- If in Immediate Copy Mode, the dual copy of logical volumes will be deferred.
- VTS I/O operations in process will continue. Upon completion of operations in process, use of the VTS associated with the failed tape library will be discontinued by all AX0 controllers.
- Performance degradation is possible because only one VTS must handle the total workload.
- Insert or eject of logical volumes is not possible.
- Preferencing is bypassed for Model AX0 controllers which were preferencing the VTS associated with the failed tape library.
- Call home support is invoked.

What happens *(3494 tape library [2] with Master VTS fails)*

- The same as for failing 3494 library[1] with VTS.
- VTS-B [1] becomes the Master VTS.

How to recover

- Contact your service representative for the activation of the failing 3494 tape library.
- Rerun the failed workload.

Note: After the failed tape library is repaired, immediate copy mode is automatically resumed by all AX0s if it was the copy mode before the failure. This starts the copy operations for the deferred copies and will impact the bandwidth for data between the host and the Peer-to-Peer VTS if there is a large backlog of copies to be made.

7.6.10 Site failure

Figure 69 shows the failing components.

If you have notice of an impending disaster such as a flood or tornado, you may wish to perform a master VTS switchover if the master VTS site is the site that could be affected. IBM support specialists can dial in to the Peer-to-Peer VTS to do this.

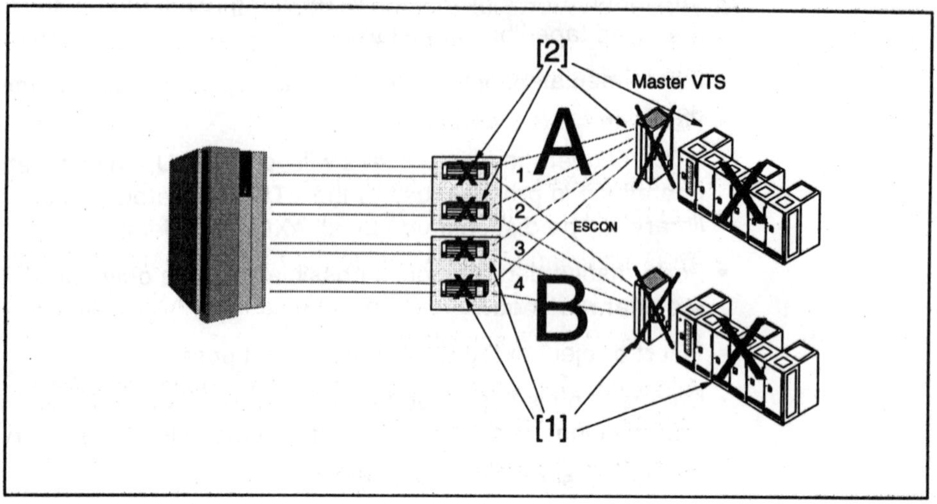

Figure 70. Site failure

What fails

All the Peer-to-Peer VTS components in one site fails. Site-A has the Master VTS. This scenario is applicable for site disasters.

What happens *(Site-B components [1] fail)*

- All remaining Peer-to-Peer VTS components continue to operate.
- Copied data remains available.
- 32 virtual tape drive addresses are not available.
- Logical volumes in VTS-B which have not been copied will not be available.
- Dual copies will be made when the failed components are repaired.
- Virtual tape drives for the failing AX0s may be boxed.
- Jobs using the virtual tape drives for the AX0s at the failed site will fail.
- Logical volumes which had failure of I/O operations in process due to the failed AX0 controllers are made available for subsequent use by other controllers.
- Performance degradation is possible because the remaining site must handle the total workload.
- Insert or eject of logical volumes is not possible.
- Call home support is invoked.

How to recover *(Site-B components [1] fails)*

- If a permanent disaster has happened, the disaster recovery procedure should be followed.
- Rerun the failed workload.

What happens *(Site-A components [2] fail)*

- Master VTS switchover fails.
- The remaining Model AX0s do not have a Master VTS connection.
- I/O operations in process on the remaining AX0 controllers with VTS-B as the I/O VTS will complete.
- All virtual tape drive addresses for the remaining AX0s will be varied off and can no longer be used.
- All further processing is stopped.
- Virtual tape drive addresses may be boxed.
- Call home support is invoked.

How to recover *(Site-A components [2] fail)*

- If a permanent disaster has happened, the disaster recovery procedure should be followed.
- Contact your service representative for repair of the failed components at Site A.
- Consider operation of the remaining Site B components in the special AX0 operational modes available. These modes can only be activated by the IBM product support specialists. See 2.6.7, "Special AX0 operational modes" on page 40.

7.6.11 Other failures

These are failures in other parts of the subsystem.

7.6.11.1 Library manager failure

When a library manager experiences a critical failure, communication with the Model B18 VTS is lost. It is also possible that the link between the Model B18 VTS and the library manager has failed.In this situation, the library manager is not able to inform the Peer-to-Peer VTS of the failure.

If the library manager is part of an HA1 configuration, the failure of the library manager causes a switchover to the standby library manager to be executed. Once the switchover completes, the new library manager informs the Peer-to-Peer VTS that is online. It may take some minutes before the

Peer-to-Peer VTS is informed of a switchover, and further minutes before the switchover is complete.

7.6.11.2 Out of empty stacked volumes

When a Model B18 VTS runs out of scratch physical volumes, many of the operations of the distributed library cannot continue. Copying the virtual volumes to the stacked volumes is no longer possible. To prevent overflow of the cache, all logical mounts are suspended to this VTS. An intervention required message is generated, indicating that the distributed library is out of empty stacked volumes.

If this occurs, the Peer-to-Peer VTS takes the following actions.

- I/O processing to active virtual addresses continues.
- If the library out of stacked volumes is the Master VTS, a Master VTS switchover is initiated.
- The dual copy operations **to** the library that is out of stacked volumes are not performed.
- The dual copy operations **from** the library that is out of stacked volumes are not performed for logical volumes that are not in the Tape Volume Cache.
- If the Peer-to-Peer VTS is in immediate copy mode, the dual copy of logical volumes will be deferred.
- When the only valid version of a logical volume is in the tape volume cache of the VTS which is out of empty stacked volumes, the logical volume is copied into the other VTS to allow a mount to be done. The mount will fail if the logical volume is not in cache as a recall is not possible.
- New mounts are accepted and processed on the other library (after a master switchover). The mount will fail if there is not yet a copy of the data in this library.

7.6.11.3 Loss of drives in Model B18 VTS

When the number of physical drives of a distributed VTS gets down to only one usable drive, the VTS will enter the *Insufficient Resources for Mount* state. Copying the virtual volumes to the stacked volumes is no longer possible. To prevent an overflow of the cache, all logical mounts are suspended to that VTS. An intervention required message is generated, indicating that the distributed library has insufficient resources.

The actions taken by the Peer-to-Peer VTS are the same as described in 7.6.11.2, “Out of empty stacked volumes” on page 190.

Chapter 8. Monitoring and reporting

Information about the Peer-to-Peer VTS can be obtained from several sources:

- By displaying library statistics directly at the library manager of the distributed library. The information obtained is solely related to the distributed library and its associated distributed VTS.
- By displaying library information at the host using the `DISPLAY SMS` command. The information obtained is related to the logical image of the Peer-to-Peer VTS, but not about the underlying hardware.
- By displaying information using the StorWatch Specialist. The information obtained is for both the logical image and for the underlying hardware components.
- By analyzing the SMF type 94 records written on the host once an hour. The SMF records contain information about both the composite library and the distributed libraries.

In this chapter, we describe how the statistics for the Peer-to-Peer VTS are created by the distributed libraries and the Model AX0 controllers and written on the hosts. We explain the enhanced reporting provided by information in the SMF type 94 records, and we highlight performance related considerations which are unique for the Peer-to-Peer VTS.

8.1 Creating Peer-to-Peer VTS statistics

As known from the stand-alone VTS and from IBM 3494 tape libraries with native tape drives installed, statistics for the Peer-to-Peer VTS are sent to the attached hosts once an hour. Because the Peer-to-Peer VTS has a logical image (composite library) as well as underlying physical components (distributed libraries), statistics are created for the composite library and for the distributed libraries. This results in three SMF94 records being created on the host once an hour. For details about the enhancements of the SMF 94 records for Peer-to-Peer VTS, please refer to D.1.14, “VTS enhanced library statistics” on page 255.

The way in which the data is created and presented to the attached hosts is different from the way in which statistics are sent to the host for non-Peer-to-Peer libraries. The actions that are taken to create the three SMF type 94 records for the Peer-to-Peer VTS on a host can be summarized in six steps:

© Copyright IBM Corp. 2000

Step 1: The library manager requests statistics; B18 returns statistics.

On the hour, both library managers of the distributed libraries prepare a statistical record for the past hour. In preparation of the record, the library managers request data from the associated distributed VTS to be included in the record.

Step 2: The library manager signals that the statistics are available.

Once each library manager has created the data for its distributed library, it sends a message indicating that statistics are available to its distributed VTS. The VTS passes this request along to all Model AX0 controllers.

Step 3: AX0 controllers exchange statistics.

In response to this message, each of the Model AX0 controllers prepares a data record containing the consolidated statistics of all Model AX0 controllers and thus for the composite library.

Step 4: The host receives notification and requests statistics.

Once all Model AX0 controllers have created their records of the statistics, each of them signals this to all attached hosts. In response, DFSMS/MVS requests statistical data for both distributed libraries and for the composite library.

Step 5: AX0 requests statistics from B18s and routes them to the host.

For host requests for statistics for the distributed libraries, the Model AX0 controller requests statistics of the distributed libraries through the VTSs and routes the data to the requesting host. On the host, the Device Services component of DFSMS/MVS initiates creation of the SMF type 94 records.

Step 6: AX0 controller sends consolidated statistics to the host.

In response to the request for statistical data for the composite library, the Model AX0 controller returns the consolidated statistics for the composite library to the requesting host. On the host, the Device Services component of DFSMS/MVS initiates the creation of the SMF type 94 record.

The steps listed above are summarized in Figure 71.

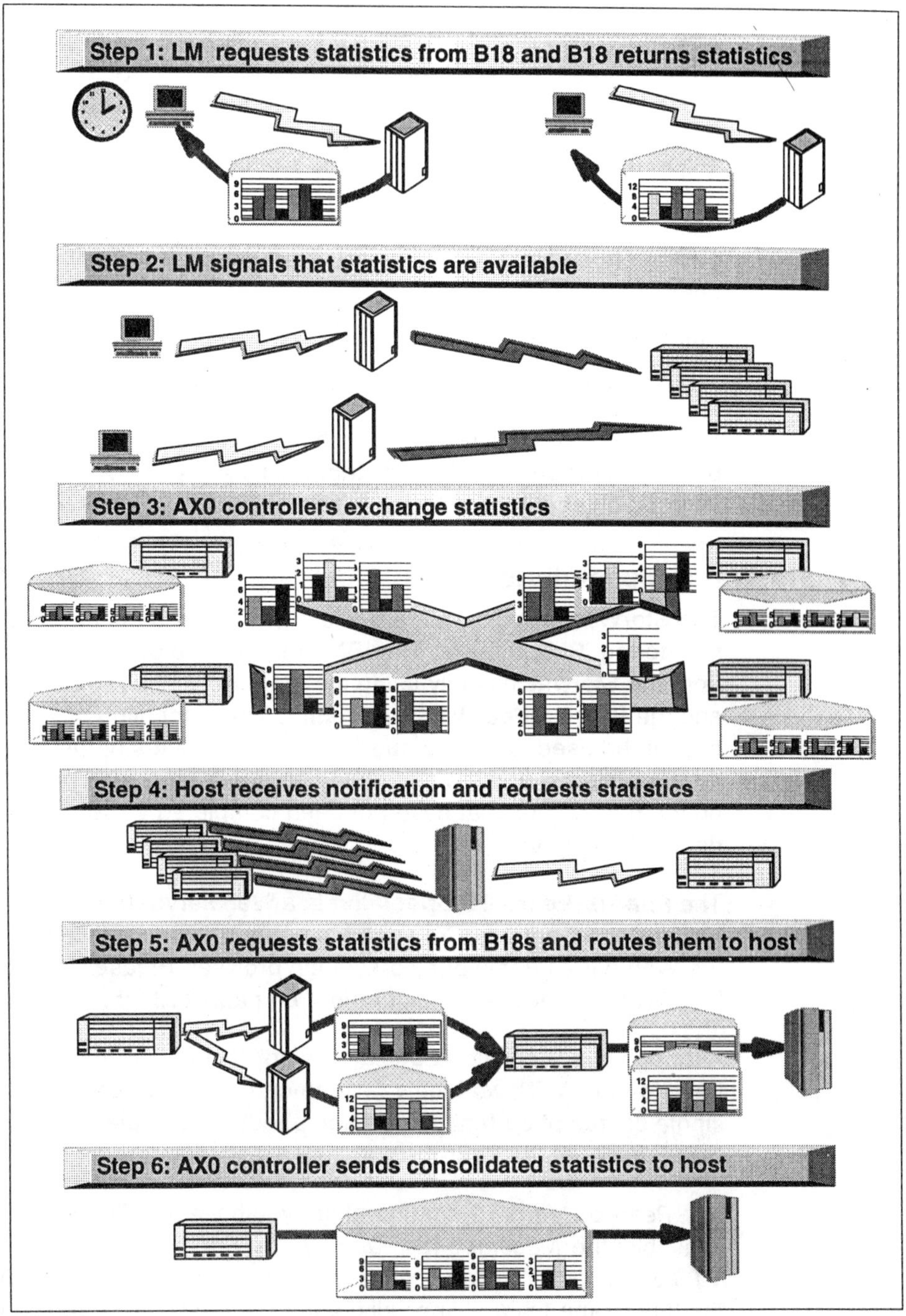

Figure 71. Creating Peer-to-Peer statistics on the host

8.2 Monitoring and reporting tools

The StorWatch Peer-to-Peer VTS Specialist, the StorWatch 3494 Tape Library Specialist, the library manager console, MVS console commands, and VTSSTATS as well as other MVS based tools can all be used to obtain information about the Peer-to-Peer VTS. The StorWatch Specialists are shipped as microcode for the VTCs and for the 3494 library manager.

Other tools are available for monitoring and reporting and may be used by customers and by IBM personnel. To check on the tools available, please see:

Internet ftp Site:	`ftp://ftp.software.ibm.com/storage/tapetool/`
IBM Intranet:	`http://w3.rmss.tucson.ibm.com/softw/tapetool.htm`

VTSLOGRP, a multiplatform reporting tool for the stand-alone VTS, can also be used for reporting of the distributed libraries. It does not provide information about the composite library.

8.2.1 StorWatch Specialists

The StorWatch Specialists are a family of tools used for reporting and monitoring IBM products. The IBM storage tape products can now benefit from the Storwatch family using the **Magstar 3494 Tape Library Specialist** and the **Peer-to-Peer VTS Specialist**. These tools do not provide reports, but can be used for online queries about the status of the Peer-to-Peer VTS, its components, and the distributed libraries. They also provide information on the dual copies that have not been completed yet and on the amount of data to be copied.

The **Peer-to-Peer VTS Specialist** is a Web server that is installed in the AX0 Virtual Tape Controller. You need to perform some installation steps to access the Web pages from your workstation browser. Please refer to 5.3.3, "StorWatch Specialist configuration" on page 113 for more information.

Although this Storwatch Specialist is not required for monitoring of the Peer-to-Peer VTS, we highly recommend that you install it, because it is a single source of current information about the complete hardware and logical components of the Peer-to-Peer VTS.

In a Peer-to-Peer VTS configuration, you have two Storwatch Specialists available: the *Magstar 3494 Tape Library Specialist* and the *Peer-to-Peer VTS Specialist.* You can access the Peer-to-Peer Specialist Web pages from the 3494 Tape Library Specialist and vice versa, as there is a link between the two products which enables you to switch between them seamlessly and hence easily find the required information.

The **Magstar 3494 Tape Library Specialist** is the Web interface to the Library Manager and the VTS of each Distributed Library.

Library Manager information includes:

- System summary
- Operational status and operator interventions
- Component availability
- Performance statistics
- Command queue
- LAN hosts status and LAN information
- Dual accessor zones (if High Availability Unit is installed)
- VOLSER ranges and cleaner masks

VTS information includes:

- Active data and active data distribution
- Data flow
- Logical mounts per hour and mount hit data
- Physical device mount history
- Category attributes
- Management policies
- Real time statistics

The real time statistics include workload and throttling statistics, the same information that has been added in the SMF 94 record.

Figure 72 shows the home page of the Magstar 3494 Tape Library Specialist.

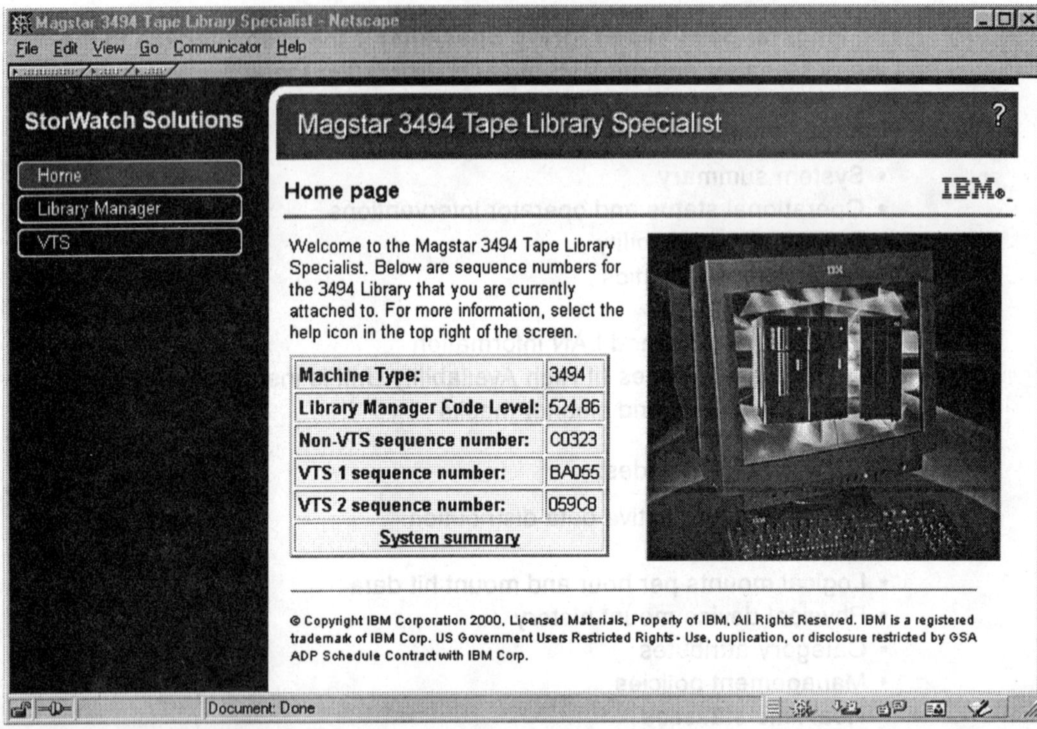

Figure 72. Magstar 3494 Tape Library Specialist: home page

The **Peer-to-Peer VTS Specialist** gives you more *Peer-to-Peer related* specific information on Virtual Tape Controllers, Composite and Distributed Library configurations, Copy workload and other useful statistics.

Figure 73 shows the home page of the Peer-to-Peer Specialist.

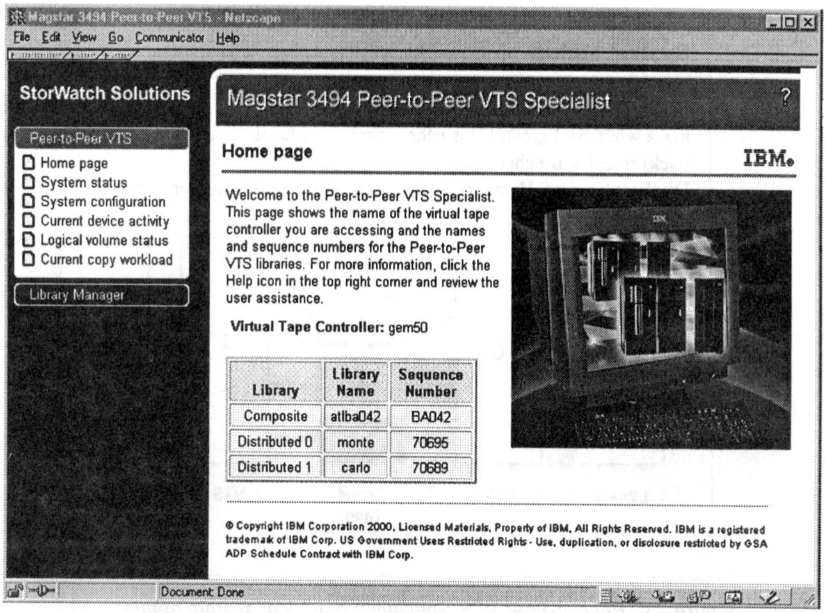

Figure 73. Peer-to-Peer VTS Specialist: home page

The page is divided into two main windows: the black window at left, where you can select the pull-down menus with the various information sources; and the right window, where the information is displayed.

From the home page, you can see the library name and sequence number of the Composite and Distributed libraries. Using the tabs in the left window, you can display the other information, detailed in the following sections.

8.2.1.1 System status

From this page, you can see the status of Virtual Tape Controllers, Distributed VTSs, Distributed Libraries and system links. For each of these components, you have a *status* column, when this column is red, either the component is *offline* or the status is *not optimal* (for distributed libraries).

There is also available a graphical view of the system status, and a detailed system status page, which gives you more detail on the status of each Peer-to-Peer VTS component.

If you need a better explanation of the fields shown on each page, click on the question mark in the upper right corner of the page. Here you can find complete help text that explains the meaning of all the information displayed.

Figure 74 is an example of the graphical system status page. Virtual Tape Controller number 3 is shown in dark shading (red) because it is offline.

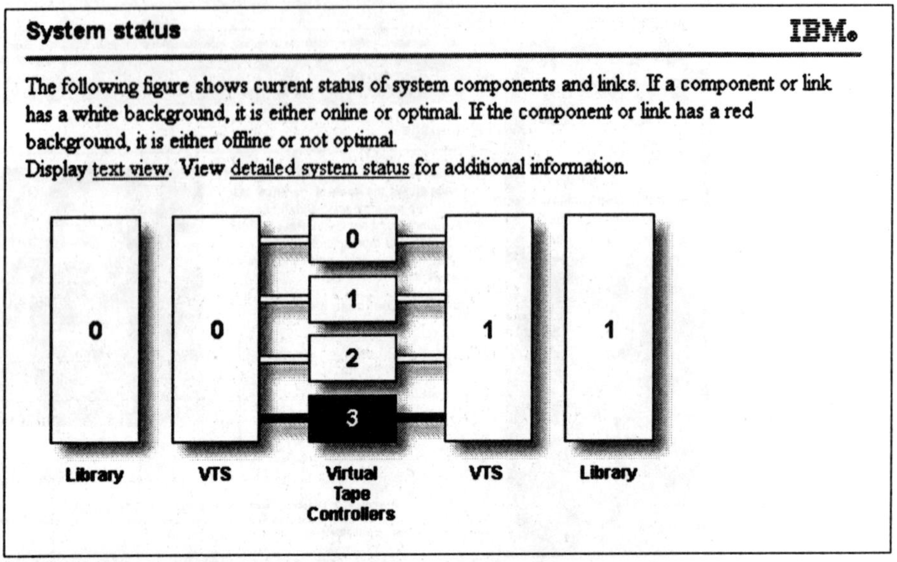

Figure 74. Peer-to-Peer VTS Specialist: graphical system status

8.2.1.2 System configuration

This page contains the following information on the configuration of every component of the Peer-to-Peer VTS complex:

- VTC name, serial number and network IP address
- Composite and distributed VTS library name, serial number, and sequence number
- Library Manager information
- Copy mode, deferred copy priority threshold, and U/I library name

An example of the information included in this page is shown in Figure 75.

System configuration

The following tables summarize the current Peer-to-Peer VTS configuration.

Copy Mode: Immediate

Deferred Copy Priority Threshold: 8 hours

Virtual Tape Controllers:

Controller	Name	Serial Number	Network IP Address
0	gem50	1060177	9.115.45.24
1	gem51	1060184	9.115.45.50
2	gem52	1060180	9.115.45.49
3	*****	******	******

VTSs:

VTS	Library Name	Serial Number
0	monte	0070927
1	carlo	0070929

Libraries:

Library	Library Name	Sequence Number	UI Library *
Composite	atlba042	BA042	-----
Distributed 0	monte	70695	Yes
Distributed 1	carlo	70689	No
* **Note:** Only one of the distributed libraries can be the UI library.			

Library	Library Name	Library Manager	Network IP Address
Distributed 0	monte	A	Not Configured
		B	Not Configured
Distributed 1	carlo	A	Not Configured
		B	Not Configured

Figure 75. Peer-to-Peer VTS Specialist: system configuration

8.2.1.3 Current device activity

For each of the four Virtual Tape Controllers (VTCs), this option shows the virtual device activity, with detailed information on:

- Mounted logical volume serial
- Written and read bytes
- Time to mount and time on drive for the mounted volume
- I/O VTS used for this logical volume

This information can be used to monitor Peer-to-Peer VTS activity, as well as evaluate performance constraints: the ratio between bytes written and read can indicate the balance between input and output, and the time to mount can give you indication of a potential performance degradation.

Figure 76 shows an example of the current device activity for VTC0.

Controller	Virtual Drive	Logical Volume	Bytes Written	Bytes Read	Time On Drive	Time To Mount	VTS In Use
0	0	XP4004	0.0 KB	319.5 MB	0:03:38	0:00:32	0
	1	XP4013	0.0 KB	283.1 MB	0:03:28	0:00:46	0
	2	XP4001	0.0 KB	364.6 MB	0:03:37	0:00:29	1
	3	XP6758	3.4 MB	0.3 KB	0:03:28	0:00:44	0
	4	XP6750	105.3 MB	2.0 MB	0:03:28	0:00:45	1
	5	XP6756	0.3 KB	0.3 KB	0:03:46	0:00:27	0
	6	XP6748	114.1 MB	0.1 KB	0:04:02	0:00:12	0
	7	XP6744	105.9 MB	0.1 KB	0:04:03	0:00:11	0
	8	XP4011	0.0 KB	427.0 MB	0:03:56	0:00:18	1
	9	XP4002	0.0 KB	38.6 MB	0:00:25	0:00:06	1
	A	XP6754	4.9 MB	0.3 KB	0:03:46	0:00:27	1
	B	XP4009	0.0 KB	281.0 MB	0:03:27	0:00:26	0
	C	XP6752	65.6 MB	292.2 KB	0:03:49	0:00:24	1
	D	XP4005	0.0 KB	40.4 MB	0:00:24	0:00:06	1
	E	XP4003	0.0 KB	276.2 MB	0:03:26	0:00:27	0
	F	XP6746	105.7 MB	2.0 MB	0:04:02	0:00:12	0

Figure 76. Peer-to-Peer VTS Specialist: current device activity

8.2.1.4 Logical volume status

Whenever you need to know specific details about a logical volume, such as its copy status, the size, or the stacked volumes where it resides, this page allows you to enter the logical volume serial number and to obtain the desired information, as detailed in Figure 77.

Logical Volume: XP5000

	VTS 0	VTS 1
Library Name	MONTE	CARLO
Stacked (Physical) Volume	RSG707	JH1262
Data Level	Current	Current
Category	000F	000F
Category Level	Current	Current
Volume in Cache	Yes	Yes
Compressed File Size	381.0 MB	381.0 MB
Last Modified Time	Mon 05/22/2000 17:13:37	Mon 05/22/2000 17:37:47
Last Access Time	Fri 06/02/2000 10:07:12	Fri 06/02/2000 10:08:11

Figure 77. Peer-to-Peer VTS Specialist: logical volume status

Note that both the *data level* and the *category level* can be ***current*** or ***downlevel***. This means that the second copy of a logical volume has already been completed for ***current***, and has not yet completed for ***downlevel.***

When the ***in transition*** keyword is present in the *Stacked Volume, Compressed File Size, Last Modified Time* and *Last Access Time* fields, this means that the specified volume is mounted on a virtual drive.

8.2.1.5 Current copy workload

This page shows the number of logical volumes that are in the process of being copied from each I/O VTS to the other Distributed VTS.

It also provides an indication if copy operations have been disabled, meaning that the Peer-to-Peer VTS is unable to make dual copies of logical volumes.

Figure 78 shows an example of this page:

Copy Work Not Yet Started:

VTS	Library Name	Number of Volumes
0	Monte	4
1	Carlo	2

Figure 78. Peer-to-Peer VTS Specialist: current copy workload.

8.2.2 StorWatch Enterprise Tape Library Expert

The StorWatch Enterprise Tape Library (ETL) Expert is a chargeable software product, program number 5648-SWV.

It complements the information that you can see from the StorWatch Specialists, and is integrated with other members of the StorWatch Expert family such as the StorWatch Enterprise Storage Server Expert.

The StorWatch ETL Expert is accessed from a suitably configured Web browser. The browser must be a graphical (that is, not text-only) browser and must be able to support Java and Javascript. It provides you with information about stand-alone VTSs and Peer-to-Peer VTSs. The StorWatch ETL Expert server runs on either AIX 4.3.3 or Windows NT 4 (with service pack 6) and maintains historical data in a database so that you can identify trends. Data is captured from the StorWatch Specialists.

For the Peer-to-Peer VTS composite library, you can view the same data that is written in the SMF type 94 records without needing to post-process the SMF data.

For a stand-alone VTS and for Peer-to-Peer distributed libraries, you can see information about the VTSs in a report form, and you can also use a Health Monitor that gives you an automatically updated view with a warning if there are unexpected conditions that need your attention. In some cases, you can also view graphs.

To start the ETL Expert, you enter the URL of the StorWatch Expert server in your Web browser. You will then see the sign-on page shown in Figure 79.

Note

Please note that the examples shown here are based on early code and are intended only to give you general information about the planned functions of the StorWatch ETL Expert. The version shipped may differ from the examples shown.

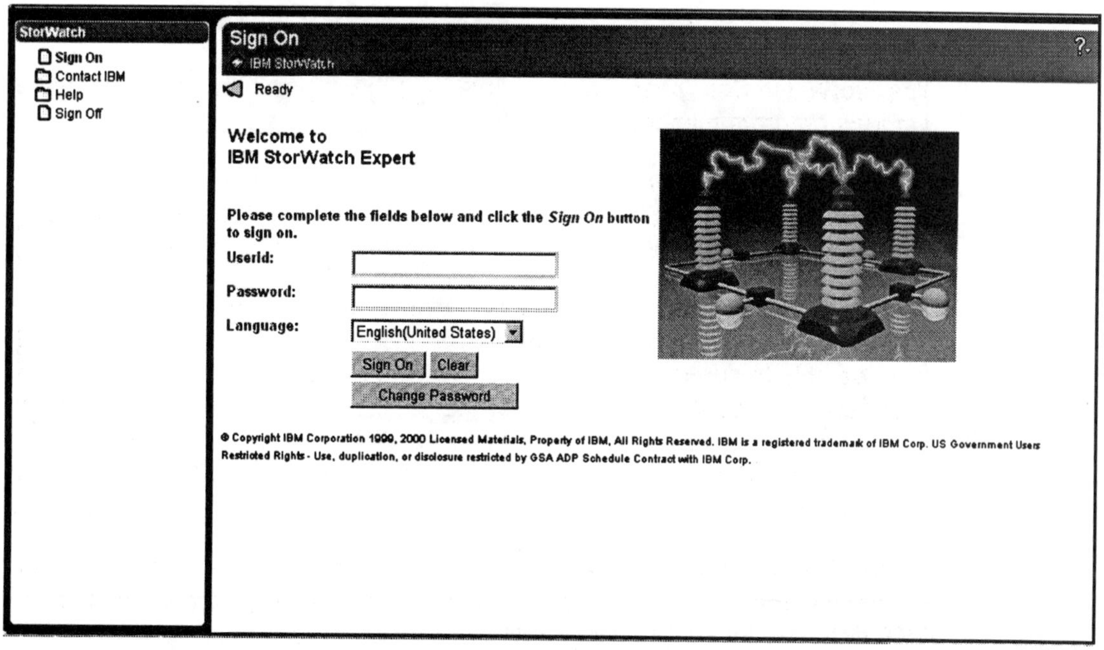

Figure 79. StorWatch ETL Expert sign-on

You need a valid userid and password to be able to access the StorWatch ETL Expert, and these must be entered on this page. When you have done so, you will see the page shown in Figure 80.

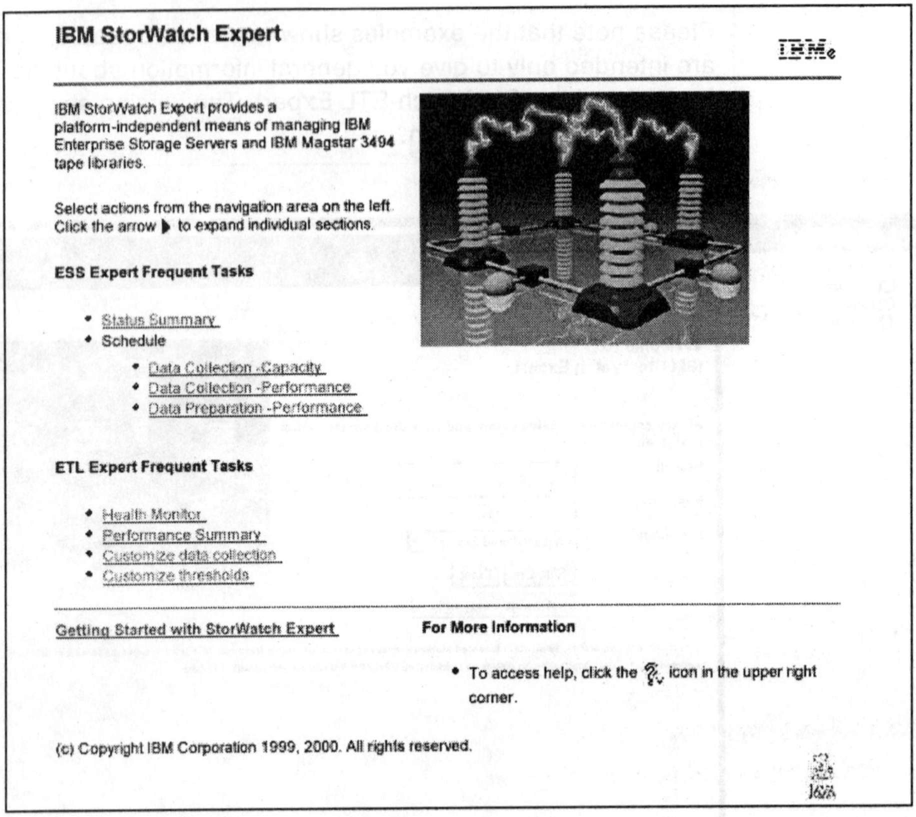

Figure 80. StorWatch ETL Expert home page

There is a navigation box on the left-hand side, as shown in Figure 81.

Figure 81. StorWatch Expert navigation bar

This will take you directly to different parts of the ETL Expert. The key choices to note are:

- Introduction
- Manage StorWatch
- Manage ETL
- Help

The small triangles within this box are used to expand or collapse the list of choice that you have. Click on a triangle that points to the right to expand the list of items underneath it.

8.2.2.1 ETL Expert introduction

This is the page that was shown in Figure 80 on page 206. You can return to this page simply by pressing the *Introduction* button in the navigation bar.

Fast paths to the tasks that you are likely to use most often are shown in the main page, rather than in the navigation box. From here, you can:

- Start the VTS Health Monitor
- View a performance summary
- Control collection of data from stand-alone and Peer-to-Peer VTSs

The VTS Health Monitor gives you a single small page which uses colors to alert you to problems (Figure 82).

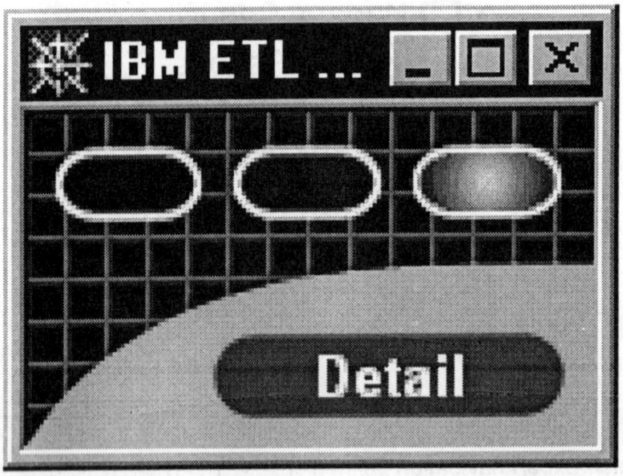

Figure 82. VTS Health Monitor

You can click on details to launch a more detailed page which will show you, by library:

- Free storage in GB
- Active data in GB
- The number of scratch and private stacked volumes
- Throughput for reads and writes
- Whether throttling is occurring
- Maximum virtual mount times
- Logical volume information
- Whether reclamation is occurring
- The number of physical and virtual drives mounted
- Component availability

8.2.2.2 Managing StorWatch

This page lets you manage the StorWatch Expert itself. You can choose one of these options:

- Management scope

  This allows you to define ranges of IP addresses that may access the StorWatch Expert.

- Administration

  Here, you can view, create, modify or delete users of the StorWatch Expert. A user may be assigned different levels of authority which you may set up.

- View Status

  This page lets you see the status of StorWatch Expert tasks that are running or scheduled. You may also see which users are signed on to the Expert.

- Customize ETL Expert

  From here, you can customize StorWatch Expert data collection and alert thresholds.

  To customize data collection, you can choose which subsystems you wish to include. You can also assign a name to the subsystems to ease identification.

  To customize thresholds, you may choose the VTS statistics for which you want to enable monitoring, and enter a warning value and a critical warning value that you want to be used for alerting you. An extract of the page is shown in Figure 83.

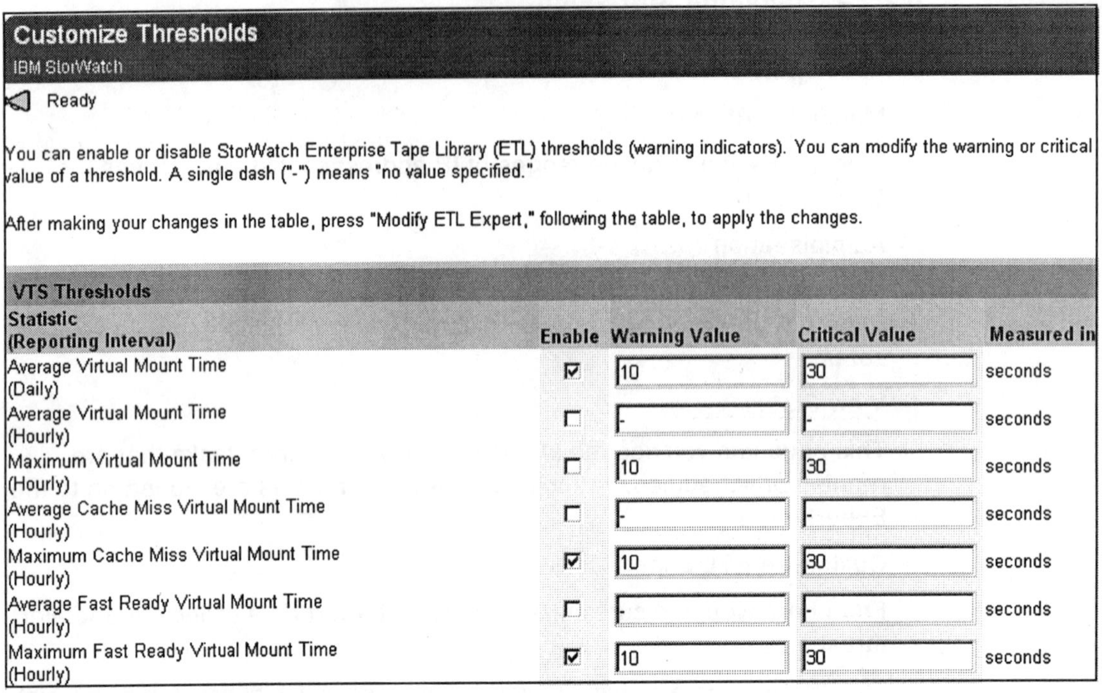

Figure 83. StorWatch Expert thresholds

8.2.2.3 Manage ETL

From here, you can:

- Manage assets

  You can see which libraries are known to the StorWatch Expert and get reports describing the library configuration (for example, the type of library and the number of drives installed).

- Manage capacity

  You can see, by library, statistics describing the actual number of logical volumes and capacities, the number of stacked volumes and the amount of free storage.

- Manage performance

  You can see, by library, statistics describing:

  - Mount times (maximum and average for overall mounts and also for cache misses and fast ready mounts)
  - The percentage of cache misses
  - The maximum cache residency time for a virtual volume

- The amount of data transferred to and from the VTS

Color coding is used to highlight values requiring further investigation.

In each case, you can refine the reports that are presented to you by choosing different subsystems, types of report, or levels of detail, as shown in Figure 84.

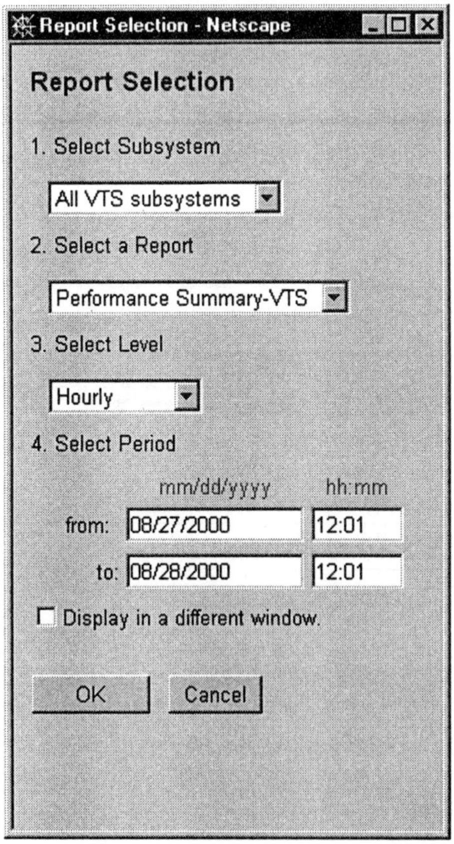

Figure 84. StorWatch Expert report selection

You can also display graphs. For example, Figure 85 is a graph showing the active data trends for one library.

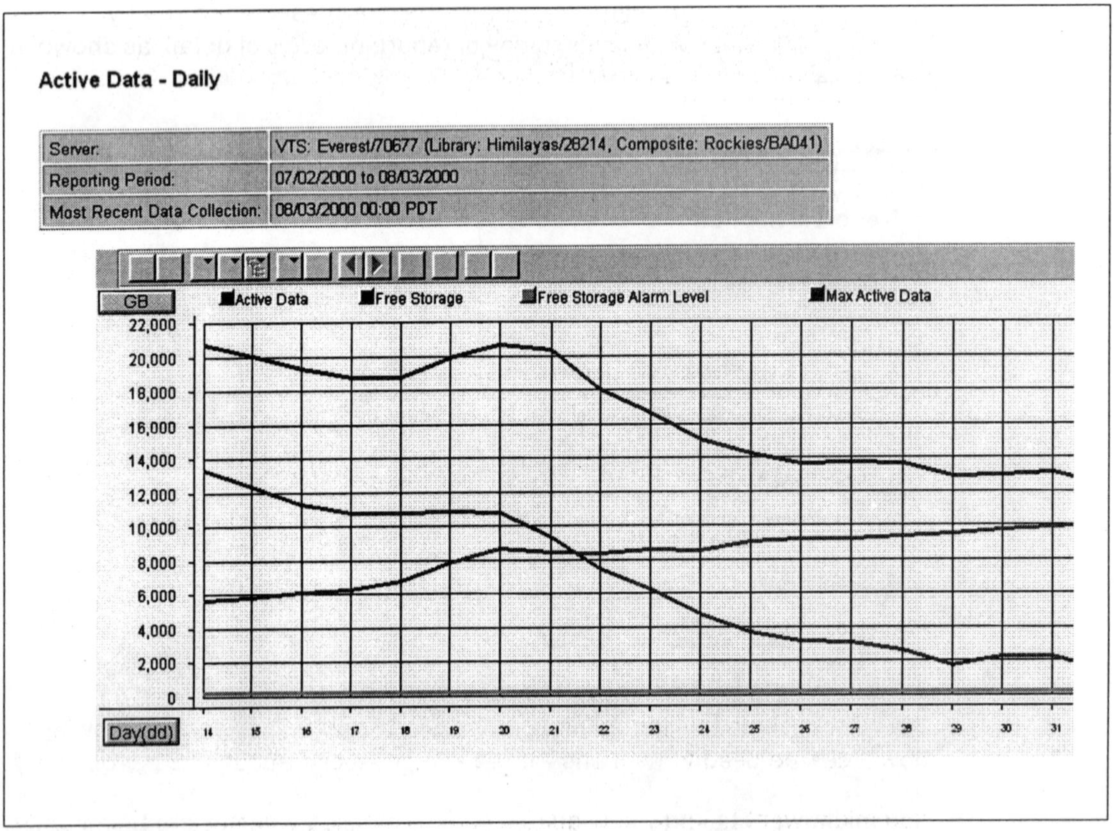

Figure 85. Active data trend graph

8.2.2.4 Help

The primary documentation for the StorWatch Expert is provided here as shown in Figure 86. There is no separate hard-copy documentation.

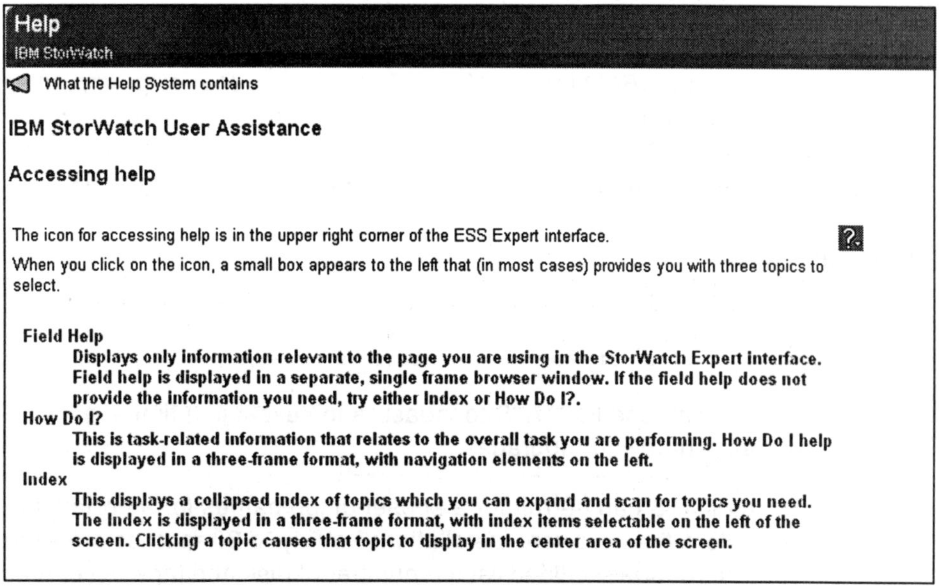

Figure 86. StorWatch Expert help page

8.2.2.5 Examples of using the ETL Expert

We will conclude this introduction to the StorWatch ETL Expert by showing how it can be used to help answer real-life questions about VTS usage.

You might want to know how quickly scratch stacked volumes are being used up. Using the Expert, you can look at the active data report for a given library and see the trend over time for the number of scratch stacked volumes. The report includes an icon to draw a graph of the active data so that you can easily see what has been happening.

8.2.3 Library manager console

The library manager provides information about the distributed library and its VTS. If the StorWatch Tape Library Specialist is installed, the library manager must still be used to perform operations.

For details about using the library manager console, please refer to the redbook *IBM Magstar Virtual Tape Server: Planning, Implementing, and Monitoring, SG24-2229*, and to the *Magstar 3494 Tape Library Operator Guide, GA32-0280*. Task related information can also be found in Chapter 7, "Operating and using the Peer-to-Peer VTS" on page 153.

8.2.4 IOSTATS

IOSTATS is part of the IBMTOOLS.EXE file which is available from:

```
ftp://ftp.software.ibm.com/storage/tapetool/
```

You can use IOSTATS to measure job execution times, especially before and after hardware upgrades.

IOSTATS can be run for a subset of job names for a certain period of time before the hardware installation. SMF type 30 records are required as input. The reports provided list the number of disk and tape I/O operations that were done for each job step, as well as the elapsed job execution time.

With the Peer-to-Peer VTS, IOSTATS can be used for different purposes:

- To evaluate the effect of the Peer-to-Peer VTS, compare job execution times before implementation of the Peer-to-Peer VTS to those after having migrated, especially if you are operating in immediate copy mode of operation.
- To evaluate the effect of hardware upgrades, compare job execution times before upgrading components of the Peer-to-Peer VTS, for example, if you are increasing the size of the tape volume cache or the number of Magstar tape drives.
- To evaluate the effect of changing the copy mode of operation on elapsed job execution time.

8.2.5 VTSSTATS

VTSSTATS is a program already used for reporting of stand-alone VTSs which has been enhanced to provide reports for the Peer-to-Peer VTS. The program can be downloaded from the Internet from:

```
ftp://ftp.software.ibm.com/storage/tapetool/
```

8.3 Enhanced VTS reporting

With the general availability of the Peer-to-Peer VTS, VTS Enhanced Library Statistics are included in the SMF type 94 records. They provide additional information in the SMF type 94 records for both the stand-alone VTS and the Peer-to-Peer VTS.

If the Statistics Format byte contains a value of X"01", Enhanced Statistics, the fields are defined.

For the complete record mapping of the SMF type 94 record, please refer to Appendix D, "SMF type 94 record layout" on page 239.

Appendix A. ESCON configurations

This appendix describes the Enterprise System CONnection (ESCON) channel architecture. It provides information on distance issues and channel configuration alternatives using fiber optics technology which can be used for a Peer-to-Peer VTS configuration.

More information on using ESCON and FICON is available in the following publications:

- *Introduction to IBM S/390 FICON*, SG24-5176-00
- *Enterprise Systems Connection (ESCON) Implementation Guide*, SG24-4662
- *Continuous Availability S/390 Technology Guide*, SG24-2086
- *S/390 I/O Connectivity Handbook*, SG24-5444
- *Enterprise Systems CONnection (ESCON) Introduction*, GA23-0383
- *ESCON Director Introduction*, GA23-0363

A.1 ESCON technology

ESCON is an IBM architecture and fiber optic technology. It is an integral part of the Enterprise System Architecture/390 (ESA/390). It allows a data center installation to replace electrical-copper cables with fiber-optic cables. Beyond this physical aspect, ESCON provides new capabilities to connect I/O equipment to a host processor at distances beyond 100 km. With these increased distances you can establish new disaster recovery methods by remote copying your DASD and tape data.

Although ESCON provides capabilities to connect over long distances, the following factors affect the distance that can be achieved:

- Physical size of fiber
- Fiber transmission mode
- Connection mode

© Copyright IBM Corp. 2000

A.1.1 Physical size of a fiber

An optical fiber functions as a kind of waveguide for light. It is usually made of silica glass. The fiber itself has a central core and a surrounding cladding of slightly different glass material. The physical size of an optical fiber is determined by the diameter of the core and cladding, expressed in microns (μ). A fiber optic cable having a core diameter of 62.5 μ and a cladding of 125 μ is designated as 62.5/125 μ optical fiber. Other fibers commonly used for ESCON are 50/125 μ and 9/125 μ.

The jumper cable has the same function as the pair of cables that make up a parallel channel. An ESCON jumper cable consists of two unidirectional fibers, one that carries data in one direction (transmit), and the other that carries data in the opposite direction (receive). The unidirectional is due to the way the fibers are connected to transmitters and receivers, not to any property of the fiber itself.

Jumper cables are typically used to connect:

- A channel to a control unit
- A channel to an ESCON director
- An ESCON director to an ESCON director
- An ESCON director to a control unit
- A channel to a Model AX0 controller
- A Model AX0 controller to a Model B18 VTS

A.1.2 Fiber transmission mode

Two modes can be used to send light signals through an optical fiber: single mode (mono mode) or multimode. The optical fibers used are called accordingly single-mode or multimode fibers. These fibers have different physical dimensions and light transmission characteristics.

The intensity of the light decreases when the light passes through the fiber. The longer the fiber, the lower the light intensity. The light intensity attenuation results in length limitations of the physical link because the receiver needs a minimum level of light intensity to correctly detect the signals.

The multimode fibers supported by IBM are either 62.5/125 μ or 50/125 μ. The light source used for multimode fiber is usually a light emitting diode (LED). LED jumpers are orange, and their duplex connectors are generally black.

The maximum distance for a multimode fiber link is 3 km if 62.5/125 µ fibers are used and 2 km if 50/125 µ fibers are used. The maximum distance for a multimode fiber link is 2 km if both 62.5/125 µ and 50/125 µ fibers are used.

Single-mode fiber usually has a core diameter of 8 to 10 µ and a cladding diameter of 125 µ. The light source used for single-mode fiber is a laser. IBM supports single-mode 9/125 µ fibers for use in an ESCON environment. The single-mode fiber must be used on links between machines with ESCON Extended Distance Feature (XDF) adapters installed. These adapters are available only on ESCON directors. They are no longer available on Host channels. XDF jumpers are yellow, and their duplex connectors are grey. The maximum distance for a single-mode fiber link is 20 km.

A.2 ESCON connection modes

You can connect an I/O control unit to a host channel through:

- A point-to-point connection
- A point-to-point connection with channel sharing
- An ESCON director as a static connection
- An ESCON director as a dynamic connection
- A FICON bridge connection

A.2.1 A point-to-point connection

A point-to-point connection is a fiber connection between a host channel and an I/O control unit (Figure 87). This is called a physical link. Through this physical link a host can communicate with only the devices attached to that I/O control unit. Figure 87 shows a point-to-point connection.

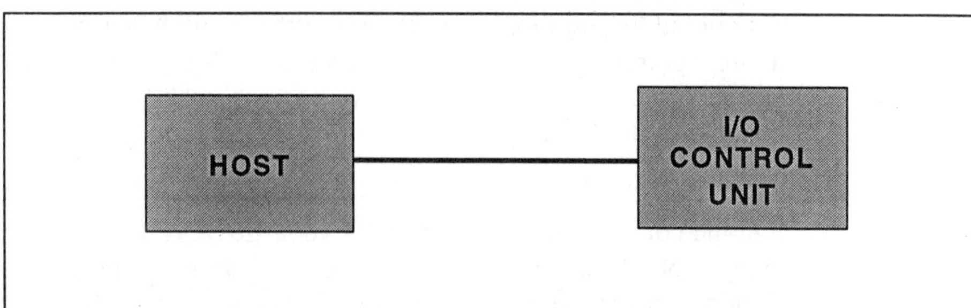

Figure 87. Point-to-point connection

A.2.2 Point-to-point connection with channel sharing

Channel sharing among Processor Resource/Systems Manager (PR/SM) logical partitions running on any IBM S/390 servers can be achieved by using the Enhanced Multiple Image Facility (EMIF or MIF).

With EMIF, the processor channel subsystem provides physical path sharing by extending the logical addressing capability of the ESCON architecture to logical partitions in host images. Each partition has its own logical channel subsystem and its own view of each shared channel and each control unit connected to the shared channel subsystem (Figure 88). Nevertheless, it is still possible to define non-shared channels.

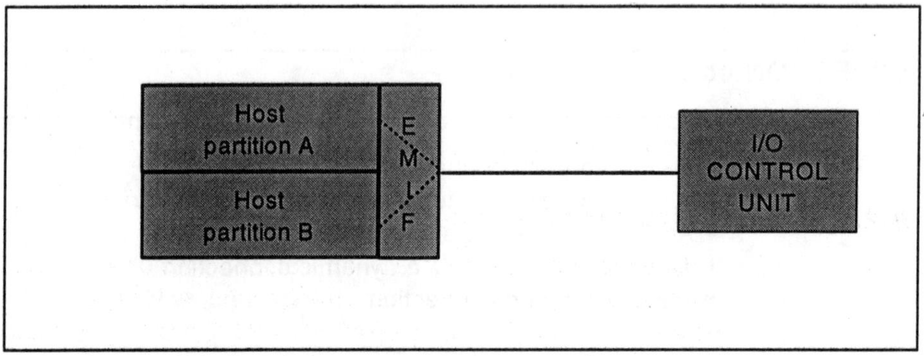

Figure 88. Point-to-point connection with channel sharing

A.2.3 ESCON director as a static connection

A static connection through an ESCON director involves having one fiber connected from a host channel to an ESCON director and a second fiber from an ESCON director to an I/O control unit. In Figure 89, the host channel is connected through ESCON director port D7 and ESCON Director port C3 to an I/O control unit. You must set up an ESCON director for a static connection (dedicated connection) of these two ports, by using the ESCON director console or the ESCON manager, a managing program running on a OS/390 server.

A static connection through an IBM 9032 ESCON director is more flexible than a point-to-point connection. You can achieve a different connection by statically switching to another port, without reconnecting the fiber.

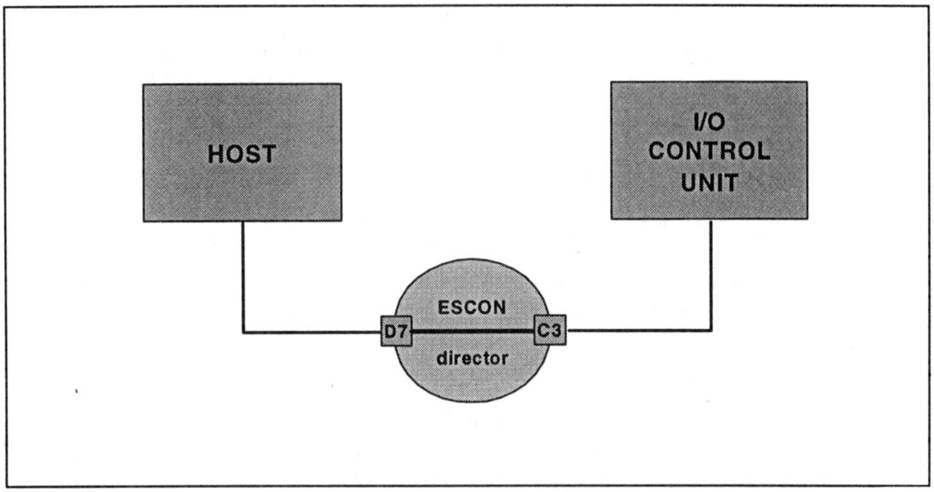

Figure 89. Static connection through an ESCON director

A.2.4 ESCON director as a dynamic connection

A dynamic connection through an ESCON director as seen in Figure 90, involves having the same fiber arrangement as for a static connection. However, instead of setting up an ESCON director for a static connection, you have to code the connections to ESCON director destination ports C3 and E5 in the link statement of the control unit macro in the IOCDS or equivalent HCD panel. In this mode, a host can communicate with multiple devices behind different I/O control units by using the same physical link between the host channel and the ESCON director. The ESCON director dynamically connects to the destination port, as required.

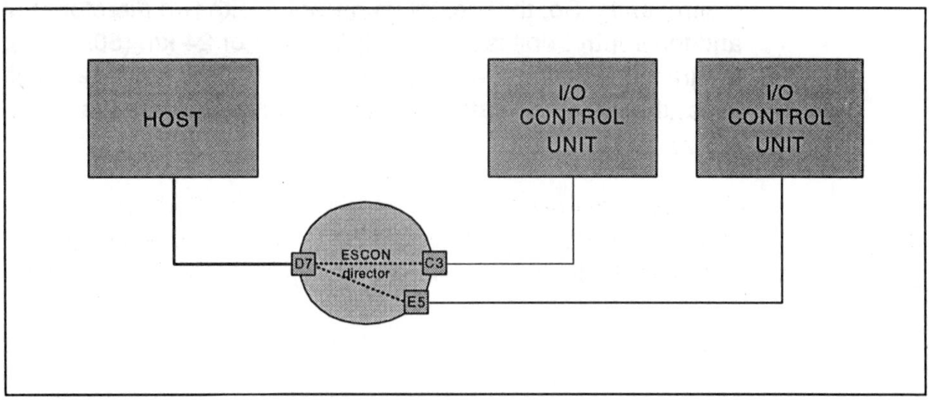

Figure 90. Dynamic connection through an ESCON director

A.3 ESCON distance alternatives

Because the light intensity is lower on increased distances, some kind of amplifier or repeater is needed to achieve distances longer than:

- 2 km for a 50/125 μ multimode fiber
- 3 km for a 62.5/125 μ multimode fiber
- 20 km for a 9/125 μ single-mode fiber

There are several options available for extending this distance:

- Using an ESCON director
- Using an ESCON channel extender
- Using a remote channel extender

A.3.1 Using an ESCON director

The main purpose of an ESCON director is to provide switching functions within an ESCON network. In addition to its switching function it acts as an amplifier or repeater, because the light signals are received on one port and transmitted by another, thus allowing distances of 2 km, 3 km or 20 km to be reached.

A connection between the host and the I/O control unit can contain two ESCON directors (Figure 91). The maximum distance between these directors is 3 km for 62.5/125 μ multimode fiber, 2 km for a 50/125 μ multimode fiber and 20 km for a 9/125 μ single mode fiber using XDF ports on the ESCON director.

Remember that there are no XDF ports available on the host and the I/O control units. So, the maximum distance with two directors between the host and the control unit is 26 km (62.5/125 μ) or 24 km (50/125 μ). Depending on the transmission mode, configuration, adapters, and the quality of the fibers used, the distance that can be reached may be less than that maximum.

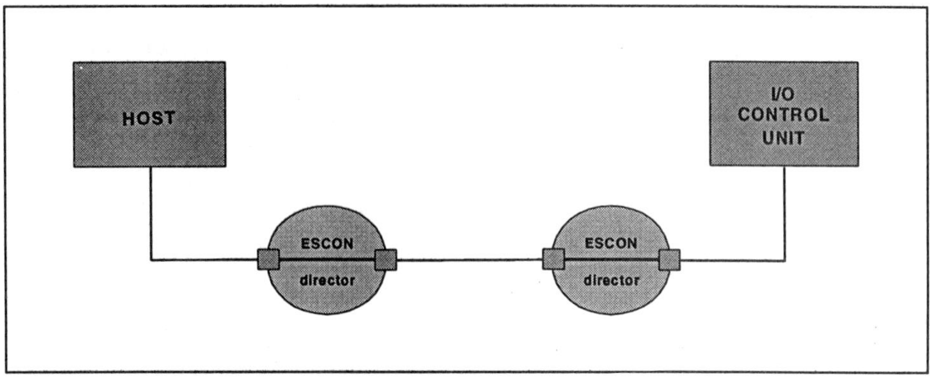

Figure 91. Connection through two ESCON directors

On the S/390 Generation 5 and Generation 6 servers, FIber CONnection (FICON) channels are available. FICON increases the link rate from 20 MB all the way up to 100 MB/sec. The effective data transfer rates are expected to be between 60 MB/sec and 80 MB/sec. The FICON implementation enables full duplex data transfer, so data travels in both directions simultaneously, rather than as with the ESCON half-duplex data transfer.

The S/390 server with FICON channels allows the accessing of control units with an ESCON interface via an ESCON director FICON bridge adapter card. Using a 9 μ single mode fiber FICON supports an unrepeated channel distance of 10 km. This can be increased to 20 KM via RPQ.

Figure 92 shows that with FICON, fewer connection are needed. A single FICON channel is able to handle more than one ESCON control unit without performance impact on the throughput of the I/O between the host and the control unit.

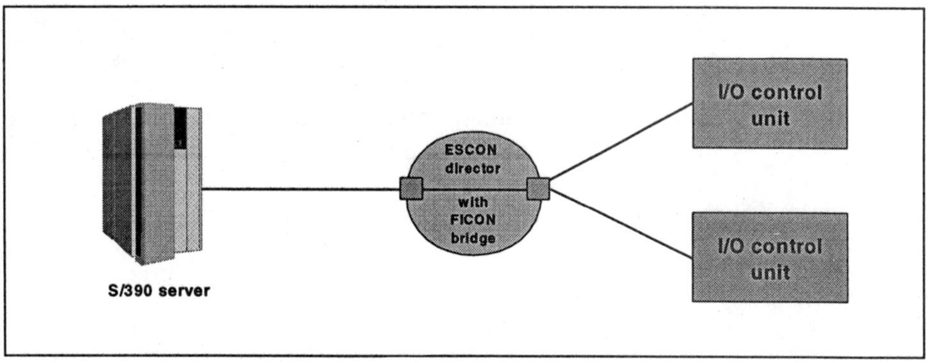

Figure 92. Connection using ESCON director with FICON bridge

A.3.2 Using an ESCON channel extender

An ESCON channel extender is a signal repeater and fiber type converter that can be used to support ESCON-XDF configurations (Figure 93). You can buy these extenders from various vendors active in this market segment.

The channel speed achieved is determined by the length of the channel. Measurement shows that a decrease of about 2% per km is experienced for data transfers of 32 KB blocks. For tape, the maximum distance between the host and the control unit should not exceed a distance of 43 km.

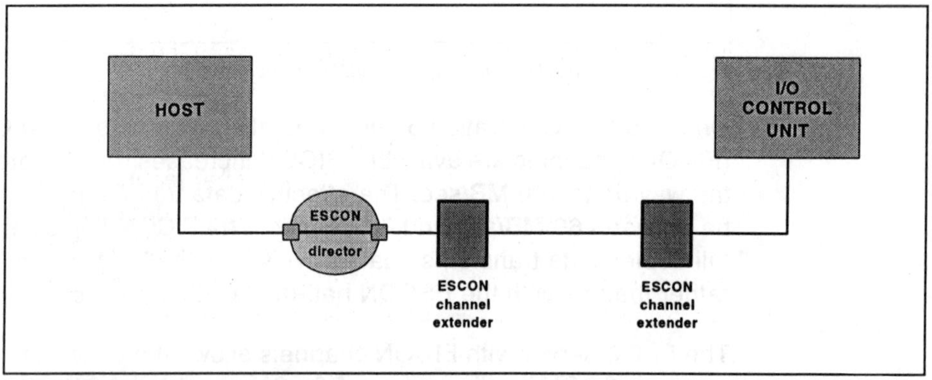

Figure 93. Connection through ESCON channel extenders

Note

The discussion of channel extenders in this book is general in nature, and you should not assume that all channel extenders will work in a Peer-to-Peer VTS environment. New commands and protocols are used, and their correct use must be verified.

You should be aware that some extenders may be certified for use between a host and AX0s but not between the AX0s and distributed VTSs.

Your channel extender vendor will be able to tell you whether particular models of extender have been tested and certified to work with a Peer-to-Peer VTS.

A.3.3 Using a remote channel extender

We use the term *remote channel extender* to group together equipment that provides switching and concentrator functions over telecommunication lines. The equipment sends the data from one or more ESCON links over one or more high speed data communication lines.

The data rates achieved are generally lower than with ESCON links. The technology used for the communication links is the limiting factor. It is, however, able to reach longer distances compared to ESCON channel extenders. The remote extenders are also a solution when ESCON links in a non-campus environment are not available or cannot be cost justified.

Although IBM does not provide remote channel extenders, we work together with various vendors implementing remote solutions at customer sites.

The justification for using remote channel extenders, the presence of the vendors, the costs and the availability of fiber technology in a non-campus environment, and the availability of high speed data communication lines varies from country to country. You may consult IBM Certified specialists for designing the best solution in your environment meeting your availability requirements within your budget limits (Figure 94).

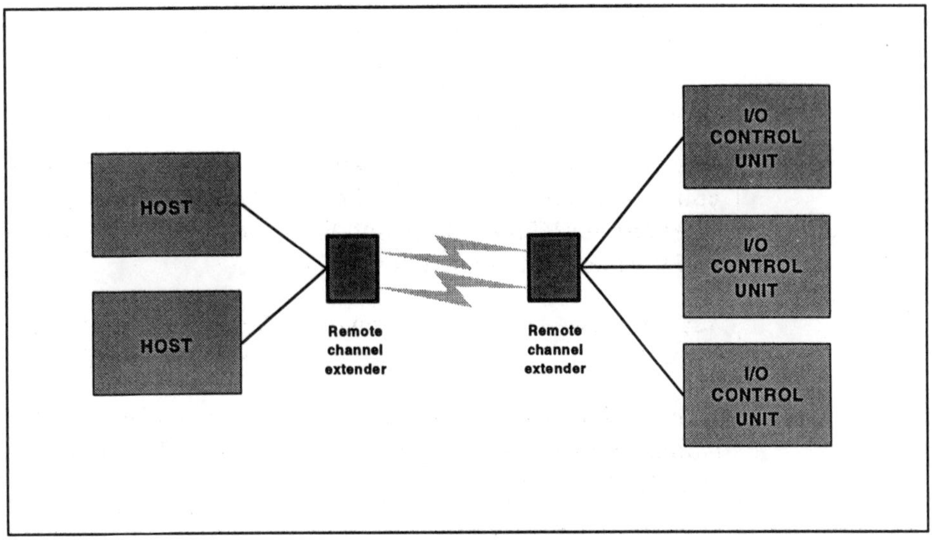

Figure 94. Connection through a remote channel extender

Appendix B. Geographically Dispersed Parallel Sysplex

With the continued decrease in Information Technology (IT) costs as well as greater emphasis on application availability and disaster recovery, more and more enterprises are adopting a two-site strategy. IBM's S/390 multi-site application availability solution, the Geographically Dispersed Parallel Sysplex (GDPS), integrates Parallel Sysplex technology and remote copy technology to enhance application availability and improve disaster recovery.

GDPS topology is a Parallel Sysplex cluster spread across two sites, with all critical data mirrored between the sites. GDPS provides the capability to manage the remote copy configuration and storage subsystem(s), automates Parallel Sysplex operational tasks, and automates failure recovery from a single point of control, thereby improving application availability. GDPS supports all transaction managers (for example, CICS and IMS) and data base managers (for example, DB2, IMS, and VSAM).

GDPS is enabled by means of the following key IBM technologies:

- Parallel Sysplex
- 9037-2 Sysplex Timer
- Coupling Facility
- Systems Automation for OS/390
- Tivoli NetView for OS/390
- Availability and Operations Manager (AOM)i
- ESS, IBM RVA, 3990-6 or 9390 DASD
- PPRC or XRC
- IBM 2029 Fiber Saver (optional)

B.1 What is a GDPS?

GDPS is a multisite management facility incorporating a combination of system code and automation that utilizes the capabilities of Parallel Sysplex technology, storage subsystem mirroring, and data bases to manage processors, storage and network resources. It is designed to minimize and potentially eliminate the impact of a disaster or planned site outage. The GDPS provides the ability to perform a controlled site switch for both planned and unplanned site outages, with no data loss, maintaining full data integrity across multiple volumes and storage subsystems, and the ability to perform a normal DBMS restart (not DBMS recovery) at the opposite site.

© Copyright IBM Corp. 2000

The GDPS manages cross-site data consistency through a combination of storage subsystem, sysplex, and environmental triggers. GDPS provides the cross-site automation that works in combination with the DASD error recovery procedures exploiting new storage subsystem functions (Freeze/Run) to manage cross-site data consistency.

The physical topology of a GDPS consists of a base or Parallel Sysplex cluster spread across two sites (known as site A and site B) with one or more OS/390 systems at each site, separated by up to 40 kilometers (km).

GDPS consists of production systems, standby systems and controlling systems.

- The production systems execute the mission-critical workload.
- The standby systems normally do not run any production work, and instead provide processing resources when a production system or a site is unavailable. A standby system may be an active member of the Parallel Sysplex cluster that will acquire processing resources from expendable systems executing in logical partitions on the same processor, or an inactive member of the Parallel Sysplex cluster.

  When additional processing resource is required, an active standby system will expand by deactivating one or more logical partitions that are executing expendable work and configure their storage resources online (processor MIPS will also be absorbed) and/or an inactive standby system will be IPLed by system resetting one or more systems executing expendable work and IPLing the inactive system in its place.

  There must be sufficient processing resource capacity, such as processor power, main and expanded storage, and channel paths, available that can quickly be brought on-line to restart a system's or site's critical workload (typically by terminating one or more systems executing expendable (non-critical) work and acquiring its processing resource).
- The controlling system coordinates GDPS processing. By convention, all GDPS functions are initiated and coordinated by one controlling system. The first active system that is specified in the controlling system list will be the primary controlling system with the others, if any, being secondary controlling systems.

All critical data resides on storage subsystem(s) in site A (the primary copy of data) and is mirrored to site B (the secondary copy of data) via PPRC synchronous remote copy or XRC asynchronous remote copy. This includes system infrastructure (for example, JES2 checkpoint and spool) and software subsystem infrastructure (for example, program libraries, PROCLIBs, control files, and DBMS data).

GDPS uses Parallel Sysplex cluster facilities to communicate between systems. Each GDPS system joins the GDPS Parallel Sysplex cluster group. When a system joins a Parallel Sysplex cluster, GDPS automation will transfer GDPS policy and all GDPS status to the joining system.

All GDPS systems, except for any inactive standby systems, are running GDPS automation based upon Tivoli NetView for OS/390 and System Automation for OS/390. Each system will monitor the Parallel Sysplex cluster, coupling facilities, and storage subsystems and maintain GDPS status. This GDPS automation can coexist with an enterprise's existing automation product.

The data center must have a survival strategy (the operations function must survive any disaster to maintain processing). Ideally, the data center is located in a third site, and the back-up operations center is located in the same site as the controlling system to help maximize survivability.

B.2 GDPS functions

GDPS provides the following functions:

- **Remote Copy Management Facility (RCMF):** Automates management of the remote copy infrastructure.
- **Planned reconfiguration support:** Automates operational tasks from one single point of control.
- **Unplanned reconfiguration support:** Recovers from an OS/390, processor, storage subsystem, or site failure.

B.2.1 Remote copy management facility

The remote copy management facility (RCMF) was designed to simplify the storage administrator's remote copy management functions by managing the remote copy configuration rather than individual remote copy pairs. This includes the initialization and monitoring of the PPRC or XRC volume pairs based upon policy and performing routine operations on installed storage subsystems.

B.2.2 Planned reconfigurations

GDPS planned reconfiguration support automates procedures performed by an operations center. These include standard actions to: (a) quiesce a system's workload and remove the system from the Parallel Sysplex cluster (stop the system prior to a change window); (b) IPL a system (start the system after a change window); and (c) quiesce a system's workload, remove the system from the Parallel Sysplex cluster, and re-IPL the system (recycle a system to pick up SW maintenance). The standard actions can be initiated against a single system or group of systems. Additionally, user-defined actions are supported (for example, a planned site switch in which the workload is switched from processors in site A to processors in site B).

B.2.3 Unplanned reconfigurations

GDPS was originally designed to minimize and potentially eliminate the amount of data loss and the duration of the recovery window in the event of a site failure; however, it will also minimize the impact and potentially mask an OS/390 system or processor failure based upon GDPS policy. GDPS uses PPRC or XRC to help minimize or eliminate data loss. Parallel sysplex cluster functions along with automation are used to detect OS/390 system, processor, or site failures and to initiate recovery processing to help minimize the duration of the recovery window.

If an OS/390 system fails, the failed system will automatically be removed from the Parallel Sysplex cluster, re-IPLed in the same location, and the workload restarted. If a processor fails, the failed system(s) will be removed from the Parallel Sysplex cluster, re-IPLed on another processor, and the workload restarted.

With PPRC there will be limited or no data loss, based upon policy, since all critical data is being synchronously mirrored from site A to site B in the event of a site failure. There will be limited data loss if the production systems continue to make updates to the primary copy of data after remote copy processing is suspended (any updates after a freeze will not be reflected in the secondary copy if data) and there is a subsequent disaster that destroys some or all of the primary copy of data. There will be no data loss if the production systems do not make any updates to the primary PPRC volumes after PPRC processing is suspended.

Depending on the type of application and/or recovery options selected by the enterprise, multiple freeze options are supported by GDPS (the freeze is always performed to allow the restart of the software subsystems):

- **Freeze and Go**
  GDPS will freeze the secondary copy of data when remote copy processing suspends and the critical workload will continue to execute making updates to the primary copy of data; however, these updates will not be on the secondary DASD if there is a subsequent site A failure in which the primary copy of data is damaged or destroyed. This is the recommended option for those enterprises that can tolerate limited data loss or have established processes to recreate the data.
- **Freeze and Stop Unconditional**
  GDPS will freeze the secondary copy of data when remote copy processing suspends and will quiesce the production systems resulting in the critical workload being stopped and thereby preventing any data loss. This option may cause the production systems executing the critical workload to be quiesced for transient events that interrupt PPRC processing, thereby adversely impacting application availability.
- **Freeze and Stop Conditional**
  GDPS inspects the reason for the suspension of remote copy processing. If the suspension is caused by the storage subsystems that contain the secondary copy of data, processing is the same as for Freeze and Go; otherwise processing is the same as for Freeze and Stop Unconditional. This function is only valid in PPRC environments. It is the recommended option for those enterprises that cannot tolerate any data loss but require maximum availability.

If a site fails, the secondary copy of data will be frozen and the workload resumed or quiesced based upon policy, the failed system(s) will be removed from the Parallel Sysplex cluster, the primary copy of data will be switched, processing resource will be acquired in the surviving site (active standby systems will expand and/or inactive standby systems will be IPLed), the network will be switched if necessary, and the critical workload restarted.

B.3 GDPS service offering

The GDPS solution is delivered as a service offering by IBM Global Services. The services provided for GDPS may vary from country to country. Consult your local IBM business contact for information on GDPS services available.

Appendix C. Peer-to-Peer VTS message support

This appendix describes the enhanced message support and the new messages related to the Peer-to-Peer VTS.

C.1 Enhanced message support

Here, we describe changes to the way that messages relating to VTSs (not just Peer-to-Peer VTSs) are provided.

C.1.1 Extended status information

Status information, error messages and user messages broadcast to the host from the library are presented at the console as follows:

CBR3750I Message from library *library-name*: **message.**

The maximum allowable number of characters is increased from 70 to 240. This will improve the information provided at the host operator console as message text will no longer be truncated.

C.1.2 Console name message routing

Today, with console name message routing support, many of the library-specific messages are only issued to the specified library console (if defined) and not to the specified routing codes.

Although this is not specific to a Peer-to-Peer VTS, the following critical, action-related messages will now be issued using the specified library console and routing codes, providing maximum visibility.

```
CBR3759E Library x safety enclosure interlock open.
CBR3764E Library x all storage cells full.
CBR3765E No cleaner volumes available in library x.
CBR3753E All convenience output stations in library x are
full.
CBR3754E High capacity output station in library x is full.
CBR3755E {Input|Output} door open in library x.
CBR3660A Enter {list of media inserts} scratch volumes into x.
```

© Copyright IBM Corp. 2000

C.2 Peer-to-Peer VTS messages

This section lists some of the new Peer-to-Peer VTS messages that you may see. For a complete and current list, please see *OS/390 System Messages, Volume 2*, GC28-1785.

The following messages can be issued for the Peer-to-Peer VTS.

CBR1100I OAM status:

Explanation: The operator has entered the following command:

```
DISPLAY SMS,OAM
```

If there are Peer-to-Peer VTS subsystems defined to the system, the following status line will be displayed reflecting the number of distributed libraries that are associated with the composite libraries.

```
There are also numvdl-lib VTS distributed libraries defined.
```

Additional status lines may appear containing one or more of the following messages:

```
Copy operations disabled.
VTS operations degraded.
Immediate Mode Copy operations deferred.
Service preparation occurring.
Library is out of empty stacked volumes.
```

CBR3016I VTS distributed library *library-name* may be offline only to host.

Explanation: Either the VTS distributed library *library-name* came up offline during OAM initialization or was varied offline using the VARY SMS,LIBRARY command. Varying the distributed library offline from the host does not by itself prevent outboard usage of the library. To prevent outboard usage of the library you must take additional outboard or host action. Use the DISPLAY SMS,LIBRARY command to verify the outboard state of the library, or if activity to the clustered VTS is to cease, use the VARY SMS,LIBRARY command to vary the associated composite library offline.

CBR3017I VTS distributed library library-name incorrectly defined to tape storage group *storage-group-name*.

Explanation: During OAM initialization processing of VTS distributed library library-name, it was detected that the library is associated with tape storage group storage-group-name. From a host perspective, since a distributed library has no tape drives and volumes associated with it, there is no need to associate a distributed library with a tape storage group. If that library is desired, verify that its composite library is also associated with that storage group. If the storage group has only distributed libraries associated with it, any scratch requests to that storage group would fail.

CBR3785E Copy operations disabled in library *library-name*.

Explanation: Copy operations in library *library-name* are disabled. The clustered VTS subsystem is in this state when the overall system is no longer capable of performing copy operations. As long as the underlying VTS subsystems and their associated distributed libraries are operational and allow data to be written to them and at least one virtual tape controller is functional, the copy function is enabled.

CBR3786E VTS operations degraded in library *library-name*.

Explanation: One or more elements in the VTS subsystem for library *library-name* are not available. The unavailable elements may include virtual device addresses, communication paths, host I/O bandwidth, etc. This message is retained until all of the resources in the subsystem are available.

CBR3787E Immediate mode copy operations deferred in library *library-name*.

Explanation: At least one immediate mode copy in library *library-name* was unable to complete before the rewind/unload that initiated the copy command completed.

CBR3788E Service preparation occurring in library *library-name*.

Explanation: An element of the clustered VTS subsystem is being prepared for service in library *library-name*. When an element of the subsystem needs to be serviced, the overall subsystem must be prepared to ensure continued host access to the data. The library remains in this state until the planned service is cancelled or until the service activity has completed in the library.

CBR3789E VTS library *library-name* is out of empty stacked volumes.

Explanation: VTS library *library-name* has used all its empty stacked volumes. Only the library partition with the VTS that has run out of stacked volumes reports this state; other library partitions are not affected.

CBR3790E VTS library *library-name* has insufficient resources to continue mount processing.

Explanation: VTS library *library-name* has determined that it does not have sufficient resources to perform mount operations. An example of this may be that the VTS does not have enough physical tape devices available. Other library partitions in the same physical library are not affected by this state.

CBR3726I Function incompatible error code *error-code* from library *library-name* for volume *volser*.

Explanation: An error has occurred during processing of volume *volser* in library *library-name*. The library returned a unit check with an error code *error-code* which indicates that an incompatible function has been requested. A command has been issued that requests an operation that is understood by the subsystem microcode, but cannot be performed due to one of the following errors:

X'00' The function requested is not supported by the subsystem to which the order was issued.

X'01' Library attachment facility not installed and allowed.

X'02' Not currently used.

X'03' High capacity input/output facility is not configured.

X'04' Reserved.

X'05' Volume requested to be mounted is not compatible with the device allocated.

X'06' The logical volume can only be ejected if it is in the insert category or is assigned to a category that has the fast-ready attribute set.

X'07' There is no pending import or export operation to cancel.

X'08' There are not enough (four are needed) physical drives available to initiate the import or export operation.

X'09' Reserved.

X'0D' The Peer-to-Peer VTS subsystem is either in service preparation mode or has an unavailable component within the subsystem such as an unavailable distributed library. Audit, eject, or entry-related commands are not being accepted at this time.

X'0E' The Peer-to-Peer VTS subsystem already has one thousand eject requests queued and is not accepting any more eject requests at this time.

X'0F' An inappropriate library function was issued to the Peer-to-Peer VTS subsystem.

X'10' The AX0 in the Peer-to-Peer VTS subsystem that the command was issued to is in read-only mode and is not accepting eject or change use attribute requests. This mode of operation is provided to support disaster recovery operations in a Peer-to-Peer VTS configuration where the configuration is split between two physical sites.

CBR4125I Valid copy of volume *volser* **in library** *library-name* **inaccessible.**

Explanation: An error has been detected during Library Automation Communication Services (LACS) processing for the MOUNT function. Library *library-name* has indicated that a valid copy of volume *volser* is not currently available. The volume cannot be retrieved using normal library automated function; operator or service representative intervention is needed. The error is reported by a unit check when the mount order is sent to the library.

CBR4126I Library *library-name* **drive is in read only mode.**

Explanation: An error has been detected during Library Automation Communication Services (LACS) processing for the MOUNT function. The requested drive in the VTS Peer-to-Peer library library-name is in read-only mode, causing the scratch mount request to this drive to fail. Read-only mode is provided at an AX0 level to prevent hosts attached to that AX0 from modifying the contents of a logical volume or its category assignment.

```
EDG0235E ERROR IN LOCDEF FOR LOCATION location - DISTRIBUTED
LIBRARIES CANNOT BE SPECIFIED
```

Explanation: This message applies only to DFSMSrmm users. A LOCDEF parameter in the DFSMSrmm PARMLIB has specified a location name which matches the name of a system-managed library which is distributed. You cannot use the names of distributed libraries with DFSMSrmm.

Appendix D. SMF type 94 record layout

The tape library accumulates statistics over a period of one hour. These statistics represent the activity of the IBM Tape Library Dataserver resulting from all hosts attached to the library.

At the end of the hour, the system calculates composite statistics about the activity of all devices in the library and writes an SMF type 94 record.

D.1 Record mapping

This section describes the mapping of the type 94 record.

D.1.1 Header and self-defining section

This section contains the common SMF record headers fields and the triplet fields (offset/length/number), if applicable, that locate the other sections on the record. The mapping macro resides in SYS1.MACLIB.

Offsets		Name	Length	Format	Description
0	0	SMF94LEN	2	binary	Record length. This field and the next field (total of four bytes) form the RDW (record descriptor word).
2	2	SMF94SEG	2	binary	Segment descriptor (see record length field).
4	4	SMF94FLG	1	binary	System indicator
5	5	SMF94RTY	1	binary	Record type 94 (X'5E')
6	6	SMF94TME	4	binary	Time since midnight, in hundredths of a second, when the record was moved into the SMF buffer.
10	A	SMF94DTE	4	packed	Date when the record was moved into the SMF buffer, in the form 0cyydddF.
14	E	SMF94SID	4	ebcdic	System identification (from SMFPRMxx PARMLIB member).
18	12	SMF94WID	4	ebcdic	Subsystem identification.
22	16	SMF94STP	2	binary	Record subtype (01 = 34XX library statistics)

© Copyright IBM Corp. 2000

D.1.2 Self-defining triplet section

Offsets		Name	Length	Format	Description
24	18	SMF94SDL	4	binary	Self-defining section length.
28	1C	SMF94POF	4	binary	Offset to product section from start of record, including record descriptor word (RDW).
32	20	SMF94PLN	2	binary	Length of product section.
34	22	SMF94PON	2	binary	Number of product sections.
36	24	SMF94HOF	4	binary	Offset to format section from start of record, including record descriptor word (RDW).
40	28	SMF94HLN	2	binary	Length of format section.
42	2A	SMF94HON	2	binary	Number of format sections.
44	2C	SMF94SOF	4	binary	Offset to self-description information section from start of record, including record descriptor word (RDW).
48	30	SMF94SLN	2	binary	Length of self-description information section.
50	32	SMF94SON	2	binary	Number of self-description information sections.
52	34	SMF94LOF	4	binary	Offset to ATL statistics section from start of record, including record descriptor word (RDW).
56	38	SMF94LLN	2	binary	Length of ATL statistics section.
58	3A	SMF94LON	2	binary	Number of ATL statistics sections.
60	3C	SMF94MOF	4	binary	Offset to mount statistics section from start of record, including record descriptor word (RDW).
64	40	SMF94MLN	2	binary	Length of mount statistics section.
66	42	SMF94MON	2	binary	Number of mount statistics sections.
68	44	SMF94DOF	4	binary	Offset to demount statistics section from start of record, including record descriptor word (RDW).

72	48	SMF94DLN	2	binary	Length of demount statistics section.
74	4A	SMF94DON	2	binary	Number of demount statistics sections.
76	4C	SMF94EOF	4	binary	Offset to eject statistics section from start of record, including record descriptor word (RDW).
80	50	SMF94ELN	2	binary	Length of eject statistics section.
82	52	SMF94EON	2	binary	Number of eject statistics sections.
84	54	SMF94AOF	4	binary	Offset to audit statistics section from start of record, including record descriptor word (RDW).
88	58	SMF94ALN	2	binary	Length of audit statistics section.
90	5A	SMF94AON	2	binary	Number of audit statistics sections.
92	5C	SMF94IOF	4	binary	Offset to insert statistics section from start of record, including record descriptor word (RDW).
96	60_	SMF94ILN	2	binary	Length of insert statistics section.
98	62	SMF94ION	2	binary	Number of insert statistics sections.
100	64	SMF94VOF	4	binary	Offset to VTS statistics
104	68	SMF94VLN	2	binary	Length of VTS statistics
106	6A	SMF94VON	2	binary	Number of VTS statistics
108	6C	SMF94XOF	4	binary	Offset to import/export statistics
112	70	SMF94XLN	2	binary	Length of import/export statistics
114	72	SMF94XON	2	binary	Number of import/export statistics
116	74	SMF942OF	4	binary	Offset to VTS enhanced library statistics
120	78	SMF942LN	2	binary	Length of VTS enhanced library statistics
122	7A	SMF942ON	2	binary	Number of VTS enhanced library statistics

D.1.3 Product section

Offsets		Name	Length	Format	Description
0	0	SMF94TYP	2	binary	Subtype for type 94 record.
2	2	SMF94RVN	2	EBCDIC	Record version number C'01'.
4	4	SMF94PNM	8	EBCDIC	Product name 'JDZ1110 '.
12	C	SMF94MVS	8	EBCDIC	MVS operating system name.

D.1.4 Format section

Offsets		Name	Length	Format	Description
0	0	SMF94HSF	1	binary	Format is either 0 or 1. Format 1 statistics include VTS enhanced library statistics.
1	1	SMF94HHI	2	binary	Hour index. Incremented every hour. Value ranges from 0 to 23.

D.1.5 Self-description information

Offsets		Name	Length	Format	Description
0	0	SMF94SLT	6	EBCDIC	System-managed tape library type number. For example, '003495' represents the IBM 3495
6	6	SMF94SLM	3	EBCDIC	System-managed tape library model number. For example, 'L30' represents model L30.
9	9	SMF94SMA	3	EBCDIC	System-managed tape library manufacturer. Always equals 'IBM'.
12	C	SMF94SPL	2	EBCDIC	System-managed tape library plant of manufacture. For example, '13' represents San Jose, California, and '77' represents Valencia, Spain.
14	E	SMF94SNO	12	EBCDIC	System-managed tape library sequence number. Uniquely identifies a ATL.
26	1A		1	binary	Reserved.

D.1.6 Managed tape library statistics

Offsets		Name	Length	Format	Description
0	0	SMF94LID	2	binary	Number of drives currently installed in a ATL.
2	2	SMF94LMD	2	binary	Number of drives currently mounted in a ATL.
4	4	SMF94LM1	2	binary	Maximum number of drives mounted during the last hour.
6	6	SMF94LM2	2	binary	Minimum number of drives mounted during the last hour.
8	8	SMF94LM3	2	binary	Average number of drives mounted during the last hour.
10	A	SMF94LT1	2	binary	Maximum amount of time, in seconds, that a tape volume was mounted on a drive during the last hour. The mount time of a volume is the time when the system completed mounting a volume on a drive until the time when the ATL receives an order from the host to demount the volume.
12	C	SMF94LT2	2	binary	Minimum amount of time, in seconds, that a tape volume was mounted on a drive during the last hour. The mount time of a volume is the time when the system completed mounting a volume on a drive until the time when the ATL receives an order from the host to demount the volume.
14	E	SMF94LT3	2	binary	Average amount of time, in seconds, that all tape volumes were mounted on drives during the last hour. The mount time of a volume is the time when the system completed mounting a volume on a drive until the time when the ATL receives an order from the host to demount the volume.

D.1.7 Mount statistics

Offsets		Name	Length	Format	Description
0	0	SMF94MPR	2	binary	The total number of mount requests currently pending.
2	2	SMF94MP1	2	binary	Maximum number of mount requests pending during the last hour.
4	4	SMF94MP2	2	binary	Minimum number of mount requests pending during the last hour.
6	6	SMF94MP3	2	binary	Average number of mount requests pending during the last hour.
8	8	SMF94MTO	2	binary	Total number of mounts during the last hour.
10	A	SMF94MIN	2	binary	Index mounts during the last hour. An index mount is a mount accomplished using the automatic cartridge loader of a 3490 tape drive.
12	C	SMF94MPM	2	binary	Pre-mounts during last hour. A single pre-mount operation causes a volume to be added to the automatic cartridge loader of a 3490 tape drive.
14	E	SMF94MT1	2	binary	Maximum amount of time, in seconds, required to perform any single mount operation during the last hour.
16	10	SMF94MT2	2	binary	Minimum amount of time, in seconds, required to perform any single mount operation during the last hour.
18	12	SMF94MT3	2	binary	Average amount of time, in seconds, required to perform a single mount operation during the last hour.

D.1.8 Demount statistics

Offsets		Name	Length	Format	Description
0	0	SMF94DPR	2	binary	The total number of demount requests currently pending.
2	2	SMF94DP1	2	binary	Maximum number of demount requests pending during the last hour.
4	4	SMF94DP2	2	binary	Minimum number of demount requests pending during the last hour.
6	6	SMF94DP3	2	binary	Average number of demount requests pending during the last hour.
8	8	SMF94DTO	2	binary	Total number of demounts during the last hour.
10	A	SMF94DIN	2	binary	Index demounts during the last hour. An index demount moves a volume from the feed station to the output stack of the automatic cartridge loader of a 3490 tape drive.
12	C	SMF94DPM	2	binary	Post-demounts during the last hour. A post-demount operation moves a volume from the output stack of the automatic cartridge loader of a 3490 tape drive.
14	E	SMF94DT1	2	binary	Maximum amount of time, in seconds, required to perform any single demount operation during the last hour.
16	10	SMF94DT2	2	binary	Minimum amount of time, in seconds, required to perform any single demount operation during the last hour.
18	12	SMF94DT3	2	binary	Average amount of time, in seconds, required to perform a single demount operation during the last hour.

D.1.9 Eject statistics

Offsets		Name	Length	Format	Description
0	0	SMF94EPR	2	binary	The total number of eject requests currently pending. An eject operation moves one volume from the ATL to an output station for an operator to remove.
2	2	SMF94EP1	2	binary	Maximum number of eject requests pending during the last hour.
4	4	SMF94EP2	2	binary	Minimum number of eject requests pending during the last hour.
6	6	SMF94EP3	2	binary	Average number of eject requests pending during the last hour.
8	8	SMF94ETO	2	binary	Totals number of ejects during the last hour.
10	A	SMF94ET1	2	binary	Maximum amount of time, in seconds, required to perform any single eject operation during the last hour.
12	C	SMF94ET2	2	binary	Minimum amount of time, in seconds, required to perform any single eject operation during the last hour.
14	E	SMF94ET3	2	binary	Average amount of time, in seconds, required to perform a single eject operation during the last hour.

D.1.10 Audit statistics

Offsets		Name	Length	Format	Description
0	0	SMF94APR	2	binary	The total number of audit requests currently pending. When the host requests an audit operation, the accessor moves to a shelf location and ensures that a volume is present.
2	2	SMF94AP1	2	binary	Maximum number of audit requests pending during the last hour.
4	4	SMF94AP2	2	binary	Minimum number of audit requests pending during the last hour.
6	6	SMF94AP3	2	binary	Average number of audit requests pending during the last hour.
8	8	SMF94ATO	2	binary	Total number of audits during the last hour.
10	A	SMF94AT1	2	binary	Maximum amount of time, in seconds, required to perform any single audit operation during the last hour.
12	C	SMF94AT2	2	binary	Minimum amount of time, in seconds, required to perform any single audit operation during the last hour.
14	E	SMF94AT3	2	binary	Average amount of time, in seconds, required to perform a single audit operation during the last hour.

D.1.11 Insert statistics

Offsets		Name	Length	Format	Description
0	0	SMF94INS	2	binary	Number of insert stores during last hour. This number is the number of volumes moved from an input station to a location inside the ATL.

D.1.12 VTS statistics

Offsets		Name	Length	Format	Description
0	0	SMF94VNO	1	binary	Library reference number. X'01', User interface library. X'02', secondary library. X'FF', composite library. X'00', non-Peer-to-Peer VTS library.
1	1	SMF94VLS	5	EBCDIC	Library sequence number for the library segment for which VTS statistics are being reported.
6	6	SMF94VTI	1	binary	Number of underlying tape drives currently installed in the VTS subsystem.[1]
7	7	SMF94VTA	1	binary	Number of underlying tape drives currently available for use by the VTS subsystem.[1]
8	8	SMF94VTX	1	binary	Maximum number of underlying tape drives mounted concurrently in this VTS during last hour.[1]
9	9	SMF94VTN	1	binary	Minimum number of underlying tape drives mounted concurrently in this VTS during last hour.[1]
10	A	SMF94VTV	1	binary	Average number of underlying tape drives mounted concurrently in this VTS during last hour. Value is determined by summing number of concurrently mounted tape drives every 10 seconds, and dividing resultant sum by 360 during hourly statistics generation.[1]
11	B	SMF94VR2	1	binary	Reserved, set to X'00'
12	C	SMF94VMX	2	binary	Maximum time in seconds used by the library to perform a mount request of a tape drive in the VTS in the last hour. Time is accrued from time mount request is accepted until it is completed. Mount time is accredited to the hour that mount is completed. [1]
14	E	SMF94VMN	2	binary	Minimum time in seconds used by the library to perform a mount request for a tape drive in the VTS in the last hour. Time is accrued from time mount request is accepted until it is completed. Mount time is accredited to the hour that mount is completed. [1]

16	10	SMF94VMV	2	binary	Average time in seconds used by the library to perform a mount request for a tape drive in the VTS in the last hour. Time is accrued from time mount request is accepted until it is completed. Mount time is accredited to the hour that mount is completed.[1]
18	12	SMF94VPS	2	binary	The number of mount requests completed in last hour to satisfy recall mounts. [1]
20	14	SMF94VPM	2	binary	The number of mount requests completed in last hour to satisfy copy requests.[1]
22	16	SMF94VPR	2	binary	The number of mount requests completed in last hour to satisfy reclamation mounts. [1]
24	18	SMF94VDC	1	binary	The number of virtual devices configured in this VTS at the time request for statistics was received (current). [2]
26	19	SMF94VDX	1	binary	The maximum number of virtual drives that were concurrently mounted in this VTS during the last hour. [2]
26	1A	SMF94VDN	1	binary	The minimum number of virtual drives that were concurrently mounted in this VTS during the last hour. [2]
27	1B	SMF94VDA	1	binary	The average number of virtual drives that were concurrently mounted in this VTS during the last hour. Value is determined by summing number of concurrently mounted virtual devices every 10 seconds, and dividing resultant sum by 360 during hourly statistics generation. [2]
28	1C	SMF94VVX	2	binary	Maximum time in seconds that a virtual drive was mounted in this VTS during the last hour. Time is accrued from completion of mount until a demount is issued. Mount time is accredited to the hour that demount is issued. [2]
30	1E	SMF94VVN	2	binary	Minimum time in seconds that a virtual drive was mounted in this VTS during the last hour. Time is accrued from completion of mount until a demount is issued. Mount time is accredited to the hour that demount is issued. [2]

32	20	SMF94VVA	2	binary	Average time in seconds that a virtual drive was mounted in this VTS during the last hour. Time is accrued from completion of mount until a demount is issued. Mount time is accredited to the hour that demount is issued. [2]
34	22	SMF94VRX	2	binary	Maximum time in seconds used to complete a mount request on a virtual drive in the last hour. Time is accrued from time mount request is accepted until it is completed. Mount time is accredited to the hour that the mount is completed. [1]
36	24	SMF94VRN	2	binary	Minimum time in seconds used to complete a mount request on a virtual drive in the last hour. Time is accrued from time it is completed. Mount time is accredited to the hour that the mount is completed. [1]
38	26	SMF94VRA	2	binary	Average time in seconds used to complete a mount request on a virtual drive in the last hour. Time is accrued from time mount request is accepted until it is completed. Mount time is accredited to the hour that the mount is completed.[1]
40	28	SMF94VFR	2	binary	The number of virtual mounts in last hour using VTS Fast-Ready facility. Fast-Ready is used for mount-from-category request for which the specified category has the Fast-Ready attribute set, or for specific volume requests for which the specified volume is, at the time the mount request is received, assigned to a category that has the Fast-Ready attribute set. [1]
42	2A	SMF94VMH	2	binary	The number of virtual mounts in the last hour that were completed for specific requested volume found resident in Tape Volume Cache (specific mount hits).[1]
44	2C	SMF94VMS	2	binary	The number of virtual mounts in last hour that were completed with specific requested logical volume recalled from a stacked tape back into Tape Volume Cache.[1]
46	2E	SMF94VMP	2	binary	The number of virtual volumes for which a copy operation was completed in the last hour. [1]

48	30	SMF94VBW	4	binary	The total number of bytes written successfully through host channels to virtual volumes in an integral multiple of 4096 bytes during the last hour. If number of bytes written is not an integer multiple of 4096, the number is rounded up. If the statistics are reported for a composite library, this field contains the sum of the values indicated for host write data transferred through each AX0.
52	34	SMF94VBR	4	binary	The total number of bytes read successfully through host channels from virtual volumes in an integral multiple of 4096 bytes during the last hour. If number of bytes read is not an integer multiple of 4096, the number is rounded up. If the statistics are reported for a composite library, this field contains the sum of the values indicated for host read data transferred through each AX0.
56	38	SMF94VTW	4	binary	The total number of bytes written successfully by VTS to its attached tape drives in an integral multiple of 4096 bytes during the last hour. If number of bytes written is not an integer multiple of 4096, the number is rounded up. Bytes are accredited to the hour in which the underlying premigrates of virtual volumes complete. [1]
60	3C	SMF94VTR	4	binary	The total number of bytes read successfully by VTS from its attached tape drives in an integral multiple of 4096 bytes during the last hour. If the number of bytes read is not an integer multiple of 4096, the number is rounded up. Bytes are accredited to the hour in which the underlying stage requests complete. [1]
64	40	SMF94VCA	2	binary	The average, in minutes, of the ages of the virtual volumes in the Tape Volume Cache as determined at the end of the reported hour. [1]
66	42	SMF94VCZ	2	binary	The average number of megabytes of data on a logical volume for the active logical volumes which are on VTS stacked volumes at the end of the reported hour. This is a calculated field (SMF94VBA divided by SMF94VLA) and represents the average size of a logical volume copied from the Tape Volume Cache. [1]

68	44	SMF94VNM	2	binary	The number of virtual volumes in Tape Volume Cache at the end of reported hour. [1]
70	46	SMF94VR3	2	binary	Reserved, set to X'00'
72	48	SMF94VBA	4	binary	The total number of megabytes of data on the active logical volumes which are on VTS stacked volumes at the end of the reported hour. The number is the integral multiple of 1,048,576 bytes. This is the number of megabytes copied from the Tape Volume Cache to the stacked volumes and may include multiple versions of logical volumes. The obsolete versions will become inactive during the next reconciliation process. [1]
76	4C	SMF94VLA	4	binary	The total number of active logical volumes which are on VTS stacked volumes at the end of the reported hour. This number may include multiple versions of logical volumes; therefore, may exceed the number of defined logical volumes. The obsolete versions will become inactive during the next reconciliation process. [1]
80	50	SMF94VEC	4	binary	The total estimated storage capacity of the empty 3590 cartridges managed by the VTS in an integral multiple of 1,048,576 bytes (1 MByte) at the end of the reported hour. Partially filled stacked volumes are not included in this calculation. The number of empty stacked volumes is multiplied by the estimated amount of data that can be stored on one of these volumes. For a 3494 Model B18 without EHPO, this amount is 20 GB for the 3590-B1A tape drives and 40 GB for the 3590-E1A tape drives which is obtained by assuming a 2:1 compression ratio. For a 3494 Model B16 this amount is 20 GB for the 3590-B1A tape drives. The 3494 Model B18 VTS with enhanced ESCON host attachments provides compression into the Tape Volume Cache (TVC); therefore, further compression when writing to the stacked volume is unlikely, and the estimated amount of data copied from the TVC to a stacked volume is 10 GB for 3590-B1A tape drives and 20 GB for 3590-E1A tape drives. [1]

D.1.13 Import/export statistics

Offsets		Name	Length	Format	Description
0	0	SMF94IM1	2	binary	count of physical volumes processed during import operations that completed in the last hour.
2	2	SMF94EX1	2	binary	count of physical volumes that contain the successfully exported logical volumes exported during the last hour.
4	4	SMF94IM2	4	binary	count of the number of logical volumes successfully imported during import operations that completed during the last hour.
8	8	SMF94EX2	4	binary	count of the number of logical volumes successfully exported for export operations that completed during the last hour.
12	C	SMF94IM3	4	binary	megabytes of data imported for import operations that completed in the last hour.
16	10	SMF94EX3	4	binary	megabytes of data exported during export operations that completed in the last hour.
20	14	SMF94IM4	4	binary	Megabytes of data that was moved from one physical stacked volume to another as part of the import operations that completed in the last hour.
24	18	SMF94EX4	4	binary	Megabytes moved from one physical stacked volume to another as part of the export operations completed in the last hour.
28	1C		8	binary	Reserved, set to X'00'
36	24	SMF94ACA	2	binary	Accessor A mounts. The count of the number of mount operations accessor A completed during the last hour.[1]
38	26	SMF94ACB	2	binary	Accessor B mounts. The count of the number of mount operations accessor B completed during the last hour. [1]
40	28		4	binary	Reserved, set to X'00'

D.1.14 VTS enhanced library statistics

Offsets		Name	Length	Format	Description
0	0	S94BSRAT	2	binary	Back-store compression ratio. Reports the compression ratio of data stored on full stacked volumes. The granularity of the value is hundredths. [1]
2	2	S94HARAT	2	binary	Host adapter compression ratio for data moved between host adapter to Tape Volume Cache in the last hour. The granularity of the value is hundredths. [1]
4	4	S94TVCS	2	binary	Tape volume cache size in gigabytes. [1]
6	6	S94ESCON	1	binary	Number of host ESCON channels installed.[2]
7	7	S94SCSI	1	binary	Number of host SCSI channels installed.[2]
8	8	S94NUMBS	4	binary	Channel blocks written in the last hour. For a composite library, this field contains the total for all AX0s.[2]
12	C	S940KB	1	binary	Percentage of 0 to 2K channel blocks written in the last hour. [2]
13	D	S942KB	1	binary	Percentage of greater than 2K to 4K channel blocks written in the last hour. [2]
14	E	S944KB	1	binary	Percentage of greater than 4K to 8K channel blocks written in the last hour. [2]
15	F	S948KB	1	binary	Percentage of greater than 8K to 16K channel blocks written in the last hour.[2]
16	10	S9416KB	1	binary	Percentage of greater than 16K to 32K channel blocks written in the last hour. [2]
17	11	S9432KB	1	binary	Percentage of greater than 32K to 64K channel blocks written in the last hour. [2]
18	12	S9464KB	1	binary	Percentage of greater than 64K channel blocks written in the last hour.[2]
19	13	S94RCPRT	1	binary	Recall predominate throttling percentage over the last hour. The percentage of 30 second intervals where there was a non-zero throttling value and recall was the predominant reason.[1]

20	14	S94WROVT	1	binary	Write overrun predominate throttling percentage over the last hour. The percentage of 30 second intervals where there was a non-zero throttling value and write overrun was the predominant reason.[1]
21	15		3	binary	Reserved
24	18	S94AVRCT	4	binary	Average recall throttle value over the last hour. Average of the non-zero throttling values where recall was the predominant reason for throttling. Granularity is milliseconds.[1]
28	1C	S94AVWOT	4	binary	Average write overrun throttle value over the last hour. Average of the non-zero throttling values where write overrun was the predominant reason for throttling. Granularity is milliseconds.[1]
32	20		4	binary	Reserved
36	24	S94TOTAT	4	binary	Overall average throttle value for the last hour. Average of all throttling values, both zero and non-zero, during the previous hour. Granularity is milliseconds.[1]
40	28	S94MAXFR	2	binary	Maximum fast-ready mount time in seconds for fast-ready mounts completed in the last hour. [2]
42	2A	S94MINFR	2	binary	Minimum fast-ready mount time in seconds for fast-ready mounts completed in the last hour. [2]
44	2C	S94AVGFR	2	binary	Average fast-ready mount time in seconds for fast-ready mounts completed in the last hour. [2]
46	2E	S94MAXCH	2	binary	Maximum cache-hit mount time in seconds for mounts completed with the requested volume in the tape volume cache in the last hour.[2]
48	30	S94MINCH	2	binary	Minimum cache-hit mount time in seconds for mounts completed with the requested volume in the tape volume cache in the last hour. [2]

50	32	S94AVGCH	2	binary	Average cache-hit mount time in seconds for mounts completed with the requested volume in the tape volume cache in the last hour. [2]
52	34	S94MAXRM	2	binary	Maximum recall-mount time in seconds for mounts where the requested volume had to be recalled from a stacked volume. The mount time is counted for the hour in which the mount completed. [2]
54	36	S94MINRM	2	binary	Minimum recall-mount time in seconds for mounts where the requested volume had to be recalled from a stacked volume. The mount time is counted for the hour in which the mount completed. [2]
56	38	S94AVGRM	2	binary	Average recall-mount time in seconds for mounts where the requested volume had to be recalled from a stacked volume. The mount time is counted for the hour in which the mount completed. [2]
58	3A	S94ADV05	2	binary	Number of volumes containing 0 to 5 percent active data. [1]
60	3C	S94ADV10	2	binary	Number of volumes containing greater than 5 to 10 percent active data. [1]
62	3E	S94ADV15	2	binary	Number of volumes containing greater than 10 to 15 percent active data. [1]
64	40	S94ADV20	2	binary	Number of volumes containing greater than 15 to 20 percent active data. [1]
66	42	S94ADV25	2	binary	Number of volumes containing greater than 20 to 25 percent active data. [1]
68	44	S94ADV30	2	binary	Number of volumes containing greater than 25 to 30 percent active data. [1]
70	46	S94ADV35	2	binary	Number of volumes containing greater than 30 to 35 percent active data. [1]
72	48	S94ADV40	2	binary	Number of volumes containing greater than 35 to 40 percent active data. [1]
74	4A	S94ADV45	2	binary	Number of volumes containing greater than 40 to 45 percent active data. [1]

76	4C	S94ADV50	2	binary	Number of volumes containing greater than 45 to 50 percent active data. [1]
78	4E	S94ADV55	2	binary	Number of volumes containing greater than 50 to 55 percent active data. [1]
80	50	S94ADV60	2	binary	Number of volumes containing greater than 55 to 60 percent active data. [1]
82	52	S94ADV65	2	binary	Number of volumes containing greater than 60 to 65 percent active data. [1]
84	54	S94ADV70	2	binary	Number of volumes containing greater than 65 to 70 percent active data. [1]
86	56	S94ADV75	2	binary	Number of volumes containing greater than 70 to 75 percent active data. [1]
88	58	S94ADV80	2	binary	Number of volumes containing greater than 75 to 80 percent active data. [1]
90	5A	S94ADV85	2	binary	Number of volumes containing greater than 80 to 85 percent active data. [1]
92	5C	S94ADV90	2	binary	Number of volumes containing greater than 85 to 90 percent active data. [1]
94	5E	S94ADV95	2	binary	Number of volumes containing greater than 90 to 95 percent active data. [1]
96	60	S94ADV00	2	binary	Number of volumes containing greater than 95 to 100 percent active data. [1]
98	62	S94THRES	1	binary	Reclaim threshold percentage set for this VTS. [1]
99	63		1	binary	reserved (set to zero)
100	64	S94SRTCT	2	binary	Scratch stacked volume count as of the end of the hour. [1]
102	66	S94PRICT	2	binary	Private stacked volume count as of the end of the hour. [1]
104	68	S94MTVCA	4	binary	Maximum age (in minutes) of any volume in the tape volume cache at the end of the last hour. [1]
108	6C		20	binary	reserved
128	80	S94CLLVC	4	binary	Number of composite library logical volumes to be copied or where the copy is in progress but has not yet completed. [3]

132	84	S94CLDTC	4	binary	Composite library data yet to be copied or in progress. Reported in integral megabytes (less than one rounded up).[3]
136	88	S94CLMT0	2	binary	Number of library mounts completed in the last hour for B18-0 where this was the I/O VTS. [3]
138	8A	S94CLMT1	2	binary	Number of library mounts completed in the last hour for B18-1 where this was the I/O VTS. [3]
140	8C		4	binary	reserved (set to zero)
144	90	S94CLDC0	4	binary	Compressed data copied by AX0 number 0 for copy operations that completed in the last hour. Reported in integral megabytes (less than one rounded up). [3]
148	94	S94CLVC0	4	binary	Number of volumes whose copy was completed by AX0 number 0 during the last hour. [3]
152	98	S94CLRD0	4	binary	Host read data (in units of 4096 bytes) transferred through AX0 number 0 in the last hour. [3]
156	9C	S94CLWD0	4	binary	Host write data (in units of 4096 bytes) transferred through AX0 number 0 in the last hour. [3]
160	A0	S94CLCM0	2	binary	Number of mounts completed in the last hour by AX0 number 0 that specified a category number rather than a specific volume serial number. [3]
162	A2	S94CLSM0	2	binary	Number of mounts completed in the last hour by AX0 number 0 that specified a volume serial number which was found in cache. [3]
164	A4	S94CLRM0	2	binary	Number of mounts completed in the last hour by AX0 number 0 that specified a volume serial number which was not found in cache and hence caused a recall from a stacked volume. [3]
166	A6		10	binary	reserved (set to zero)

176	B0	S94CLDC1	4		binary	Compressed data copied by AX0 number 1 for copy operations that completed in the last hour. Reported in integral megabytes (less than one rounded up). [3]
180	B4	S94CLVC1	4		binary	Number of volumes whose copy was completed by AX0 number 1 during the last hour. [3]
184	B8	S94CLRD1	4		binary	Host read data (in units of 4096 bytes) transferred through AX0 number 1 in the last hour. [3]
188	BC	S94CLWD1	4		binary	Host write data (in units of 4096 bytes) transferred through AX0 number 1 in the last hour. [3]
192	C0	S94CLCM1	2		binary	Number of mounts completed in the last hour by AX0 number 1 that specified a category number rather than a specific volume serial number. [3]
194	C2	S94CLSM1	2		binary	Number of mounts completed in the last hour by AX0 number 1 that specified a volume serial number which was found in cache.[3]
196	C4	S94CLRM1	2		binary	Number of mounts completed in the last hour by AX0 number 1 that specified a volume serial number which was not found in cache and hence caused a recall from a stacked volume. [3]
198	C6		10		binary	reserved (set to zero)
208	D0	S94CLDC2	4		binary	Compressed data copied by AX0 number 2 for copy operations that completed in the last hour. Reported in integral megabytes (less than one rounded up). [3]
212	D4	S94CLVC2	4		binary	Number of volumes whose copy was completed by AX0 number 2 during the last hour. [3]
216	D8	S94CLRD2	4		binary	Host read data (in units of 4096 bytes) transferred through AX0 number 2 in the last hour. [3]
220	DC	S94CLWD2	4		binary	Host write data (in units of 4096 bytes) transferred through AX0 number 2 in the last hour.[3]

224	E0	S94CLCM2	2	binary	Number of mounts completed in the last hour by AX0 number 2 that specified a category number rather than a specific volume serial number. [3]
226	E2	S94CLSM2	2	binary	Number of mounts completed in the last hour by AX0 number 2 that specified a volume serial number which was found in cache. [3]
228	E4	S94CLRM2	2	binary	Number of mounts completed in the last hour by AX0 number 2 that specified a volume serial number which was not found in cache and hence caused a recall from a stacked volume.[3]
230	E6		10		reserved (set to zero)
240	F0	S94CLDC3	4	binary	Compressed data copied by AX0 number 3 for copy operations that completed in the last hour. Reported in integral megabytes (less than one rounded up). [3]
244	F4	S94CLVC3	4	binary	Number of volumes whose copy was completed by AX0 number 3 during the last hour. [3]
248	F8	S94CLRD3	4	binary	Host read data (in units of 4096 bytes) transferred through AX0 number 3 in the last hour. [3]
252	FC	S94CLWD3	4	binary	Host write data (in units of 4096 bytes) transferred through AX0 number 3 in the last hour.[3]
256	100	S94CLCM3	2	binary	Number of mounts completed in the last hour by AX0 number 3 that specified a category number rather than a specific volume serial number. [3]
258	102	S94CLSM3	2	binary	Number of mounts completed in the last hour by AX0 number 3 that specified a volume serial number which was found in cache.[3]
260	104	S94CLRM3	2	binary	Number of mounts completed in the last hour by AX0 number 3 that specified a volume serial number which was not found in cache and hence caused a recall from a stacked volume.[3]

262	106		10	binary	reserved (set to zero)

The values for the superscripts represent:

- [1] This field will be zero if the statistics are reported for a composite library (SMF94VNO=X'FF')
- [2] This field is a composite of all AX0s when reported for a composite library (SMF94VNO=X'FF')
- [3] This field is only valid when reported for a composite library (SMF94VNO=X'FF'). For other than a composite library, the field will contain zero.

Appendix E. VTS tape volume cache management

In many installations, much of the data written to a VTS is for backup or long-term archival purposes, and the likelihood of reading it again is extremely low. There is no significant benefit in keeping such data in cache; indeed, it is undesirable to retain it, as it may not allow data which does have some chance of reuse to be retained in cache. Informal studies suggest that the proportion of data that does not benefit from being cached may be as high as 80% of the data written to a VTS (Figure 95).

A tape volume cache management function was added to the existing Advanced Functions feature, #4000, in December 2000. The tape volume cache management function provides the ability, using DFSMS policy controls, to influence how long data remains in the tape volume cache. You may assign data to one of two groups, where the contents of one group are preferentially removed from cache. This means that the data in the other group will tend to stay in cache much longer, and therefore you would expect to improve the average mount response time because data does not need to be recalled from a stacked volume into the tape volume cache.

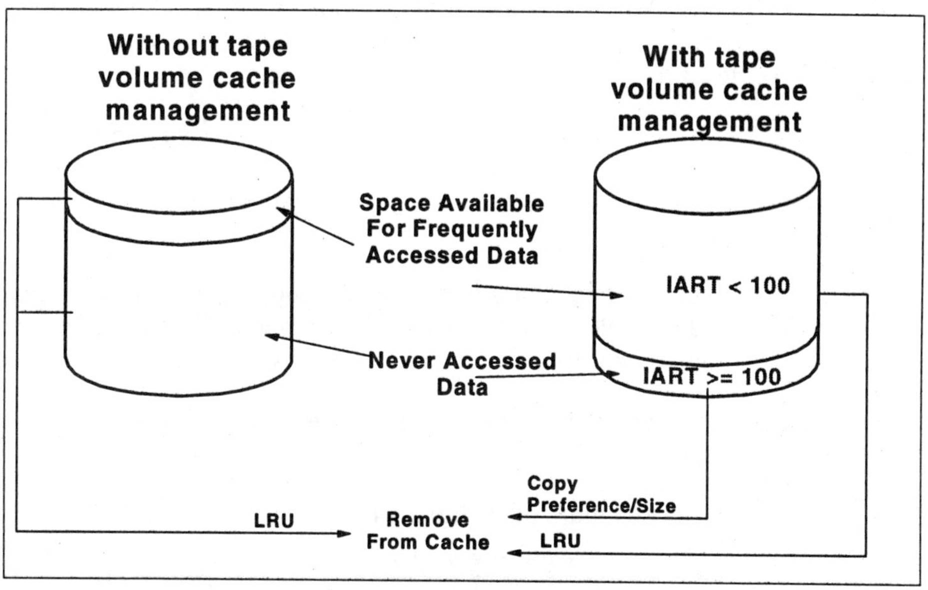

Figure 95. Effect of cache management on TVC use

When the tape volume cache management function is installed, the VTS controller recognizes a new command that is issued by a host to tell the VTS how a virtual volume should be managed. DFSMS now uses the Initial

© Copyright IBM Corp. 2000

Access Response Time (IART) attribute of the storage class as the external control of the cache and issues the command to the VTS according to the IART value.

The IART is an existing storage class attribute, currently used to determine where an OAM object should be placed. A non-zero IART value is also used by DFSMS as an indicator to use randomization algorithms when selecting volumes for allocation or extension of SMS-managed data sets.

E.1 Tape volume cache management overview

The function provides two Cache Preference Groups, 0 and 1. Data falls in one of these two groups, depending on the IART setting.

If the IART is set to 100 seconds or more, the data is assigned to cache preference group 0 and the VTS controller removes this data from cache, largest volumes first, in preference to data in cache preference group 1. The largest volume is processed first so that the maximum amount of tape volume cache space is freed for each volume removed.

If the IART is less than 100 seconds, the data is assigned to cache preference group 1 and is managed in the same way as now by removing the least recently used volumes from cache.

The host informs a VTS of the IART value at open time for file position 1 and, for multi-volume data sets, during end of volume processing. When a volume is closed, the VTS then assigns the data to a cache preference group based on the IART value.

When it is necessary to remove volumes from the tape volume cache, the VTS controller now chooses to remove virtual volumes in cache preference group 0 before any in cache preference group 1.

Note that a virtual volume must have been copied to a stacked volume before it may be removed from cache.

This is summarized in Table 14.

Table 14. Cache preference group summary

Cache preference group	IART	Management technique
0	100 seconds or more	Preferential removal of volumes from cache, largest first.

Cache preference group	IART	Management technique
1	Less than 100 seconds	Removal of volumes after group 0, least recently used first.

E.2 Prerequisites

Tape volume cache management requires:

- The Advanced Functions feature, #4000, together with its prerequisites (3494-B18 VTS, at least four 3590 drives, convenience I/O station and either feature #3200 or #3400/#3412 to provide ESCON attachment with data compression in the channel cards)
- Licensed internal code at a level providing tape volume cache management
- PTFs to DFSMS/MVS 1.4, 1.5 and DFSMS 2.10
- At least one storage class with an IART of 100 seconds or more

Volumes created by a host without the software support will be assigned to cache preference group 1. A volume previously placed in cache preference group 0 by a host with the software support will be assigned to cache preference group 1 if a write operation is performed at the beginning of the tape by a host without the software support.

Tape volume cache management is available on stand-alone VTSs and Peer-to-Peer VTSs with the Advanced Functions feature. You may now choose whether to enable or disable the import/export function at the library manager. For Peer-to-Peer VTSs, import/export must be explicitly disabled as the default is for it to be enabled. In a Peer-to-Peer VTS configuration, feature #4000 must be installed on both distributed VTSs.

E.3 Software support for cache management

The support is provided by APARs OW45956 and OW45959 for DFSMS/MVS 1.4 and 1.5 and for DFSMS 2.10.

No toleration support is needed.

E.4 Exploiting tape volume cache management

To make use of VTS tape volume cache management, you will need to:

- Review your storage class ACS routine to identify storage classes assigned to tape allocations.
- Change or define storage classes so that you have at least one storage class with an IART greater than or equal to 100 seconds and at least one with an IART less than 100 seconds.
- Identify the data suitable for preferential removal from cache.
- Change and test your storage class ACS routine.
- Monitor the effects of the change.

E.4.1 Storage class

You set the Initial Access Response time in the ISMF storage class definition, as shown in Figure 96. If you do not specify a value for the IART, the default is zero seconds.

```
 Panel  Utilities  Scroll  Help
------------------------------------------------------------------
                    STORAGE CLASS DEFINE                Page 1 of 2
Command ===>

SCDS Name . . . . . : USER8.TEST.SCDS
Storage Class Name  : VTSPURGE
To DEFINE Storage Class, Specify:
 Description ==> DEFINE STORAGE CLASS
             ==>
 Performance Objectives
 Direct Millisecond Response . . . .     (1 to 999 or blank)
 Direct Bias . . . . . . . . . . . .     (R, W or blank)
 Sequential Millisecond Response . .     (1 to 999 or blank)
 Sequential Bias . . . . . . . . . .     (R, W or blank)
 Initial Access Response Seconds . .100 (0 to 9999 or blank)
 Sustained Data Rate (MB/sec)  . . .     (0 to 999 or blank)
Availability . . . . . . . . . . . . N   (C, P ,S or N)
Accessibility  . . . . . . . . . . . N   (C, P ,S or N)
 Backup  . . . . . . . . . . . . . .     (Y, N or Blank)
 Versioning  . . . . . . . . . . . .     (Y, N or Blank)
```

Figure 96. Storage class Initial Access Response

E.4.2 Identifying suitable data

It would be wise to move data gradually to storage classes that enable cache management. The objective is to identify data that need not stay in cache. We can break data into three categories:

1. Expected to be suitable for early removal from cache.

We would expect to include database logs, image copies, archival data and long-term backups.

2. Not certain whether suitable or not.

   This is data that does not fall into the other two categories. It is likely that the effort of identifying candidates from this category would outweigh the benefits.

3. Not suitable for early removal from cache.

   This type of data would have a high chance of reuse. It could include DFSMShsm migration data or application data written directly to the VTS.

E.4.3 Tools

A new analysis tool, VOLREUSE, is available via anonymous FTP from:

`ftp://ftp.software.ibm.com/storage/tapetool`

It will take SMF type 14, 15, 21 and 30 records as input and will show what percentage of VTS write activity (at both an hourly and daily level) is never read again and therefore is an ideal candidate for early removal from cache. The TGROUP control statement allows you to keep data together for address ranges that you specify. This will allow you to produce separate reports for different VTSs.

It will also provide a list of data set names for write-only data sets. At a later stage, this list can be provided to Batch Magic to allow a simulation showing the improvements in read hits by using cache management.

E.4.4 Storage class ACS routine

Because tape volume cache management is requested by assigning storage classes with the IART attribute set, you are able to use all of the information available to you in an ACS routine (data set names, qualifiers, program names, job names and so on) to select only the data you want.

Figure 97 shows an example of a storage class ACS routine that chooses cache management for DFSMSdss backups and DB2 archive logs.

```
FILTLIST TVC_early_remove_PGM INCLUDE(ADRDSSU)
FILTLIST TVC_early_remove_DSN INCLUDE(DB2*.**.LOG*)
FILTLIST TAPE                 INCLUDE(349*,359*)
.
SELECT
.
  WHEN (&DSN = &TVC_early_remove_DSN && UNIT = &TAPE)
    DO
    SET &STORCLAS = VTSPURGE
    EXIT
    END
.
  WHEN (&PGM = &TVC_early_remove_PGM && UNIT = &TAPE)
    DO
    SET &STORCLAS = VTSPURGE
    EXIT
    END
.
.
```

Figure 97. Example ACS fragment for cache management

E.4.5 Monitor effects

If you have data that is suitable for early removal from cache and you have enabled the cache management function, you would expect to see an increase in the proportion of read hits. You can get this information from the SMF type 94 record via VTSSTATS and from the StorWatch ETL Expert.

Appendix F. Altering TCDB entries after merging VTSs

The REXX exec in Figure 98 shows how you might correct the TCDB entries for one of the VTSs merged to form a Peer-to-Peer VTS. You would use this to alter the TCDB entries for the library whose library name is *not* reused for the Peer-to-Peer composite library.

```
Arg parms
Dsn=''; Lib=''
If pos('DSN(',parms)>0 then do
   parse var parms front 'DSN(' dsn ')' back
   parms = front || back
   end
If pos('LIB(',parms)>0 then do
   parse var parms front 'LIB(' lib ')' back
   parms = front || back
   end
If dsn='' | lib='' then do
   'Usage:   ALTERVOL DSN(volserlist) LIB(libname) '
   exit 4
   end
/***************************************************************/
/*  Get volume serials from source input dsn                   */
/***************************************************************/
Address TSO "FREE FI(INDD)"
Address TSO "ALLOCATE FI(INDD) DA("dsn") SHR"
Address TSO "EXECIO * DISKR INDD (STEM X."
Alter1 = "ALTER '"
Alter2 = "' VOLUMEENTRY LIBRARYNAME("lib")"
Volumes = 0
Do N=1 to X.0
   If Pos("VOLUME-ENTRY----",x.n)>0 then do
      Volumes = Volumes + 1
      Parse var x.n "VOLUME-ENTRY----" volser .
      Address TSO Alter1||volser||Alter2
   end
End
Say "Lines Read:       " format(x.0,9)
Say "Volumes Altered: " format(Volumes,9)
Address TSO "EXECIO * DISKR INDD (FINIS"
Address TSO "FREE FI(INDD)"
Exit 0
```

Figure 98. ALTERVOL exec

© Copyright IBM Corp. 2000

Appendix G. Special notices

This publication is intended to help storage systems technical professionals such as customers, Business Partners, and IBM to plan, configure, install, and implement the Magstar Peer-to-Peer VTS solution. The information in this publication is not intended as the specification of any programming interfaces that are provided by the Magstar 3494 Tape Libraries or the supporting host software. See the PUBLICATIONS section of the IBM Programming Announcement for the Magstar Peer-to-Peer Virtual Tape Server for more information about what publications are considered to be product documentation.

References in this publication to IBM products, programs or services do not imply that IBM intends to make these available in all countries in which IBM operates. Any reference to an IBM product, program, or service is not intended to state or imply that only IBM's product, program, or service may be used. Any functionally equivalent program that does not infringe any of IBM's intellectual property rights may be used instead of the IBM product, program or service.

Information in this book was developed in conjunction with use of the equipment specified, and is limited in application to those specific hardware and software products and levels.

IBM may have patents or pending patent applications covering subject matter in this document. The furnishing of this document does not give you any license to these patents. You can send license inquiries, in writing, to the IBM Director of Licensing, IBM Corporation, North Castle Drive, Armonk, NY 10504-1785.

Licensees of this program who wish to have information about it for the purpose of enabling: (i) the exchange of information between independently created programs and other programs (including this one) and (ii) the mutual use of the information which has been exchanged, should contact IBM Corporation, Dept. 600A, Mail Drop 1329, Somers, NY 10589 USA.

Such information may be available, subject to appropriate terms and conditions, including in some cases, payment of a fee.

The information contained in this document has not been submitted to any formal IBM test and is distributed AS IS. The information about non-IBM ("vendor") products in this manual has been supplied by the vendor and IBM assumes no responsibility for its accuracy or completeness. The use of this information or the implementation of any of these techniques is a customer responsibility and depends on the customer's ability to evaluate and integrate them into the customer's operational environment. While each item may have been reviewed by IBM for accuracy in a specific situation, there is no guarantee that the same or similar results will be obtained elsewhere. Customers attempting to adapt these techniques to their own environments do so at their own risk.

Any pointers in this publication to external Web sites are provided for convenience only and do not in any manner serve as an endorsement of these Web sites.

Any performance data contained in this document was determined in a controlled environment, and therefore, the results that may be obtained in other operating environments may vary significantly. Users of this document should verify the applicable data for their specific environment.

This document contains examples of data and reports used in daily business operations. To illustrate them as completely as possible, the examples contain the names of individuals, companies, brands, and products. All of these names are fictitious and any similarity to the names and addresses used by an actual business enterprise is entirely coincidental.

Reference to PTF numbers that have not been released through the normal distribution process does not imply general availability. The purpose of including these reference numbers is to alert IBM customers to specific information relative to the implementation of the PTF when it becomes available to each customer according to the normal IBM PTF distribution process.

The following terms are trademarks of the International Business Machines Corporation in the United States and/or other countries:

IBM ®	Redbooks
AIX	Redbooks Logo
AT	DB2
DFSMS	DFSMS/MVS
DFSMSdss	DFSMShsm
DFSMSrmm	DFSORT
ESCON	Magstar
OS/390	Parallel Sysplex
RS/6000	S/390
SP	StorWatch
Enterprise Storage Server	FICON
PR/SM	Processor Resource/Systems Manager
Sysplex Timer	System/390
RAMAC	

The following terms are trademarks of other companies:

Tivoli, Manage. Anything. Anywhere.,The Power To Manage., Anything. Anywhere.,TME, NetView, Cross-Site, Tivoli Ready, Tivoli Certified, Planet Tivoli, and Tivoli Enterprise are trademarks or registered trademarks of Tivoli Systems Inc., an IBM company, in the United States, other countries, or both. In Denmark, Tivoli is a trademark licensed from Kjøbenhavns Sommer - Tivoli A/S.

C-bus is a trademark of Corollary, Inc. in the United States and/or other countries.

Java and all Java-based trademarks and logos are trademarks or registered trademarks of Sun Microsystems, Inc. in the United States and/or other countries.

Microsoft, Windows, Windows NT, and the Windows logo are trademarks of Microsoft Corporation in the United States and/or other countries.

PC Direct is a trademark of Ziff Communications Company in the United States and/or other countries and is used by IBM Corporation under license.

ActionMedia, LANDesk, MMX, Pentium and ProShare are trademarks of Intel Corporation in the United States and/or other countries.

UNIX is a registered trademark in the United States and other countries licensed exclusively through The Open Group.

SET, SET Secure Electronic Transaction, and the SET Logo are trademarks owned by SET Secure Electronic Transaction LLC.

Other company, product, and service names may be trademarks or service marks of others.

Appendix H. Related publications

The publications listed in this section are considered particularly suitable for a more detailed discussion of the topics covered in this redbook.

H.1 IBM Redbooks

For information on ordering these publications see "How to get IBM Redbooks" on page 277.

- *IBM Magstar Virtual Tape Server: Planning, Implementing, and Monitoring,* SG24-2229
- *IBM Magstar Tape Products Family: A Practical Guide*, SG24-4632
- *Guide to Sharing and Partitioning IBM Tape Library Dataserver,* SG24-4409
- *Continuous Availability — Systems Design Guide*, SG24-2085
- *Continuous Availability — S/390 Technology Guide*, SG24-2086
- *IBM Fiber Saver (2029) Implementation Guide*, SG24-5608
- *S/390 I/O Connectivity Handbook*, SG24-5444
- *Introduction to IBM S/390 FICON* , SG24-5176

H.2 IBM Redbooks collections

Redbooks are also available on the following CD-ROMs. Click the CD-ROMs button at `ibm.com/redbooks` for information about all the CD-ROMs offered, updates and formats.

CD-ROM Title	Collection Kit Number
IBM System/390 Redbooks Collection	SK2T-2177
IBM Networking Redbooks Collection	SK2T-6022
IBM Transaction Processing and Data Management Redbooks Collection	SK2T-8038
IBM Lotus Redbooks Collection	SK2T-8039
Tivoli Redbooks Collection	SK2T-8044
IBM AS/400 Redbooks Collection	SK2T-2849
IBM Netfinity Hardware and Software Redbooks Collection	SK2T-8046
IBM RS/6000 Redbooks Collection	SK2T-8043
IBM Application Development Redbooks Collection	SK2T-8037
IBM Enterprise Storage and Systems Management Solutions	SK3T-3694

© Copyright IBM Corp. 2000

H.3 Other resources

These publications are also relevant as further information sources:

- *DFSMS/MVS OAM Planning, Installation and Storage Administration Guide for Tape Libraries*, SC26-3051
- *IBM 3494 Tape Library Dataserver Introduction and Planning Guide*, GA32-0279
- *IBM 3494 Tape Library Dataserver Operator Guide*, GA32-0280
- *OS/390 MVS System Messages, Volume 2*, GC28-1785

H.4 Referenced Web sites

These Web sites are also relevant as further information sources:

- `ftp://ftp.software.ibm.com/storage/tapetool`

  Customer FTP site for tape tools.
- `http://w3.rmss.tucson.ibm.com/softw/tapetool.htm`

  IBM internal site for tape tools.
- `http://www.storage.ibm.com/hardsoft/tape/3494_vts/ptp.html`

  Product specifications and information.
- `http://www.s390.ibm.com.bkserv`

  Product manuals, including OAM, SMF and messages.
- `http://www.ibm.com/support/techdocs`

  Technical flashes concerning VTS.

How to get IBM Redbooks

This section explains how both customers and IBM employees can find out about IBM Redbooks, redpieces, and CD-ROMs. A form for ordering books and CD-ROMs by fax or e-mail is also provided.

- **Redbooks Web Site** ibm.com/redbooks

  Search for, view, download, or order hardcopy/CD-ROM Redbooks from the Redbooks Web site. Also read redpieces and download additional materials (code samples or diskette/CD-ROM images) from this Redbooks site.

  Redpieces are Redbooks in progress; not all Redbooks become redpieces and sometimes just a few chapters will be published this way. The intent is to get the information out much quicker than the formal publishing process allows.

- **E-mail Orders**

  Send orders by e-mail including information from the IBM Redbooks fax order form to:

	e-mail address
In United States or Canada	pubscan@us.ibm.com
Outside North America	Contact information is in the "How to Order" section at this site: http://www.elink.ibmlink.ibm.com/pbl/pbl

- **Telephone Orders**

United States (toll free)	1-800-879-2755
Canada (toll free)	1-800-IBM-4YOU
Outside North America	Country coordinator phone number is in the "How to Order" section at this site: http://www.elink.ibmlink.ibm.com/pbl/pbl

- **Fax Orders**

United States (toll free)	1-800-445-9269
Canada	1-403-267-4455
Outside North America	Fax phone number is in the "How to Order" section at this site: http://www.elink.ibmlink.ibm.com/pbl/pbl

This information was current at the time of publication, but is continually subject to change. The latest information may be found at the Redbooks Web site.

IBM Intranet for Employees

IBM employees may register for information on workshops, residencies, and Redbooks by accessing the IBM Intranet Web site at http://w3.itso.ibm.com/ and clicking the ITSO Mailing List button. Look in the Materials repository for workshops, presentations, papers, and Web pages developed and written by the ITSO technical professionals; click the Additional Materials button. Employees may access MyNews at http://w3.ibm.com/ for redbook, residency, and workshop announcements.

© Copyright IBM Corp. 2000

IBM Redbooks fax order form

Please send me the following:

Title	Order Number	Quantity

First name

Last name

Company

Address

City

Postal code

Country

Telephone number

Telefax number

VAT number

☐ Invoice to customer number

☐ Credit card number

Credit card expiration date

Card issued to

Signature

We accept American Express, Diners, Eurocard, Master Card, and Visa. Payment by credit card not available in all countries. Signature mandatory for credit card payment.

Index

© Copyright IBM Corp. 2000

IBM Redbooks review

Your feedback is valued by the Redbook authors. In particular we are interested in situations where a Redbook "made the difference" in a task or problem you encountered. Using one of the following methods, **please review the Redbook, addressing value, subject matter, structure, depth and quality as appropriate.**

- Use the online **Contact us** review redbook form found at **ibm.com**/redbooks
- Fax this form to: USA International Access Code + 1 914 432 8264
- Send your comments in an Internet note to redbook@us.ibm.com

Document Number **Redbook Title**	SG24-6115-00 Magstar Peer-to-Peer Virtual Tape Server Planning and Implementation Guide
Review	
What other subjects would you like to see IBM Redbooks address?	
Please rate your overall satisfaction:	O Very Good O Good O Average O Poor
Please identify yourself as belonging to one of the following groups:	O Customer O Business Partner O Solution Developer O IBM, Lotus or Tivoli Employee O None of the above
Your email address: The data you provide here may be used to provide you with information from IBM or our business partners about our products, services or activities.	O Please do not use the information collected here for future marketing or promotional contacts or other communications beyond the scope of this transaction.
Questions about IBM's privacy policy?	The following link explains how we protect your personal information. **ibm.com**/privacy/yourprivacy/

© Copyright IBM Corp. 2000